Black Ethos

Black Ethos

NORTHERN URBAN NEGRO LIFE AND THOUGHT, 1890-1930

David Gordon Nielson

Contributions in Afro-American and African Studies, Number 29

GREENWOOD PRESS
WESTPORT, CONNECTICUT • LONDON, ENGLAND

Library of Congress Cataloging in Publication Data

Nielson, David Gordon.
    Black ethos.

    (Contributions in Afro-American and African studies; no. 29)
    Bibliography: p.
    Includes index.
    1. Afro-Americans—Psychology. 2. Afro-Americans—Social life and customs.
    3. Afro-Americans—Social conditions—To 1964. I. Title. II. Series.
    E185.625.N53   301.45'19'6073   76-47169
    ISBN 0-8371-9402-4

Library of Congress Catalog Number: 76-47169
ISBN: 0-8371-9402-4

First published in 1977

Greenwood Press, Inc.
51 Riverside Avenue, Westport, Connecticut 06880

Printed in the United States of America

Copyright Acknowledgments

The following material is reprinted with permission:

Lines from the poem "I Met a Little Blue-Eyed Girl," by Bertha Johnson, *Crisis*, 4 (July 1912), p. 147. Reprinted with the permission of the National Association for the Advancement of Colored People.

Extracts from *The Best of Simple*, by Langston Hughes. Copyright © 1961. Reprinted with permission of Hill & Wang.

Extracts from *The Big Sea*, by Langston Hughes. Copyright © 1963. Reprinted with permission of Hill & Wang.

"We Wear the Mask," by Paul Laurence Dunbar, in *The Complete Poems of Paul Laurence Dunbar*, Copyright © 1962. Reprinted with permission of Dodd, Mead & Company.

Extract from John H. Burma, "Humor as a Technique in Race Conflict," *American Sociological Review* 11 (December 1946), p. 713.

Extracts from Alden Bland, *Behold a Cry*. Copyright© 1947. Reprinted with permission of Charles Scribner's Sons.

Extracts from *On Being Negro in America*, copyright © 1951 by J. Saunders Redding. Reprinted by permission of the publisher, The Bobbs-Merrill Company, Inc., and by permission of The Harold Matson Company, Inc.

For Gladys

CONTENTS

PREFACE

IN SPITE of the manyfold increase in studies focused upon black America in the late 1960s and early 1970s, few have been directly concerned with the ordinary black American. Fewer still have centered upon the ordinary black of the urban North and the development of a sense of community in the black districts of northern cities as America became an urban nation. Modern black America came into being between 1890 and 1930. And despite the difficulties involved, it is possible to gather at least some insights into the ethos of ordinary black America.

From the perspectives of the late 1960s and early 1970s, it seemed that the nation had been offered second chance after second chance for social reform, but to no real advantage. In the early 1960s Michael Harrington in *The Other America* (1963) was striking the same chords as were played by Jacob Riis in *How the Other Half Lives* in 1890. How far removed is the violence of the 1890s, when there were almost 200 lynchings a year over the decade, from the murder-from-ambush of the 1960s? Claude Brown in *Manchild in the Promised Land* (1965) and Piri Thomas in *Down These Mean Streets* (1967) make black urban existence come alive in today's white world. How much different are their descriptions from the account of growing up black in the urban north in *His Eye Is on the Sparrow* by Ethel Waters, who was born more than a generation earlier?[1] By such measures the social changes wrought in America over more than three generations are pretty meager.

The recitation here is obviously foreshortened and inflated, but certainly white America should not have been overly surprised at the raised, clenched black fist. Yet, as Harrington noted, in 1960 "the United States found cause for celebration in the announcement that Negro workers had reached 58 per cent of the wage level of their white co-workers."[2] What of the black Americans whose "progress" was so celebrated? They, or their parents, are the topic of this study.

Basically the study rests upon two rather simple assumptions. First, it is accepted that "blackness" really did matter, that "blackness" was in the very warp and woof of the Negro's experience. Given this, it is understood that the life experiences of the Negro around the turn of the century were singularly different from those of any other group in the American culture. So they are today. Second, because the Negro's role in the larger society was narrowly restricted, it also is accepted that the life experiences of the members of this group contained many similarities. The tone of sentiment or ethos of the black masses of the northern urban community, therefore, should be discernible in spite of the fact that they were generally quite inarticulate and left few records.

Ordinary black life in the urban North had its mundane features, of course. It was not just a sequence of one damn thing after another brought about by "Negroness." It was not (and is not) "piss in the halls and blood on the stairs" of some ghetto tenement, as novelist Ralph Ellison so powerfully paraphrased it in his charge to Negro authors, even if there is a certain reality to be acknowledged there.[3] The concern here is with the attitudes of the janitor walking down South Parkway toward Washington Park in Chicago after buying his son an ice cream cone. It is with the thoughts of the tired black domestic hanging on a subway strap, her feet aching, thinking of her black family and the food she must buy before going home. It is with the young couple emerging from the subway exit on Lenox Avenue and walking up 135th Street toward Seventh Avenue, each thinking Lord knows what. All just ordinary Americans in so many ways, but nevertheless black in white America. None of these people appear as distinct individuals on the following pages. In a common portraiture, though, they all are present in large numbers, sketched through the perceptions of writers and other observers who had known them as parents, neighbors, friends, brothers and sisters, or—as was not so rare—their earlier selves. We are concerned with the ethos of such people as Langston Hughes made come alive in his poems and stories: "people up today and down tomorrow, working this week and fired the next, beaten and baffled, but determined not to be wholly beaten, buying furniture on the installment plan, filling the house with roomers to help pay the rent, hoping to get a new suit for Easter—and pawning that suit before the Fourth of July."[4]

The time frame of 1890 to 1930 is especially pertinent; 1890 and 1930 can each be regarded as a milestone along the long road of the black American experience. In the 1890s, the nature and pressure of his experience forced the Negro into a new racial awareness. A nadir in race relations had been reached, in the North as well as in the South. That apt representation of American racism, Jim Crow, had a home in the North as well as in the South. By the end of the century new Jim Crow dictates, brought about by a number of forces, had fairly well fixed the standards of interracial relations. The most important of these forces were migrations of other peoples from abroad, which caused social and economic disturbances in the slowly growing black communities, and a search by white Americans for a social order more in keeping with a modern urban industrial society. Such pressures urged upon the black community a realignment of thought of self and of "whiteness." In a way, black America turned inward in the 1890s; the ordinary Afro-American, quietly, unconsciously perhaps, no longer concerned himself with fighting the forces in the interrelationship that delimited him from the dominant group or dreamed of their fading away. Now a new measure of racial consciousness, pervasive "we-group" feelings, a distinct sense of "peoplehood," was given full leave to develop.[5] It was to percolate its way upward as a nascent middle class developed, one that was founded upon providing services to the growing black communities.

To be sure, the World War era brought to some in black America the hope that the color line would at least fade somewhat if it were not to be swept away. Even the small black elite, though it saw itself more class akin to the dominant white majority than race akin to the mass of the black minority, made use of the rhetoric of black solidarity in this instance. Black America would demonstrate its worthiness if that was what was required. But the hoped-for improvements all along the color line were to be frustrated.

Racial consciousness was swept upward to a new level as a result of the wartime and the especially bitter postwar experiences. In spite of the fact that the black social structure became more than ever a mirror image of the white, this heightened sense of community was to be maintained. Further reinforced by new waves of migration from the South, black Americans in the urban North were possessed of a sense of peoplehood as the 1930s and the Great Depression dawned that was strong enough to sustain them even through these hard years. This alone was not the answer to being black in a white America, but class awareness came to nourish racial awareness, and the black community entered World War II determined that the disappointments of the post-World War I era would not be repeated. The 1930s mark the beginning of an "eruption from the bottom" that would boil up in the World War II period and after.[6] Between the white man's "nigger" characterized by the "Uncle Tom" epithet and the Black Panthers, there must have been some rather drastic change in the black ethos.[7] It occurred during these years.

Implicit in this study, then, is the idea that the antecedents of the black revolution of the 1960s and early 1970s are discernible in the changing ethos of the earlier time. The period saw a restructuring of the northern Negro's outlook regarding not only his black world but also the white world about him. But it is not particularly the purpose of this study to offer another watershed theme; it is rather to describe, with as much precision as possible, the characteristic spirit woven into the web of northern black urban existence during the time while analyzing how it changed.

The research for this study was conducted primarily in the New York Public Library and within the Schomburg Collection of the New York Public Library, as well as at the libraries of Cornell University and the State University of New York at Binghamton. I am grateful for the assistance furnished by the many individuals of these institutions. Special thanks are due to Janet Brown of the last-mentioned library for her efforts on my behalf.

Grateful acknowledgment must also be offered to the Ford Foundation for the Ethnic Studies Fellowship that so smoothed the way toward completion of this study.

I am especially indebted to Professor Charles B. Forcey, State University of New York at Binghamton, for the suggestions and assistance that did so much to give form and focus to my efforts. Professor Richard Dalfiume also provided criticisms stemming from his own years of study of Negro America and, with Professor Walter Hugins, gave a critical reading to the entire study. But in the end, the greatest debt to be acknowledged is to my wife Gladys, to whom this study is dedicated.

NOTES

[1] Ethel Waters, with Charles Samuels, *His Eye Is on the Sparrow* (Doubleday and Co., 1951). The listing of the place of publication in the bibliographical data of a study based upon American sources is not a very helpful inclusion since most such sources are published in New York City. Therefore the place of publication will be shown only where it is not New York or apparent from the publisher's name. Instead the publisher's name, often very informative of itself, as well as the date of original publication, if applicable, will be provided.

[2] Michael Harrington, *The Other America*: *Poverty in the United States* (Penguin Books, 1963), 74.

[3] Ralph Ellison, "A Very Stern Discipline," *Harper's Magazine* 234 (March 1967): 76.

[4] Langston Hughes, *The Big Sea* (1940; reprint ed., Hill and Wang, 1963), 264. At this time, it is doubtful that these Americans can be made much more "visible" individually than they are revealed in such sources. When the oral history work that has been started under the direction of Professor Herbert Gutman is further along, a more definitive picture perhaps will be possible. Such a portrait, in any case, would result in an entirely different kind of study than I attempted here.

[5] The approach here obviously sees the black American community as a distinct subculture within the American society. Those panhuman features of American life that span the whole of the subcultures that are the larger society are not denied; they simply are not within the scope of this study. The concern is with being black in white America and what it meant during this period. See J. Milton Yinger, "Contra-culture and Subculture," *American Sociological Review*, 25 (October 1960): 627-628. See also Milton M. Gordon, *Assimilation in American Life*: *The Role of Race, Religion, and National Origins* (Oxford University Press, 1964), 34 and passim. Gordon provides here a cogent and forceful discussion of subsociety, subculture, and group awareness in American life. The expression *peoplehood* as a synonym for ethnic group and awareness is suggested here. Race consciousness and "we-group" feelings will be explored in some detail in the study.

[6] Hugh H. Smythe, "Negro Masses and Leaders: An Analysis of Current Trends," *Sociology and Social Research* 35 (September-October 1950): 34; S.P. Fullinwider, *The Mind and Mood of Black America: 20th Century Thought* (Homewood, Illinois: Dorsey Press, 1969), 173.

[7] Stephen H. Bronz, *Roots of Negro Racial Consciousness, The 1920's: Three Harlem Renaissance Authors* (Libra Publishers, 1964), 9.

ABBREVIATIONS

AJS	*American Journal of Sociology*
Annals	*Annals, American Academy of Political and Social Science*
ASR	*American Sociological Review*
JAH	*Journal of American History*
JNE	**Journal of Negro Education**
JNH	**Journal of Negro History**

Black Ethos

1

THE VIEW
FROM THE BOTTOM

Yet do I marvel at this curious thing:
To make a poet black, and bid him sing![1]

THE YEARS between 1890 and 1930 saw a drastic and dramatic reorientation of the northern black urban community.[2] Industrialization and urbanization had been in the process of reshaping white America and its image of itself for a generation. They changed black America as well—especially during these years. A Negro America possessed of a distinct sense of community had emerged by the late 1920s. At the same time, its social structure had been molded into a distorted facsimile of white society, a Negro middle class rising out of the single social class that was typical of the black districts of the northern industrial cities in the 1890s. The ethos of the black community, however, was shaped by the overwhelming majority of the black population that still formed a more-or-less homogeneous mass at the bottom of the social structure. It is the collective minds and beliefs of these Americans, of those the "farthest down," to borrow from the title of one of Booker T. Washington's publications, that is the focal point of this study.[3]

"All classes of a people," said the scholarly Alain Locke of Howard University, who are "under social pressure are permeated with a common experience; they are emotionally welded as others cannot be. With them, even ordinary living has epic depth and lyric intensity, and this, their material handicap, is their spiritual advantage."[4] It is in this sense that the term *ethos* is used here. The basic assumption, to combine several dictionary definitions, is that it is

possible to speak of and to seek "the characteristic spirit, the pre-
valent tone of sentiment, of a people or a community"; that it is possible to reconstruct "the characteristic and distinguishing" tones "of
a racial, political, occupational, or other group."

The opinions of the great mass of people at the bottom of the
black social pyramid—a markedly truncated pyramid—were given
shape in large part by the color line. It was *their* view of the dominant white society, for instance, that had much to do with how the
Negro community as a whole defined its own structure and roles.
Thus to gain meaningful perspective on these opinions, one must try
to go inside—to become part of the group and look outward.[5] But
going inside is not easy since the members of this segment of society,
while not inarticulate, did little writing. Memoirs and diaries are ap-
parently nonexistent, as would be expected, but some oral history
material is being collected. Some letters of the participants in the
Great Migration of the World War I years and after have been
preserved, but little else of this nature seems to have survived.[6]
Nevertheless, the threshold at least can be crossed.

How things looked from the inside finds its fullest expression in
the literature and poetry of black artists. The Negro newspapers of
the day also permit glimpses inside. When these two sources are supplemented by selections from the literature of the social sciences, an
outline of the black world and the surrounding white world of this
"man the farthest down" can be sketched, albeit with a fairly broad
brush.

The imaginative literature of and on the Negro is best capable
of providing the kind of historical insights being sought here. Statistics of urban growth, or mortality rates resulting from the "white
plague" (tuberculosis), of occupational limitations, and the like are
only the bones of a skeleton at best, upon which one must flesh out
the black experience. *Such data, essential as they are, cannot relate
the psychic impact of being black in a white society.* In this instance
one must agree with literary critic Nick Aaron Ford's assertion that
"history records the deeds of a people, but literature registers their
hopes, fears, and dreams. If we wish to understand the motives behind action, literature is more profitable than history; for it reflects
the thought which later produces the act. Most literature is a com-

mentary on life."[7] The basic assumption here is, as psychologist David McClelland so aptly puts it, that "successful authors are in part successful because they manage to put into writing what is in everyone's mind, the hopes, dreams, strivings and motives of their audience. Their own motives may be less important than their ability to project the feelings of their readers."[8]

Critics seem to agree because, as Seymour Gross and John Hardy say, "writers of fiction and poetry tend to grope for meanings rather than superimpose them, . . . [and] can bring to the surface what otherwise might be buried in the culture's subconscious."[9] An author is subjected, of course, to the same multitude of pressures that impinge upon the rest of the society, and his dreams, drives, and disappointments can get in the way of reality. But there is a consensus, nevertheless, as to the historical worth of literature. When considering the Negro author, however, one enters a sort of literary no-man's-land.

From about the turn of the century the "place" of the Negro American author in American literature has been periodically debated—much as if "Negro author" and "American literature" were mutually exclusive categories.[10] Of course, the contention that Negro writing is somehow distinctive is one that cuts both ways; on the one hand it restricts the Negro author's subject matter to the black experience, and on the other hand it argues that there is in blackness a host of subtleties that cannot be presented by other than the black artist.[11] There is no one brand of literary output "that automatically goes with a flat nose while another brand automatically goes with aquiline features," as Nick Ford so well puts it.[12] There is, however, an added responsibility when the black author addresses the reality of blackness in white America. "Like any other artist," writes a leading authority on the matter, "the Negro novelist must achieve universality through a sensitive interpretation of his own culture. The American Negro, however, has not one but two cultures to interpret. He bears a double burden, corresponding to the double environment in which he lives."[13]

After one insists upon the ability of an author to interpret his culture as well as the capacity of the Negro author to interpret his double environment, one still must be cautious in using this literature as an historical source. For instance, Claude McKay, Countee

Cullen, and Langston Hughes, all celebrated artists of the 1920s, dealt much with the highly charged, romantic side of black life during the period. The subject matter, as two anthologists have recently noted, provided these authors with effective counterpropaganda to white racial stereotypes but thus necessarily "avoided a description of all those Negroes who were simply trying to survive and improve themselves economically.[14] This is an accurate enough generalization. The more colorful characters created by these authors are certainly not typical of the ordinary black city dweller in the North in the early decades of this century. On the other hand, these artists could hardly have avoided such description entirely and remained faithful in their interpretations. The "general ambience" of black life, as these anthologists term it, is still to be found there.[15]

Problems of identity and self-esteem suffered by the author further complicate the use of this literature as an historical source. Richard Wright, who is found on any modern list of accomplished American authors, provides an excellent example. "After the emergence of Richard Wright the double standard for Negro writers was over," says one anthologist. "Hereafter Negro writers had to stand or fall by the same standards used to evaluate the work of white writers."[16] But some critics of the late Richard Wright say he wrote as if he thought he were white. A comparison of his values as revealed in his autobiography *Black Boy* (1973) discloses a "doubtful identification with other Negroes," argues one psychological study.[17] "There is the fact that 79 per cent of his descriptions of Negroes are unfavorable," the statistical analysis in this study showed, and, ". . . the fact that the characteristics he attributes to Negroes as such are radically different from those he attributes to himself, and in which he takes pride." In all, Wright, in even his autobiography, is charged in this investigation with a "surprising infrequency of explicit concern for the welfare of Negroes as a group."[18]

Wright's most famous character creation, Bigger Thomas in *Native Son* (1940), is also the product of a "white" interpretation, a recent study argues, for Bigger lacks even a single redeeming feature. What is more striking, Bigger has been seen by some critics as representing black America.[19] But *Native Son* is part of the literary heritage of Dos Passos, Farrell, and Steinbeck and may well have come from the mold of Theodore Dreiser's *An American Tragedy* (1925). And certainly the flow of black life around Bigger's tragic existence mirrors the day-to-day life of the ordinary Negro in the black urban community.[20]

Selecting and using the literature of black American artists is further confounded by the fact that in the 1890-1930 period much of their work was of a propaganda-counterpropaganda nature. From the last decade of the nineteenth century many black artists were highly race conscious.[21] Then, starting in the 1920s, Negro literature picked up tones of class consciousness as well, the two being melded in the works of such authors as Richard Wright and Ann Petry. Black writing was, generally, protest writing. "Some agreed with Booker Washington, more with DuBois," critic and author Sterling Brown writes, "but all stressed the Negro's persecution and his achievement."[22] One author said Brown, in "answering Booker T. Washington's conciliatory school of thought," asked, "What are houses, land and money to men who are women?"[23] In 1889, by way of further example, Sutton Griggs in *Imperium in Imperio* offered the first novel that suggested direct political action and the use of violence as a solution to the Afro-American's condition in America. In his novels, Griggs weighed open revolt versus exodus versus the Booker Washington approach, forecasting the arguments of the twentieth century.[24]

Stereotyping was a major weapon in white propaganda missives and in these black countermissives. For the most part, white characterizations of the Negro tended to range between "The Contented Slave" and "The Exotic Primitive" on the one hand, to "The Tragic Mulatto" and "The Local Color Negro" on the other.[25] The more "Negroes showed themselves as seeking economic advancement and civil rights," Sterling Brown wrote, the more white "authors portrayed them as insulting brutes and rapists," a stereotype that came to full flower in the early years of this century.[26]

Even the muckrakers, those reform-minded publicists of the Progressive era, fell short in this area. Today Ray Stannard Baker's famous *Following the Color Line* (1908) is seen as a product of the national climate of the times. "The book," historian Carl Resek asserts, "was typical in its readiness to accept the Southern view of 'the millions of inert, largely helpless Negroes who, imbued with a sharp sense of their rights, are attaining only slowly a corresponding appreciation of their duties and responsibilities.'"[27] The implicit attitude in Baker's much praised work was not lost on the black community. Even the conservative *Colored American Magazine*, while reviewing *Following the Color Line* favorably, pointed out that there were "many things the Negro . . . knows about this question that Mr. Baker will never know, because the Negroes fear to tell him."[28]

The black author's propaganda counterattack also used stereotypes, as noted. Sutton Griggs, for example, in an addendum to his novel *The Hindered Hand: or, The Reign of The Repressionists* (1905) attacked the popular racist novelist Thomas Dixon, attributing Dixon's dislike of the Negro to his poor-white extraction.[29] This, the notion of the cracker, is one of the major pre-World War I stereotypes that survived the period. Other major types, in addition to the poor-white villain, were "the benevolent white father of mulattoes, the kind aristocrat, the mean planter, the brutal overseer, and the Northern champion of the Negro."[30]

Even so, such propagandizing by writers on both sides does not keep their literature from being useful as a window on the black experience. There are flaws in the glass, but the view is not wholly obscured—not even by white prejudices. It was quite possible for white authors to interpret the black man with fidelity.[31] A leading authority, for example, considers George Washington Cable "one of the finest creators of Negro character in the nineteenth century," while Mark Twain's Jim in *Huckleberry Finn* (1884) is cited as "the best example in nineteenth century fiction of the average Negro slave."[32] After the turn of the century one can point to Stephen Crane, Theodore Dreiser, and William Faulkner as further examples. They and others grasped that the Negro during encounters with the white man wore a mask that mirrored to the white world what it desired to see. "A nigger is not a person so much as a form of behavior," Faulkner wrote in *The Sound and the Fury*; "a sort of obverse reflection of the white people he lives among."[33] It was in fact such authors as Cable, Twain, and Crane who many times attacked the rabid racism of the times.[34]

The selection and use of literature as a historical source, then, is confounded by a number of considerations, not the least of which is their protest nature and widespread use of stereotypes. There is an additional problem concerning the Negro in the urban North to carry this topic but one step further. Before the flood of migration from the South began to swell the northern urban centers during World War I, a cityward movement that continued into the 1920s, there was little imaginative writing concerning black life in these cities. Paul Laurence Dunbar's *The Sport of the Gods*, published in 1902, is generally considered the first novel about northern urban life by a Negro author.[35] One has to wait for the 1920s really—and the stories of Rudolph Fisher, Claude McKay, Langston Hughes, and others—before the northern black scene is capitalized upon. Here Richard Wright is again worth mention, especially for his writings on the quests of the migrants to the northern promised land.[36]

The novel perhaps presents the greatest problems when using it as a historical source, but cautions quite similar in nature to those outlined above are applicable to other types of literary works as well. Of the poetry of the early years of the twentieth century, it has been noted that the thrust of propaganda and protest was not quite as pronounced as in the novel. But, wrote Sterling Brown, it "was difficult in a period of conciliation and middle class striving for recognition and respectability" to break out of the traditional molds. "Their poetry seeks escape from a burdensome reality, but almost never is the burden explicitly stated, or the protest more than a vague dissatisfaction." But then, he continued, "in comparison to the Negro masses they [the black poets] did not have so very much to forgive."[37] This would change as the century wore on, however, and some of the most bitter black protest of the period would be expressed in poetry.[38]

A somewhat parallel situation existed in the theater. To play successfully to a white audience looking to be entertained not propagandized, any protest offerings had to be tempered with reminders of the familiar, a situation that did much to perpetuate the stereotypes of black life.[39] This is especially the case with that American peculiarity, the minstrel show. It had much to do with establishing the comic Negro stereotype—the shuffling Negro all gawdied up in outlandish clothes and spilling big words and malapropisms at every turn.[40] The Negro like the white, of course, attended the theater as an escape, not to be propagandized. He cared not at all for drama as protest, much to the despair of the small black elite who saw in the popular stage presentations and in the newer mass media of radio and movies the perpetuation of racial stereotypes.[41]

Other kinds of writings are capable of providing glimpses inside, of course, and the problems encountered in using them as historical sources are not so very different in many ways from those met in using imaginative literature. For instance, the public utterance of the black leader, like that of the politician, "in most instances, has been altered in the interest of policy," as W.T. Fontaine put it.[42] Obviously the caution would be applicable to the essays of Booker T. Washington and W.E.B. DuBois. The public image of Washington may be one of an altruistic man, but he appears also—at least in his public image—to have been somewhat color blind. W.E.B. DuBois, on the other hand, although at the pinnacle of the black intellectual elite, was anything but optimistic as far as color and the American culture were concerned. Of DuBois, author Claude McKay wrote that meeting him

was something of a personal disappointment. He seemed possessed of a cold, acid hauteur of spirit, which is not lessened even when he vouchsafes a smile. Negroes say that Dr. DuBois is naturally unfriendly and selfish. I did not feel any magnetism in his personality. But I do in his writings, which is more important.[43]

At times, it seems, DuBois could really touch the blackness of the ordinary Negro—polemics aside, of course.

Autobiography, a field of literature to which DuBois contributed a number of times, is another avenue into the culture of black America. Autobiographies are especially valuable in exploring the motivations and the policies of black leaders, but some also are capable of providing insights into the other end of the black social spectrum. Excellent comment on being black in America is to be found here. This is especially the case since Booker Washington's *Up From*

Slavery (1901). The Horatio Alger image so explicit there was more often rejected by black writers after that time. Look, these later writers seem to have said during this period of growing race consciousness, the Alger-like success of Washington hinged upon white help.[44] Thus, the autobiographical sketch, in addition to the formal autobiographies of such notables as Langston Hughes, Claude McKay, and W.E.B. DuBois, is especially useful in gaining insights into the black "characteristic spirit."

Before turning to the Negro newspaper and periodical as mirrors of black life, it remains only to comment on the use of the literature of the social sciences—especially sociological studies—in exploring the ethos of the black northern community. An ever-increasing number of studies was generated during this period, many of which must be approached with caution because of the highly racist climate of the time. It would appear, for instance, that the noted Atlanta University Studies, a research program inaugurated by W.E.B. DuBois for the study of Negro life in all its facets, became mired in questionable methodology as well as a morass of insufficient funds and a dearth of able personnel.[45] Moreover the later studies evidently suffered from a lack of objectivity.[46] But this type of material is not rendered useless by such shortcomings. And the studies of the later decades of this century—those of such respected researchers and writers as E. Franklin Frazier, St. Clair Drake, and Horace Cayton—may be used with confidence.

The case for Negro newspaper and periodicals being at least partial mirrors of the black community is somewhat the same as that for those classes of writing already mentioned. During the period being considered here, all Negro newspapers were weekly publications, and all were "additional papers, ... largely supplement[ing] the ordinary [white] papers with Negro news and opinions."[47] They have been likened to "a huge sounding board" of the black community, and it is the general consensus of scholars that "the [Afro-American] press defines the Negro to the Negroes themselves."[48] "His newspaper is the voice of the Negro," critic Robert T. Kerlin said.

Those who would honestly seek to know the Negro must read his papers. It is in them that the Negro speaks out with freedom, with sincerity, with justice to himself, for there he speaks

as a Negro to Negroes, and he is aware that the white people do
not so much as know of the existence of his papers.

    To know the Negro do not quiz the cook in your kitchen,
or the odd-job, all-service menial . . . . In general they will tell
you what they know you wish to hear, or on difficult matters,
remain noncommittal.[49]

    Negro newspapers were—and still are—almost the only source
of race news; that the white press "rarely gives space for anything
concerning him [the Negro] except an all too frequently overdrawn
description of his bad qualities" was a fact continually noted in the
black press.[50] Such a suspicision within the black community that
the white press—even in the North—could not be trusted to give the
Negro an even break was well founded. By far the greatest portion of
the coverage devoted to black Americans was to antisocial news
items. White newspapers were simply indifferent to the Negro unless
he thrust himself upon the white consciousness by interfering in
some manner with the habitual patterns of the white community.[51]
Conversely the white press did yeoman service in perpetuating black
stereotypes, as shown by the following filler item from a northern
paper.

    "Why is it, Sam, that one never hears of a darky committing
suicide?" inquired the Northerner.

    "Well, you see, it's disaway, boss; when a white pusson
has any trouble he sets down an' gets to studyin' 'bout it an'
aworryin'. Then firs' thing you know he's done killed hisse'f.
But when a nigger sets down to think 'bout his troubles, why,
he jes nacherly goes to sleep."[52]

    The need of the black community for its own communications
media was obvious. The black newspaper did not, however, take on
its role as propagandist for the Negro community until the last years
of the nineteenth century. Prior to this time Negro papers were
mainly religious and denominational in nature, although before the
Civil War they had functioned as potent propaganda organs.[53] And
it was not until the makeup of the urban black communities was
altered by the northward migration of southern Negroes that the

Negro newspapers took up their role as organs of counterpropaganda in earnest.[54] It was in this role that these papers mirrored the image of the Negro communities of the urban North in these years, a role that made protest, black achievements, and a sense of common identity regular features.[55]

Over a period of time, of course, a paper altered the image it reflected by changing makeup and tone. The striking exception to this is the constancy of the race progress and "social uplift" type of coverage. Examine almost any issue of any black newspaper or other periodical (for example, *The Crisis*), and these themes in the form of stories about property accumulations, new business ventures, individual achievements—no matter how mundane and unnewsworthy they would have been in the white world—will be found. "It is characteristic of the Negro newspaper that a great deal of space goes for various sorts of welfare and uplift effort," Frederick Detweiler wrote in his definitive study of black newspapers. "It is a group that keeps on saying: 'Tell them we are rising.'"[56]

The Negro press, in short, was—and remains today—almost a "peculiar institution." As Arnold Rose emphasized, their main strength rested in the fact that almost all blacks turned to them at some time or another.[57] It has been noted that the "jus' among ourselves" tone of the Negro paper changed when the country newspapers became urban journals as their audiences moved cityward. This within-the-group tenor continued, however, even into the 1940s, sustained by the fact so few whites knew these papers even existed.[58]

It is just because the Negro newspaper was able to talk without whites listening that it was one of the better mirrors of the black community. But in spite of its protest nature, in spite of its counterassertion role, the Negro press of the time was, at bottom, conservative. Quick to attack where racial inferiority may have been implied, the black press basically followed the lead of the white: it reflected the values of the dominant society—values those in control of the black press had adopted and that the Negro community as a whole accepted. Of course many of these values were inappropriate because of the color line, but this fact was more appreciated by those at the bottom of the social heap than the members of the rising middle class.[59] From this point of view, it would perhaps be better to see the Negro press as an organ of reform rather than protest, as Maxwell Brooks has suggested in his study. The suggestion does not mean the papers were not the voice of black America. It was just here, on the "question of questions for America—the race question"— that the Negro made his voice heard so clearly.[60]

Much of what has been noted here concerning the Negro press is equally applicable to the last class of source material to be mentioned, Negro magazines. Polemical from the start, they reflected the challenge the rising racial consciousness of the black community would be offering to the dominant cultural ideas of the nation. Some would maintain this polemical stance; others would be born as black replicas of white periodicals.[61]

Like many of the newspapers, the Negro magazine was apt to suffer a short life span. Charles S. Johnson, in an early article regarding Negro magazines, noted that support from white subscribers often made the difference between life and death to these magazines. It was easy to lose such support if the material appealed too much to its black readership.[62] The *Colored American Magazine* ceased publication in 1909 after almost a decade, for instance. At least part of its troubles stemmed from a failure to satisfy the demands of white supporters.[63] In spite of their susceptibility to outside pressures, however, the magazines are an important source into the life of the black community and are especially rich as a source of the short story form of fiction. Several, especially *The Crisis* and *Opportunity*, are notable for their encouragement of this form of expression.[64]

There are, in summary, quite a number of avenues leading inside, leading to openings into the ethos of the northern black community of the times. The poetry, short stories, novels, and drama of black artists provide the best insights because as artists, they could search for and find the meanings within the life of the black American community. Individually, the black American wore a mask that presented to the white world only a mirror. No matter how closely the individual may have guarded his share of the "characteristic spirit" of the black world, however, the imaginative literature of his artists, his newspapers, and his magazines turn the mirror into a window.

NOTES

[1] "Yet Do I Marvel," by Countee Cullen, in *On These I Stand: An Anthology of the Best Poems of Countee Cullen* (Harper & Brothers, 1927), 3.

[2] *Community* is used here in its general sense of a social grouping at large, rather than in the specific, physical sense. In this manner it is also used to refer to a *composite* of black districts of the northern urban industrial centers—to a composite of New York's Harlem, Chicago's Bronzeville, and the burgeoning black areas of such cities as Detroit, Philadelphia, Boston, Pittsburgh, Toledo, and Buffalo—just as the portrait of the ordinary black American of the period that has been attempted here is also a composite.

[3] Booker T. Washington, *The Man Farthest Down: A Record of Observation and Study in Europe* (Doubleday, Page & Co., 1912). Washington here compared the lot of the black American favorably to that of the European peasant—a comparison that had caused sparks in black America before it saw print here. See *Crisis* 1 (January 1911): 9-11. It is doubtful that Washington's comparison made black Americans feel much better about their assigned role at the social mudsill in America.

[4] Alain Locke, ed., *The New Negro: An Interpretation* (1925; reprint, Arno Press, 1968) 47.

[5] The approach here, then, strives to get away from the elitist orientation that the late Robert Starobin noted has plagued even the post-World War II revisionists' interpretations in American Negro history. See Robert Starobin, "The Negro: A Central Theme in American History," *Journal of Contemporary History* 3 (April 1968): 41-43.

[6] See Emmett Scott, "Letters of Negro Migrants of 1916-18," JNH 4 (July 1919): 290-340, and "Additional Letters of Negro Migrants," ibid. (October 1919): 412-465.

[7] Nick Aaron Ford, *The Contemporary Negro Novel: A Study in Race Relations* (Boston: Meador Publishing Co., 1936), 17

[8] David C. McClelland, *The Achieving Society* (Princeton: D. Van Nostrand Co., 1961), 112-113. See also Carl Milton Hughes [John Milton Charles Hughes], *The Negro Novelists: A Discussion of the Writings of American Negro Novelists, 1940-1950* (Citadel Press, 1953), 23; Harold A. Farrell, "Theme and Variation: A Critical Evaluation of the Negro Novel, 1919-1947" (Ph.D. diss., Ohio State University, 1949), 190; Hugh Morris Gloster, *Negro Voices in American Fiction* (University of North Carolina Press, 1948), vii; Walter L. Daykin, "Social Thought in Negro Novels," *Sociology and Social Research* 19 (January-February 1935): 247-252. Several of the works cited here are unable to avoid racist overtones in spite of the interpretative power they are willing to acknowledge.

[9] Seymour L. Gross and John Edward Hardy, eds., *Images of the Negro in American Literature* (University of Chicago Press, 1966), 1.

[10] Saunders Redding, "The Problems of the Negro Writers," *Massachusetts Review* 6 (Autumn-Winter 1964-1965): 58. See also James Weldon Johnson, "The Dilemma of the Negro Author," *American Mercury* 15 (December 1928): 477-481; Charles I. Glicksberg, "Negro Fiction in America," *South Atlantic Quarterly* 45 (October 1946): 477-488, and "Negro Poets and the American Tradition," *Antioch Review* 6 (Summer 1946): 243-253. In the first article, Glicksberg submits that "the ultimate aim of Negro literature is to destroy itself, to become an indivisible part of American literature," evidently not recognizing that it is just this in any case.

[11] Langston Hughes, "The Negro Artist and the Racial Mountain," *Nation* 122 (June 23, 1926): 692-694; Arnold Mulder, "Wanted: A Negro Novelist," *Independent* 112 (June 21, 1924): 341-342; M. J. C. Echerno, "American Negro Poetry," *Phylon* 24 (Spring 1963): 62-68; Cedric Dover, "Notes on Coloured Writing," *Phylon* 8 (Third Quarter 1947): 213-224; Philip Butcher, "The Younger Novelists and the Urban Negro," *CLA Journal* 4 (March 1961): 196-203. In both Harry A. Overstreet, "The Negro Writer as Spokesman," *Saturday Review of Literature* 27 (September 2, 1944): 5-6, 26-27, and Blyden Jackson, "The Negro's Negro in Negro Literature," *Michigan Quarterly Review* 4 (Fall 1965): 290-295, the Negro author is seen limited by his racial consciousness in the creation of black characters.

[12] Nick Aaron Ford, "The Negro Author's Use of Propaganda in Imaginative Literature" (Ph.D. diss., University of Iowa, 1946), 302. See also Theodore L. Gross, "Our Mutual Estate: The Literature of the American Negro," *Antioch Review* 28 (Fall 1968): 293-303.

[13] Robert Bone, *The Negro Novel in America*, rev. ed. (New Haven: Yale University Press, 1965), 2. See August Meier, "Some Reflections on the Negro Novel," *CLA Journal* 2 (March 1959): 168-177, for a critique of Bone's work. Meier is critical of Bone in some areas and sees the study as unhistorical in places but finds the study still superior to most others. On the other hand, Darwin T. Turner, "The Negro Novel in America: In Rebuttal," *CLA Journal* 10 (December 1966): 122-134, charges Bone with everything from selective quotation and misinterpretation to lapses in good taste. See also James W. Byrd, "The Portrayal of White Character by Negro Novelists, 1900-1950" (Ph.D. diss., George Peabody College for Teachers, 1955), 364; Gloster, *Negro Voices in American Fiction*, vii; Ford, "Negro Author's Use of Propaganda," 146-147, 160.

[14] James A. Emmanuel and Theodore L. Gross, eds., *Dark Symphony: Negro Literature in America* (Free Press, 1968), 66.

[15]Ibid., 67. See, for example, Claude McKay, *Home to Harlem* (Harper & Brothers, 1928). For an evaluation of McKay as an interpreter of the ordinary black American and his role in American literature, see Wayne Cooper, "Claude McKay and the New Negro of the 1920's," *Phylon* 25 (Third Quarter 1964): 297-306, and *The Passion of Claude McKay: Selected Prose and Poetry, 1912-1948* (Schocken Books, 1973), passim. See also Emmanuel and Gross, eds., *Dark Symphony*, 87.

[16]John Henrick Clarke, ed., *American Negro Short Stories* (Hill and Wang, 1966), xviii. The standards of literary criticism and the Negro novel is still a much discussed topic. See Gross, "Our Mutual Estate," 297-299.

[17]Ralph K. White, "Black Boy: A Value Analysis," *Journal of Abnormal and Social Psychology* 42 (October 1947): 454 (emphasis removed).

[18]Ibid., 455. See also Thomas F. Pettigrew, *A Profile of the Negro American* (Princeton: D. Van Nostrand Co., 1964), 9; Steven Marcus, "The American Negro in Search of Identity; Three Novelists: Richard Wright, Ralph Ellison, James Baldwin," *Commentary* 16 (November 1953): 456-463; Ralph Ellison, *Shadow and Act* (Signet Books, 1966), 89-104.

[19]S. P. Fullinwider, *The Mind and Mood of Black America: 20th Century Thought* (Homeward, Illinois: Dorsey Press, 1969), 187-193. See also James Baldwin, *Notes of a Native Son* (Boston: Beacon Press, 1955), 30-45. *Native Son* has been subjected to much critical examination. Of the many such studies encountered, one of the earliest and still one of the best general discussions, is found in Gloster, *Negro Voices in American Fiction*, 228-234.

[20]Bone, *Negro Novel in America*, 142-143; Nelson Manfred Blake, *Novelists' America: Fiction as History, 1910-1940* (Syracuse University Press, 1969), 226-253.

[21]Gloster, *Negro Voices in American Fiction*, 98-99. Ford, "Negro Author's Use of Propaganda," ii, would date the "literary awakening," as he terms it, a little later, on the basis that the founding of *The Crisis* in 1910 "marks the first external evidence of a conscious united aid . . . [toward] literary propaganda in behalf of the race." See also Walter L. Daykin, "Attitudes in Negro Novels," *Sociology and Social Research* 20 (November-December 1935): 152-160, and "Race Consciousness in Negro Poetry," Ibid. 21 (September-October 1936): 45-53; Sterling A. Brown, "The American Race Problem as Reflected in American Literature," 8 (July 1939): 275-290.

[22]Sterling Brown, *The Negro in American Fiction* (1937; reprint ed., Atheneum, 1969), 100.

[23]Ibid., 102. See also Arnold M. Rose, *The Negro's Morale: Group Identification and Protest* (University of Minnesota Press, 1949), 8; Ford,

"Negro Author's Use of Propaganda," 17; Farrell, "Theme and Variation," 51; J Saunders Redding, "American Negro Literature," *American Scholar* 18 (Spring 1949): 137-140; Edward Bland, "Social Forces Shaping the Negro Novel," *Negro Quarterly* 1 (Fall 1942): 241-248.

[24]For an evaluation of Grigg's work see Hugh M. Gloster, "The Negro in American Fiction," *Phylon* 4 (Fourth Quarter 1943): 335-350.

[25]Sterling A. Brown, "Negro Character as Seen by White Authors," *JNE* 2 (April 1933): 180. See also Walter L. Daykin, "Negro Types in American White Fiction," *Sociology and Social Research* 22 (September-October 1937): 45-52; Benjamin Brawley, "The Negro in American Fiction," *Dial* 60 (May 11, 1916): 445-450, and "The Negro in American Literature," *Bookman* 56 (October 1922): 137-141; Harry A. Overstreet, "Images and the Negro," *Saturday Review of Literature* 27 (August 26, 1944): 5-6; Gross, "Our Mutual Estate," 294.

One study of the Negro in American literature, John Herbert Nelson, *The Negro Character in American Literature* (1926; reprint ed., College Park, Maryland: McGrath Publishing Co., 1968) 118, went so far as to assert that "the whole range of the Negro character is revealed thoroughly" in one of Joel Chandler Harris's Uncle Remus stories. He went on in the same vein, stating "From a purely artistic standpoint, it is doubtful whether any real advance in portraying the negro has been made since the publication of Harris's first books." Ibid., 120. Here also see Brown, "Negro Character as Seen by White Authors," 181, and Gross and Hardy, eds., *Images of the Negro in American Literature*, 5.

The "tragic mulatto" is perhaps the most infamous stereotype. "The statement is clear: black Negroes, contented with serving and worshipping whites; mixed Negroes, discontented, aspiring and therefore tragic. Alas, the poor mulatto!" Brown, *Negro in American Fiction*, 144.

[26]Ibid., 93.

[27]Carl Resek, ed., *The Progressives* (Bobbs-Merrill Co., 1967), xiii.

[28]*Colored American Magazine* 12 (July 1907): 8-9.

[29]Farrell, "Theme and Variation," 32-33.

[30]Byrd, "Portrayal of White Character," 111, and James A. Byrd, "Stereotypes of White Characters in Early Negro Novels," *CLA Journal* 1 (November 1957): 29.

[31]W. T. Fontaine, "The Mind and Thought of the Negro of the United States as Revealed in Imaginative Literature, 1876-1940," *Southern University Bulletin* 28 (March 1942): 5-50; Brown, "Negro Character as Seen by White Authors," 200-203.

[32]Brown, *Negro in American Fiction*, 67, 68.

[33]Blake, *Novelists' America*, 103.

[34]Thomas F. Gossett, *Race: The History of an Idea in America* (Schocken Books, 1965), 431-439.

[35]Paul Laurence Dunbar, *The Sport of the Gods* (1902; reprint., Arno Press, 1969) introduction; Emanuel and Gross, eds., *Dark Symphony*, 37; Brown, *Negro in American Fiction*, 131; Eugene Arden, "The Early Harlem Novel," *Phylon* 20 (Spring 1959): 25-31. The novel is, it seems, more a reflection of Dunbar's negative attitudes toward urban life in general and of his suspicions about the North than of life in the city, however.

[36]Blake, *Novelists' America*, 8. See, for example, Richard Wright, *Eight Men* (1961; reprint ed., Pyramid Books, 1969) and *Uncle Tom's Children* (Harper & Row, 1940).

[37]Sterling Brown, *Negro Poetry and Drama* (1937; reprint ed., Atheneum, 1969), 43, 58, 59.

[38]See, for example, Claude McKay's "The Lynching," or "If We Must Die." Both are found in many anthologies.

[39]Alain LeRoy Locke and Montgomery Gregory, eds., *Plays of Negro Life: A Source-Book of Native American Drama* (Harper, 1927). This anthology of twenty plays, ten by white playwrights and ten by black, hit upon every Negro stereotype in the book. An excellent example of casting protest against a background of the familiar is found in Paul Green's "The No 'Count Boy: A Folk Comedy in One Act," 69-96. Pheelie can dream and understand the dreams of wider horizons that "No 'Count Boy" spins for her, but the reality of Enos, her boy friend and "good, respectable Negro beholden' to his white benefactor," soon buries the dreams.

[40]Brown, *Negro Poetry and Drama*, 106.

[41]Ibid., 140. Royal D. Colle, "The Negro Image and the Mass Media" (Ph.D. diss., Cornell University, 1967), chap. 4, provides a most readable summary of the Negro image in the movies.

[42]Fontaine, "Mind and Thought of the Negro," 5.

[43]Claude McKay, *A Long Way from Home* (1937; reprint ed., Harcourt, Brace and World, 1970) 110.

[44]Frederick W. Turner, "Black Jazz Artists: The Dark Side of Horatio Alger," *Massachusetts Review* 10 (Spring 1969): 341-353.

[45]Elliott M. Rudwick, *W. E. B. DuBois: Propagandist of the Negro Protest* (1960; reprint ed., Atheneum, 1969) 40-41. Rudwick notes here how the program started and how DuBois described its start.

[46]Ibid, 41-53; Fullinwider, *Mind and Mood of Black America*, 50-51. See also William T. Fontaine, " 'Social Determination' in the Writings of Negro Scholars," 49 (January 1944): 302-315. Fontaine asserts that selection of data and theories, scope, and methodology are all affected to some degree by the author's blackness—by his social condition.

[47]Gunnar Myrdal, *An American Dilemma: The Negro Problem and Modern Democracy*, 20th anniversary ed. (Harper & Row, 1962), 915; E. Franklin Frazier, *Black Bourgeoisie: The Rise of a New Middle Class in the*

United States (The Free Press, 1957), 140; Maxwell R. Brooks, "Content Analysis of Leading Negro Newspapers" (Ph.D. diss., Ohio State University, 1953), 49. The "supplementary" nature of the black press can be appreciated by even a casual examination of almost any Negro newspaper file. The *Pittsburgh Courier* of the 1920s is an excellent example. To find out "what really happened" in that story that was reported in the white press, the Negro turned to his own papers. Ibid.

[48]Myrdal, *American Dilemma*, 911 (emphasis removed). See also, E. Franklin Frazier, "Race Contacts and the Social Structure," *ASR* 14 (February, 1949), 6; Brooks, "Content Analysis of Negro Newspapers," 49; Lewis H. Fenderson, "The Negro Press as a Social Instrument," *JNE* 20 (Spring 1951): 181-188.

[49]Robert T. Kerlin, *Voice of the Negro: 1919* (1920; reprint ed., Arno Press, 1968) ix, x.

[50]This comment from the Chicago *Broad Ax* April 10, 1909, is typical.

[51]Frazier, *Black Bourgeoisie*, 149; Ira B. Bryant, "News Items about Negroes in White Urban and Rural Newspapers," *JNE* 4 (April 1935): 169-178; Noel P. Gist, "Racial Attitudes in the Press," *Sociology and Social Research* 17 (September-October 1932): 25-36; and "The Negro in the Daily Press," *Social Forces* 10 (March 1932): 405-411; George E. Simpson, *The Negro in the Philadelphia Press* (University of Pennsylvania Press, 1936), 57 and passim, and "Race Relations and the Philadelphia Press," *JNE* 6 (October 1937): 628; Myrdal, *American Dilemma*, 37, 48, 655-656, 1184. Excellent examples of this are found periodically in *The Crisis* under the general rubric "Manufacturing Prejudice." These usually consist of a series of headlines or column leads, the first charging the "brute" Negro with some crime, the last noting the guilt of a white for the crime but with no mention of the earlier charges. See, for example, *Crisis* 13 (March 1917): 239.

Bryant, in the article cited above, attempts to demonstrate that the political status of Negroes directly correlates to the amount of anti-social news coverage and that there may be a correlation between the percentage of Negroes engaged in domestic service in a locale and the amount of anti-social news coverage. Bryant also attempts to correlate press treatment in 1932 with that in 1912 and concludes that there was little difference. His sample is restricted, however, to Texas newspapers.

That nothing much really has changed in respect to the kinds of coverage found in the white press over the first half-dozen decades of this century is demonstrated in Colle, "The Negro Image and the Mass Media," chap. 3. See also Elliott M. Rudwick, "Race Labeling and the Press," *JNE* 31 (Spring 1962): 177-188.

[52]Quoted in Simpson, *Negro in the Philadelphia Press*, 46-47. One function of dialect, it has been noted, is that of "a general characterizing
device . . . ; thus . . . 'Massa' is cheerful, trivially dishonest, faithful and
childlike." "It finds a formal and traditional role for him [the Negro] to play
in society—though it is on the lowest rank." Jules Zanger, "Literary Dialect
and Social Change," *Mid-Continent American Studies Journal* 7 (Fall
1966): 40, 44.

[53]Brooks, "Content Analysis of Negro Newspapers," 79, 81.

[54]Richard Robbins, "Counter-Assertion in the New York Negro Press,"
Phylon 10 (Second Quarter 1949): 126-136; Frederick G. Detweiler, *The
Negro Press in the United States* (1922; reprint ed., College Park, Maryland: McGrath Publishing Co., 1968) 13; Eugene Gordon, "The Negro
Press," *American Mercury* 8 (June 1926): 208. As will be noted in a later
chapter, the Negro press of the North was an agent of migration through its
exortations and encouragements.

[55]Detweiler, *Negro Press in the United States*, 58, 79; Myrdal, *American
Dilemma*, 903; Robbins, "Counter-Assertion in the New York Negro
Press," 127.

[56]Detweiler, *Negro Press in the United States*, 91. For a general
description of the themes and make-up of the Negro newspaper
at the time, see ibid., 79-100; Eugene Gordon, "The Negro Press,"
207-215, and an article by the same title in the *Annals* 140 (November 1928): 248-256; and "Outstanding Negro Newspapers," *Opportunity* 3 (December 1924): 365-367, which became something of a
regular yearly *Opportunity* feature. See also, Myrdal, *American Dilemma*, 915-920; Doxey A. Wilkerson, "The Negro Press," *JNE*
16 (Fall 1947): 511-521; Armistead Scott Pride, "Negro Newspapers;
Yesterday, Today and Tomorrow," *Journalism Quarterly* 28 (Spring
1957): 179-188.

Another often noted ubiquitous feature of the Negro newspaper of the
times was the advertisements devoted to beauty preparations (among them
skin lighteners, and hair straighteners), patent medicines, charms, clair-
voyance, and so forth. For an early study of this feature and its relation to
the black community, see Guy B. Johnson, "Newspaper Advertisement and
Negro Culture," *Social Forces* 3 (May 1925): 706-709. See also Myrdal,
American Dilemma, 922-923.

[57]Rose, *Negro's Morale*, 103; L.M. Hershaw, "The Negro Press in
America," *Charities* 15 (October 7, 1905): 67. Within the Negro press,
assertions to the contrary are not unusual. Most often these are to the effect
that the Negro does not support the race papers but buys the white
newspapers instead and that the average Negro is ignorant of activities

within the race because he fails to read the Negro weeklies. See, for instance, Chicago *Broad Ax*, May 29, 1909, and *New York Age*, May 13, 1909. Such assertions are at least partially explained by the additional role of the Negro press pointed to above.

[58] Bertram Wilber Doyle, "Racial Traits of the Negro as Negroes Assign Them to Themselves" (Master's thesis, University of Chicago, 1924), 15; Rose, *Negro's Morale*, 107; Kerlin, *Voice of the Negro,* x; Detweiler, *Negro Press in the United States*, 2-3. Detweiler noted that even some of the members of the Chicago Commission on Race Relations, which came into existence after the bloody riot of the summer of 1919, did not know of the Negro press in Chicago. See also Richard M. Dalfiume, "The 'Forgotten Years' of the Negro Revolution," *JAH* 55 (June 1968); 101.

[59] Frazier, *Black Bourgeoisie*, 158-161; Myrdal, *American Dilemma*, 920-922; Elizabeth Atkinson Green, *The Negro in Contemporary American Literature* (1928; reprint ed. McGrath Publishing Co., 1968).

[60] Brooks, "Content Analysis of Negro Newspapers," 83, 86-87; Kerlin, *Voice of the Negro,* v.

[61]Charles S. Johnson, "The Rise of the Negro Magazine," *JNH* 13 (January 1928): 7-21; Sidney J. Reedy, "The Negro Magazine: A Critical Study of Its Educational Significance," *JNE* 3 (October 1934): 604; Lewis H. Fenderson, "Development of the Negro Press, 1827-1948" (Ph.d. diss., University of Pittsburgh, 1949), 30; Emanuel and Gross, eds., *Dark Symphony*, 6.

[62]Johnson, "Rise of the Negro Magazine," 9.

[63]Ibid., 12-13.

[64]Emanuel and Gross, eds., *Dark Symphony*, 6.

2

THE VIEW
FROM OUTSIDE

Why should it be my *loneliness,*
Why should it be my *song,*
Why should it be my *dream*
  deferred
  overlong?[1]

IN LATE 1916 an elephant was hanged in Erwin, Tennessee. The
"lynching," reported by the Louisville, Kentucky, *News* and quoted
in *The Crisis*, took place after the brute had "murdered" its circus
keeper. The truth of the report cannot be fully vouched for, but its
significance here lies in the wide-swinging satire with which the
Negro newspaper greeted it. The paper related how the circus crowd
had surged forward to collect souvenirs from the carcass of the sus-
pended brute, as was usual at such southern spectacles. But a true
son of the South stopped the celebrants. In the name of all that was
holy to southern dignity, out of respect for its heritage and heroes,
he pleaded that shame not be heaped upon the good name of the
South by carving up an elephant for souvenirs as if it were a "common Negro."[2]

Today such an event and the resulting comment sound bizar-
re—from a white point of view. From a black viewpoint, however,
they document the national climate of the times. The last decade of
the nineteenth century and the first three decades of this century
were, literally, the Negro American's modern "time of troubles." In
spite of gains over former conditions in many spheres, their status in

the society as a whole had deteriorated markedly. Black America realized by the 1890s that the hopes and promises of emancipation were empty ones. As a result, Negro America became institutionalized; it became a society within a society, coming into existence and growing to early maturity during the period, while white society played the dual role of parents and midwife.[3]

The social and intellectual forces produced by industrialization, urbanization, and foreign immigration all merged in the last years of the nineteenth century to bring about a restructuring of American life by the early years of the twentieth. As so aptly expressed by historian Robert Wiebe, these forces brought forth a "search for order" that threw up a new middle class in white America.[4] The change was of a fundamental nature; a large portion of the old values, encased as they were in nineteenth-century small-town America, had to be reworked or discarded. New values—grounded in economic and social imperatives that had been in the process of changing for years because of industrialization and urbanization—had to be tailored to meet new needs. It was a dramatic time, these decades between 1890 and 1930.

Racial thought, like social thought, was moderated during these years. The shift may be described as a transition from the ideas of Social Darwinism to those of the Social Gospel.[5] It was a shift from a biological kind of explanation of individual, social, and racial hierarchies to an explanation of these hierarchies that, while based on inherited traits, made them responsive to society's control. "Confronted with an ideological tension between the doctrines of brotherhood and inequality," writes Curtis Grant, a recent student of the Social Gospel movement, "the Social Gospelers formulated a pragmatic program of Christian service and duty which made room for both."[6]

The great spokesmen of the Social Gospel, however, were never particularly explicit on the racial aspects of their theorizing. The more notable spokesmen—Washington Gladden, Lyman Abbott, and Walter Rauschenbusch—seemed especially unsure here. The ties between the apparent ordering of the races and evolutionary theory were just too striking, and these clergymen accepted the evidence of modern science.[7] Only Josiah Strong, a crusading clergyman in the West in his younger days and the earliest of the Social

Gospelers, gave any special thought to the Negro in his theme of Nordic supremacy. Curtis Grant writes of him:

> Strong compared the situation of the American Negro immediately after the Civil War with that of the Anglo-Saxon emerging from barbarism centuries ago. Because the Negro was thrown into the midst of an advanced social order blessed with matured industrial, political, and religious institutions, he lacked the opportunity to develop himself by creating his own civilization; he had no alternative but to accept the existing society and adjust to it in a passive spirit. On the other hand, our Anglo-Saxon ancestors, without the machinery of an advanced culture, were driven by necessity to invent new tools and processes. Devoid of pampering luxuries and confronted with a climate and conditions of life that challenged his ingenuity, the Anglo-Saxon had to struggle for survival, thereby developing a robust nature and character not possible under more salubrious conditions. Using Lamarckian language, Strong added [in *Our Country*]: "It is those qualities, slowly acquired through long ages of struggle, and *born in* Anglo-Saxons to-day, rather than the lands, the riches, the industrial, social and political institutions *into which they are born*, that make Anglo-Saxons free and mighty."[8]

For the most part, though, it was the pioneer social themes of the Social Gospelers that interested the new middle class being formed in urban-industrial white America. These themes attacked the use of popularized Darwinian ideas as a rationale for existing conditions, especially in the economic and political spheres. Reform Darwinists, historian Eric Goldman termed these young progressives.[9] This new middle class of professionals and business specialists sought change and found in new "scientific" attitudes toward society the rationale for an organized attack on the deplorable conditions of the urban poor and the like. A responsible society, one that used the tools that efficient bureaucratic organization could bring to bear on its problems, was their goal. Mastery, not the drift of lassez-faire government and competitive business, to paraphrase Walter Lippmann, was the key.

At the same time, this new middle class had to look beyond its immediate concern as it sought to identify its place in the national scheme of things. They were the leaders of the "search for order" that began in the last years of the nineteenth century. Traditional standards no longer sufficed. The bureaucratic needs of urban-industrial development and reform could be met only through a social system that measured worth by a yardstick of skill and talent instead of wealth and ethnic background.[10]

The practical consequences of the search as a whole need not be rehearsed. Beginning in the 1890s and continuing throughout the Progressive era and beyond, changes in local and state governments, in tenement laws, enforcement of public health regulations, settlement house movements and public education drives, as well as changes in business methods and organization, wrought modifications of the American scene. And, of course, the black American reaped some benefits from the reforms, especially at the lower political levels. Better urban traction service, for instance, helped him as well as the white urban dweller. Still, the search and the changes it wrought largely bypassed the Negro, especially in the South, although change in the dominant white society—particularly when coupled with growing racial antipathy—automatically meant change in the black community.[11]

Much of the period seems to have been characterized by temporary and constantly changing coalitions of pressure groups whose immediate common goals often had different motives. But on "the problem"—the race problem—these groups, whether northern or southern, found an area of essential agreement. The end of the century capped some twenty-five years of effort to exclude the Negro from the white social structure.[12] This is not to say that the American color caste system that assigned the Negro his permanently inferior role on the basis of race emerged full blown in the 1890s as a product of the "search for order" in white America. The free Negro's status before the Civil War cast a shadow before it and at least outlined modern segregation. In fact, the racist nature of American society seems in retrospect to have been foreshadowed from the first settlements on the North American continent. Reconstruction, one noted historian has remarked, was "only an interruption" in the task of assigning the Negro to his new "place" in the system after the Civil War.[13] How his new place would be shaped, its metes and bounds, was to be determined by the changes taking place in the white world. At the popular level, moreover, biological interpretations of the Negro's inferiority, along with the even older theological explanations, persisted into the 1920s and beyond and further set the limits of his place.

In the northern urban centers, the years after the Civil War had been a time of relatively relaxed interracial contact. The "old settlers" in the northern cities, as the old black elite has been termed, supposed that they had worked out a fairly comfortable settlement with the old white middle class. They had, in fact, adopted the values and manners of white urban America and looked forward to their acceptance by the larger society in the not too distant future.[14] Living as they did in isolation from white society as well as from the mass of the ordinary black population in the cities, perhaps the old settlers' insistence on this optimistic theme is understandable. At any rate, they did not seem to be aware that the old strongholds of interracial support were no longer being manned. Since the 1880s, the former adherents to the abolitionist tradition had been otherwise occupied and, as Arnold Rose notes, were no longer interested in the Negro and his cause, if they had not come to regard him as a hopeless case as well.[15]

Not all white militancy on the black man's behalf ceased, of course. The National Citizen's Rights Association (NCRA) was organized in 1890, for example, but it foundered by 1894.[16] That a condition of disinterest among former supporters of black rights existed by the 1890s, as Arnold Rose noted, would perhaps be the best way of putting it. Such disinterest was prerequisite to the adjustment of interracial affairs that took place in the South and that is so well described by C. Vann Woodward in his *Strange Career of Jim Crow* and *The Origins of the New South*. Extreme racism became the mode in the South, a mode that little disturbed the North and its growing new "liberal" middle class and that was in fact reflected in the North's own interracial affairs.[17]

The "revolution of the red-necks" in the South, underway by 1890, made it seem as if the race war had already begun there. "Have American Negroes Too Much Liberty?" asked an article in *The Forum* in 1893. Obviously, yes. "Some radical change will have to be made . . . . The negro will have to be disfranchised and a separate code enacted that will fit him. Corporal punishment," the article added, "is the only kind that has ever reformed him."[18] Refashioning the Negro's place through disfranchisement took most of the decade to complete, however. What Mississippi had managed to accomplish by constitutional convention in 1890 could not be done elsewhere until after the collapse of Populism in the South. But once the power of Populism was broken, once the ingenious "grandfather clause" was devised in Louisiana, once the Hoke Smiths and Ben Tillmans emerged, once Jim Crow roosts were constructed by local and state laws, the black man's place became clear enough. Popularly, the racial creed became, "Let the lowest white man count for more than the highest Negro."[19]

It is little wonder, then, that a mood of bitterness emerged— that distrust of whites and frustration over their actions pervaded the black community as a whole, both North and South. From the black viewpoint, the painful conditions that had existed since the end of Reconstruction now deteriorated further. Even among many of the spokesmen of the race, who were remote from the far more intolerable conditions of the ordinary Negro, hope gave way to bitterness. Black America turned inward. The ordinary Negro sought refuge from white racism within the comparative safety of the black community.[20]

By the end of the century the Negro's place had thus been defined, not just in the South but within the national scheme of things.[21] The southern view of the Negro's place is chronicled in the response of Senator Tillman when in 1901, President Theodore Roosevelt invited Booker T. Washington, principal of Tuskegee Institute, to the White House. It would cost a thousand dead "niggers" to get them back into their place, the South Carolina senator raged. The threat was made good in the next fourteen years.[22]

The South had, of course, been reminding the North for years not to object too loudly to its ways: do not point at our refusal to have black postmasters when you refused to employ Negroes even as clerks in department stores.[23] That the North had accepted such southern preachments is suggested by the fact that the Lincoln Day speeches of 1904, as *Harper's Weekly* noted, reflected no support in the North for further enforcement of the Fourteenth and Fifteenth amendments. Industrialist Andrew Carnegie agreed, for instance, that the ignorant southern black could not be safely enfranchised. President Eliot of Harvard agreed that racial admixture must certainly be avoided.[24] The logic of the southern argument was obvious when the conditions in the South were realized when it was real ized that white womanhood was trembling in terror while the black woman was safe from the "Potomac to Texas."[25] South and North, white America seemed to have gone mad, or at the very least to have been struck by a kind of "color fever."

Book titles can serve as sort of a fever thermometer of the racial climate. In 1881 a southern clergyman published *Our Brothers in Black*. A quarter-century later another southern clergyman, the Reverend Thomas Dixon, Jr., put into print *The Leopard's Spots: A Romance of the White Man's Burden—1865-1900* and two other contributions to the stream of racist tracts for the times. Among the many other titles, more striking if less noted than Dixon's works, are: *The Color Line: A Brief in Behalf of the Unborn*, a book that "proved" the Negro's inferiority, and *"The Negro a Beast."*[26] The Reverend Dixon, a recent study of *The Leopard's Spots* by Maxwell Bloomfield notes, "added a new dimension to the [race] problem by carrying his readers northward for a look at the threat which the black race allegedly offered to an urban-industrial society."[27]

Little is to be found that would ameliorate this view even in liberal middle-class America. Rarely did even the muckrakers, as noted earlier, transcend the racism of the times. The Negro seldom concerned these publicists of reform liberalism, except for Ray Stannard Baker. When he did, he was seen only as confirming the old stereotypes.[28]

In short, racism reached pandemic proportions in the United States by the first decade of the twentieth century. Obviously the nation's adventures on the international scene—the Spanish-American War, the acquisition of the Philippines and the Hawaiian Islands, Theodore Roosevelt's "big stick" in the Caribbean, the Panama Canal construction—gave new dimensions to America's racial thinking at the ordinary citizen's level. The controversies over immigration provided added fuel. Beyond these developments, though, the nation seemed to be taking on some of the South's preoccupation

with the "problem of problems."[29] It was as if some of its consciousness of the "Negro problem" had leaked throughout the land. "Can
it be said," asked one racist tract, "that America is falling prey to
the collective soul of the negro?" The fear that the "inferior thought-
expression" of the Negro's "collective soul" would infect white
America candidly indicates the extent of the nation's color fever.[30]

Controversy continued, to be sure, but the black American
knew that for most of his former white friends in the North, "the
whole Negro problem resolved itself into the matter of their getting a
cook or a maid." They realized that most whites, as W.E.B. DuBois
put it, were "tired of the persistence of 'the Negro problem,'"
wondering "not when [they could] . . . settle this problem, but
when [they would] . . . be well rid of it."[31]

Not that white America was short of solutions. William Dorsey
Jelks, an ex-governor of Alabama, shuddered at the horrors of social
and political equality when he wrote an article for the *North American Review* in 1907. If only the blacks would depart en masse; but
he realized that all such deportation-colonization schemes were but
wishful thinking. The only reasonable solution Jelks saw was white
control of Negro education. Provide just an elementary education
that inculcated well the worthiness of labor, place the Negro in agriculture where he belonged, and the black "army of vagrants" would
melt away. Black agricultural serfdom, in other words, was the
answer.[32] Another suggestion called for worldwide racial segregation
and, in the United States, a separate Negro state.[33] More original
was the idea that all blacks below a "certain grade of citizenship" be
"enlisted" into an agricultural-industrial army by each of the states.
Maintained by the several states, these armies would be trained for
the good of the nation as a whole. The individual Negro recruit
would be "graduated" into the larger society only when he was "fitted to take his place in the community."[34] Such suggestions, especially the latter, not only demonstrate the pervasiveness of white
American racism but open to question the bases of American reform
thought.

Such suggestions—these are but a sampling—obviously could
not have been offered if the Negro's disabilities had not had legal
sanction. In spite of constitutional guarantees, the Negro was legally
inferior, as demonstrated by the fact that twenty-eight states in 1913

had laws against interracial marriage, while six states prohibited
intermarriage in their constitutions.[35]

The powerful hold of racism grasped even the intellectual community of the nation. It held sway there well into the first decade of
the twentieth century, Thomas Gossett notes in his study of race in
America, largely because alternatives were not available. "If racism
did not explain why one race was bold and adventurous and another
was submissive and sedentary," he writes rhetorically in discussing
the lack of other theories, "what did explain it?"[36]

With the rise of cultural anthropology, however, the needed
alternative to race theory was provided, and the study of culture and
society was shifted away from racial channels. One man is eminently
important here, anthropologist Franz Boas. Boas had worked for
some years on the premise that social processess, not biology, explained cultural differences. His arguments, summed up in *The
Mind of Primitive Man* (1911), demonstrated that race was irrele-
vant in a cultural context. Culture was not a function of biological
heredity.[37]

Of course racists' arguments did not simply crumble before
Boas's logic. In fact they continued on strongly and were given a re-
juvenating shot in the arm by the massive intelligence testing conducted by the U.S. Army during World War I.[38] Experimental testing to identify racial differences had been going on continuously
since the latter years of the nineteenth century.[39] This widespread
testing provided just the evidence of hereditary racial differences
needed to bolster the scientific racists' position. But these arguments
failed too and fell from respectability under Boas's attacks during
the 1920s.[40]

At the same time that the discipline of anthropology under
Boas's leadership was conducting its campaigns against racism,
Robert Ezra Park was leading the discipline of sociology away from
the practice of seeing race relations in terms of race differences. The
racial framework that served such noted liberals as sociologist E. A.
Ross during the late nineteenth and early twentieth centuries was
soon to be replaced by one based on class distinctions and conflicts.[41] In a short time the combined assault of the two disciplines
dealt heavy blows to racism within the scholarly community. By
1930, a survey of "'competent scholars in the field of racial differ-

ences' revealed that only 4 per cent of the respondents believed in race superiority and inferiority."[42]

But clearly there was a marked distinction between racial thought in the scholarly community and in the ordinary one, just as there was between the race theorizing of the biologist and "scientific" racism.[43] In the first year of President Wilson's administration the color line in America was termed by one sociologist a "comprehensive designation" of the inevitable separation of two racially distinct groups. The Negro's disabilities were being further institutionalized. Jim Crow had been given the sanction of the Supreme Court in 1896 in *Plessy* v. *Ferguson*, and separation of the races spread widely in federal facilities during the years of the Wilson administration.[44]

There were a number of reasons for the increased strain in race relations—for the "Gathering Clouds Along the Color Line," as Ray Stannard Baker expressed it.[45] Some of the reasons were products of the national "overconsciousness" of the problems of race. The reported remarks of a white jurist at a 1917 meeting of the Alabama Sociological Congress are suggestive here:

> From the top of his bone head to the bottom of his flat foot, there isn't a chance to educate a Negro. God almighty made them to hew wood and draw water and I'm opposed to educating them. Booker Washington has done more harm in Alabama than tuberculosis.
>
> There's just as much difference in human nature and Negro nature as there is between the smell of Limberger [*sic*] cheese and a bunch of roses. I believe in keeping him on the farm.[46]

Other reasons, however, were the by-products of the very sources of a rising optimism in the black community, for, paradoxically, these were the same years that provided a boost to Negro hopes that they would be shed of at least the worst of the many disabilities they were forced to carry.

Before the outbreak of war in Europe in 1914, the northward migration of the Negro was barely a trickle. With European emigration cut off by the war, opportunities opened up to the huge pool of black labor struggling in the South—opportunities not just for more jobs but for better jobs. New horizons opened up as Negroes now flooded north, horizons that were made even brighter when America itself entered World War I. The black man's contribution to the war effort was not always welcomed, but it was accepted. Fundamental changes seemed the promise of the future. Carl Sandburg observed at the time:

> Walk around this district [Chicago's Negro district] and talk with the black folk and leaders of the black folk. Ask them, "What about the future of the colored people?" The reply that comes most often and the thought that seems uppermost is: "We make the supreme sacrifice; they didn't need any work or fight law for us; our record, like Old Glory, the flag we love because it stands for our freedom, hasn't got a spot on it; we 'come clean'; now we want to see our country live up to the constitution and declaration of independence."
>
> Soldiers, ministers, lawyers, doctors, politicians, machinists, teamsters, day laborers—this is the inevitable outstanding thought they offer when consulted about tomorrow, next week, next year, or the next century for the colored race in America. [47]

A scattering of small victories won in northern courts under state civil-rights statutes helped sustain such hopes as these during these years. There were even two rather substantial victories for black America in Supreme Court decisions that knocked down a residential segregation ordinance and the infamous grandfather clause. [48]

The hopes turned to dust in the mouths of black Americans, however. Banjo, a character created by poet and novelist Claude McKay, expressed well the wave of disappointment that struck soon after victory had been won in Europe.

> "When I enlisted in the Army during the war," said Banjo, "mah best buddy said I was a fool nigger. He said the white man nevah would ketch him toting his gun unless it was to rid the wul' of all the crackers, and I done told him back that the hullabaloo was to make the wul' safe foh democracy and there

wouldn't be no crackers when the war was 'ovah and ended,' as
was done said by President Wilson, as crackers didn't belong
in democracy. But mah buddy said to me I had a screw loose,
for President Wilson wasn't moh'n a cracker. He was bohn one
and he guineta live and die one, and that a cracker and a
Democrat was one and the same thing. And mah buddy was
sure right. For according to my eyesight, and Ise one sure-
seeing nigger, the wul' safe for democracy is a wul' safe foh
crackerism."[49]

Real race war threatened in the spring and summer of the year
after the war ended. In a *Crisis* editorial that stirred racist America,
W. E. B. DuBois proclaimed that America was the black American's "fatherland." "But by the God of Heaven, we are cowards
and jackasses if now that the war is over, we do not marshal every
ounce of our brain and brawn to fight a sterner, longer, more un-
bending battle against the forces of hell in our own land."[50] These
were troubling words to a nation running close to panic. Violent
strikes and rumors of radical revolution were sweeping the country.
Race riots erupted in Washington, D.C., Chicago, Knoxville,
Omaha, and Elaine, Arkansas. To the members of white middle-
class America who had led the "search for order," these clashes ap-
peared, in Walter Lippmann's words, "a by-product of our planless,
disordered, bedraggled, drifting democracy. . . . We shall have to
work out with the Negro a relationship which gives him complete
access to all the machinery of our common civilization, and yet
allows him to live so that no Negro need dream of a white heaven and
of bleached angels."[51]

To black America the causes of these racial clashes were ever
apparent and everywhere the same regardless of the triggering incident. "Scratch the surface of public opinion in Washington," wrote
Herbert J. Seligman of the National Association for the Advancement of Colored People (NAACP), "and you found beneath the talk
of assaults upon women and of 'crime waves,' a determination to put
the Negro back where he was before the war. White workmen would
tell you that Negroes were getting too high wages and were becoming
'independent,' i.e., were no longer as servile as the southern white
man wished."[52]

Race relations dipped to a nadir at the end of the war and from it recovered but slowly. The revival of the Ku Klux Klan after the war might be taken as one measure of the interracial climate. In the 1920s the Klan was a city-born phenomenon as well as a rural one—it was an offspring of all of the disruptive forces loose in a nation that had just become more urban than rural. Anti Catholic and anti-Semitic, as well as anti-Negro, the revived Klan was an evanescent organization. Nevertheless even its momentary triumphs show that America was still preoccupied with race. In New York, Indiana, Michigan, and New England, it flourished. In some places, North as well as South, it even became a semiofficial organ of government. Because of it, as one historian has noted, the "color line seemed marked more indelibly than before."[53]

Perhaps an even better example of the preoccupation with race that had seized the nation is provided by the city of Johnstown, Pennsylvania, and the so-called Johnstown expulsion. Prompted by a fatal shoot-out between a Negro and police, Johnstown's mayor Joseph Cauffiel in August 1922 issued an order through the local press to the effect that all Negroes (and Mexicans as well) were to depart Johnstown immediately if they had not resided there for at least seven years. The mayor said later that he really only "advised" them to leave, but this was after a wave of indignation had coursed through the national press and the governor had promised state intervention.[54]

There was little change in American race relations during the 1920s; if they did not improve much over the new low they had reached after the war, at least the Negro's disabilities were no more severe. There were an ever-increasing number of interracial councils and committees, and some of the more optimistic saw them as evidence that the color line was not indelible.[55] Yet nothing much changed. There was in fact, as J. Saunders Redding has noted, a deadly sameness to the tenor of American race relations over the whole first half of this century.[56] The public reaction that greeted Mrs. Hoover's entertaining of Mrs. Oscar DePriest (wife of Chicago's first Negro congressman) at quite an ordinary congressional tea in June 1929 highlights that sameness. It was reminiscent of that following Booker Washington's visit to the White House a generation earlier.[57]

Popularizers of racist themes still flourished, the most noted being the formidable Theodore Lathrop Stoddard. He was almost a one-man propaganda agency. Stoddard's favorite theme was that a tide of color would surely wash over the Nordic nations of the world if they did not exercise both caution and vigorous policies toward inferior peoples.[58]

The old stereotypes remained about the same, although they were carried over into the wider-reaching media, as in radio's "Amos 'n' Andy."[59] Not even the white middle class's "discovery" of the Negro in the so-called Negro or Harlem Renaissance of the 1920s brought much change, except perhaps to enhance the "exotic primitive" stereotype.[60]

The Renaissance, which is discussed in greater detail in a later chapter, began gathering momentum after the war. "Can it be," wrote the noted editor and arbiter of everything in America, H. L. Mencken, "that the Republic emerging painfully from the Age of Rotary, comes into a Coon Age? For one, I am not above believing it."[61] The Renaissance gave many Negro artists their chance, but it did not last long. Nor did it reach very far down into the black world. Of the Rennaissance, one of the participants wrote:

> I was there. I had a swell time while it lasted. But I thought it wouldn't last long. . . . For how could a large and enthusiastic number of people be crazy about Negroes forever? But some Harlemites thought the millennium had come. They thought the race problem had at last been solved through Art plus Gladys Bentley [an entertainer who rose to fame]. They were sure the New Negro would lead a new life from then on in green pastures of tolerance created by Countee Cullen, Ethel Waters, Claude McKay, Duke Ellington, Bojangles, and Alain Locke.
>
> I don't know what made any Negroes think that—except that they were mostly intellectuals doing thinking. The ordinary Negroes hadn't heard of the Negro Renaissance. And if they had, it hadn't raised their wages any.[62]

When America tumbled into the Great Depression at the end of the decade, the Negro's position, as Langston Hughes said, had not

changed so much that he had more than a peg or two to fall.[63] The
depression hit the Negro first (effectively starting back in the mid-
1920s) and the hardest.[64] For those at the bottom of the heap, the
crush was almost unbelievable. The black community everywhere
took on a haunting look of desperation. And while the depression
was a most potent force in melding racial consciousness with class
consciousness, black America was hard pressed to think in the latter
terms at times. "Look Out, Brown Man!" said novelist Sherwood
Anderson. These are tough times and second-rate whites are edgy.
Hide behind your mask again, because "the fellow who has to look
out now is the Negroes' Negro."[65] Police nightsticks and black heads
automatically equaled "red agitation."[66] "The pattern for the ghetto
was set," S. P. Fullinwider writes; "desperation checked by police
power. The law became the enemy." The depression reinforced the
ordinary Negro's reading of white America: it was a rather hopeless
society for the black American to aspire to join.[67]

Obviously, then, there had been significant changes in both
white and black America over these years. The white search for
order had not been entirely futile, and the changes reflected into the
black community reshaped it as well. But the significance of the
changes for the nation as a whole remained hidden under the
blanket of sameness spread by America's racial climate of the times.
The sense of community that developed in the black urban centers of
the North would not become visible for another decade or more.
Only then would the significance of the period become apparent.

NOTES

[1]"Tell Me," by Langston Hughes, in *Montage of a Dream Deferred* (Henry Holt, 1951), 15.

[2]*Crisis* 13 (November 1916): 25.

[3]Lynn Adelman, "A Study of James Weldon Johnson," *JNH* 52 (April 1967): 128; Robert Hayden in the preface to Alain Locke, ed., *The New Negro* (1925; reprint ed., Atheneum, 1969), ix; C. Vann Woodward, *Origins of the New South, 1877-1913* (Louisiana State University Press, 1951), 363-366. See also, Thomas Gossett, *Race: The History of an Idea in America* (Schocken Books, 1965), chaps. 4-16.

[4]Robert Wiebe, *The Search for Order, 1877-1920* (Hill and Wang, 1967), 111-112. "The new middle class," as Wiebe notes, "was a class only by courtesy of the historian's afterthought" in many respects. The expression is used to denote the loose collection of professional and business aspirants who saw in the forces disrupting traditional America not only opportunities to enhance their social standing but the chance to apply their skills to the shaping of the new America. Ibid., 112. See also John D. Buenker, "The Progressive Era: A Search for a Synthesis," *Mid-America* 51 (July 1969): 175-193.

[5]The Social Gospel movement was perhaps too special and limited a movement to justify this generalization entirely. Its spokesmen, however, gave good voice to the ideas and ideals being transformed.

[6]Curtis Robert Grant, "The Social Gospel and Race" (Ph.D. dissertation, Stanford University, 1968), 154.

[7]Ibid., 1-2, 20-21, 23; Gossett, *Race*, 177, 197; Bernard Magubane, "The American Negro's Conception of Africa: A Study in the Ideology of Pride and Prejudice" (Ph.D. diss., University of California, Los Angeles, 1967), 95-96.

[8]Grant, "Social Gospel and Race," 89-90. Grant notes that acceptance of Lamarckian theories concerning the inheritance of acquired traits was widespread among American social scientists and intellectuals until well into the twentieth century. Ibid., 23. See also Ralph Henry Gabriel, *The Course of American Democratic Thought*, 2d ed. (Ronald Press Company, 1956), 368-369; Gossett, *Race*, 197.

[9]Eric F. Goldman, *Rendezvous with Destiny: A History of Modern American Reform*, rev. ed., abridged (Vintage Books, 1956), passim.

[10]Wiebe, *Search for Order, 13-14, 112-113.*

[11]Gilbert Osofsky, "Progressivism and the Negro: New York, 1900-1915," *American Quarterly* 16 (Summer 1964): 153; Dewey W. Grantham, Jr.,

"The Progressive Movement and the Negro," *South Atlantic Quarterly* 54 (1955): 461-477; Carl Resek, ed., *The Progressives* (Bobbs-Merrill, 1967), xii; August Meier, "Negro Class Structure and Ideology in the Age of Booker T. Washington," *Phylon* 23 (Fall 1962): 259; Richard Hofstadter, *The Age of Reform* (Vintage Books, 1955), chaps. 5-6; Arthur S. Link, "What Happened to the Progressive Movement in the 1920's?" *American Historical Review* 64 (July 1959): 845ff.

[12]Wiebe, *Search for Order*, 58-59; Goldman, *Rendezvous with Destiny*, 96-97.

[13]Woodward, *Origins of the New South*, 209. See also Robert Starobin, "The Negro: A Central Theme in American History," *Journal of Contemporary History* 3 (April 1968): 51-53; Arnold A. Sio, "Interpretations of Slavery: The Slave Status in the Americas," in Allen Weinstein and Frank Otto Gatell, eds., *American Negro Slavery* (Oxford University Press, 1968), 331 n.79; Edward G. Olsen, "Racism, a Modern Invention," *Journal of Human Relations* 17 (Summer 1969): 173-184; Dante A. Puzzo, "Racism and the Western Tradition," *Journal of the History of Ideas* 25 (October-December 1964): 578-586; C. Vann Woodward, *The Strange Career of Jim Crow*, 2d ed., rev. (Oxford University Press, 1966), 6-7, 52-56, 59, and chap. 30.

A syllabus of racial thought and racism in America is provided by Winthrop D. Jordan, *White over Black: American Attitudes Toward the Negro, 1550-1812* (Baltimore: Penguin Books, 1969); Leon F. Litwack, *North of Slavery: The Negro in the Free States, 1790-1860* (University of Chicago Press, 1961); I. A. Newby, *Jim Crow's Defense: Anti-Negro Thought in America, 1900-1930* (Louisiana State University Press, 1965); and Gossett, *Race.*

[14]See, for instance, St. Clair Drake and Horace R. Cayton, *Black Metropolis: A Study of Negro Life in a Northern City* (1945; revised ed., Harper Torchbook edition, 1962; originally published 1945), 51; Gilbert Osofsky, *Harlem: The Making of a Ghetto: Negro New York, 1890-1930* (Harper & Row, 1963), 37; Elliot Rudwick, "Black Metropolis—The Making of the Ghetto, A Review Essay," *Wisconsin Magazine of History* 51 (Spring 1968): 245.

[15]Arnold Rose, *The Negro's Morale: Group Identification and Protest* (University of Minnesota Press, 1949), 32. See also Gosset, *Race,* 265.

[16]Otto H. Olsen, "Albion W. Tourgee and Negro Militants of the 1890s," *Science and Society* 28 (Spring 1964): 183-208. Olsen notes that the organization drew surprisingly little support from Negroes in the North, probably because of the growing potency of accommodationist philosophy. Ibid., 187-188. See also, Emma Lou Thornbrough, "The National Afro-American

League, 1877-1908," *Journal of Southern History* 27 (November 1961): 494-512.

[17]These brief comments do not do justice to Woodward's thesis, of course. See also, Gossett, *Race*, 174; Grant, "Social Gospel and Race," 1-2.

[18]Charles H. Smith, "Have American Negroes Too Much Liberty?" *Forum* 16 (October 1893): 182. There were many such racist tracts for the times. See, for instance, John T. Morgan, "Shall Negro Majorities Rule," *Forum* 6 (February 1889): 586-599; Alice Bodington, "The Importance of Race and Its Bearing on the 'Negro Question,' " *Westminster Review* 134 (December 1890): 415, 427. For an outline of the idea of Negro inferiority as it grew up and was applied in the South, see James Wilfred Zanden, "The Ideology of White Supremacy," *Journal of the History of Ideas* 20 (July-September 1958): 385-402.

[19]See, for instance, S. P. Fullinwider, *Mind and Mood of Black America* (Dorsey Press, 1969), 13; Woodward, *Origins of the New South*, 332-349, and *Strange Career of Jim Crow*, chap. 3; E. Franklin Frazier, *Black Bourgeoisie* (Free Press, 1957), 120-122; John Hope Franklin, *From Slavery to Freedom: A History of American Negroes,* 3d ed., (1966; reprint ed., Vintage Books, 1969; 1st ed. published 1947), 335-338; "Phases of the Negro Problem," *Nation* 69 (August 31, 1899): 163-164.

[20]Woodward, *Origins of the New South*, 355-356; Gossett, *Race*, 266; Frazier, *Black Bourgeoisie*, 22, 123. It would not be very fruitful to enter into a discussion here of just how tolerable or intolerable conditions might actually have been for the Negro in the South during these years. Woodward, for instance, evidently reconsidered his earlier estimates of conditions,

[21]Republican and Democratic national policy are not directly relevant to this discussion. See Stanley P. Hirshon, *Farewell to the Bloody Shirt: Northern Republicans and the Southern Negro, 1877-1893* (Chicago: Quadrangle Books, 1968); August Meier, "The Negro and the Democratic Party, 1875-1915," *Phylon* 17 (Second Quarter 1956): 173-191; Woodward, *Origins of the New South*, 270ff.

[22]Goldman, *Rendezvous with Destiny*, 137; *Crisis* 17 (February 1919): 181. The change in the interracial climate in these years is also indicated by the fact that when President Cleveland had Frederick Douglass (and his white wife) to the White House on several occasions, no particular notice was taken. Goldman, *Rendezvous with Destiny*, 137. There seems to have been perennial interest in Washington's White House visit. An article in *Harper's* several years later noted, for instance, that perhaps Thomas Jefferson did sit down at his dining table with a Negro in 1815, but it was as a private citizen and in no way set any precedence for Roosevelt's faux pas in

this affair. "Recent Comments on the Negro Problem," *Harper's Weekly*, 48 (June 11, 1904): 892-893.

[23]For an example see "Color Prejudice," *Nation* 49 (July 11, 1889): 26-27.

[24]"Recent Views on the Negro Problem," *Harper's Weekly* 48 (February 27, 1904): 312-313.

[25]"Mr. Washington and the Negro Problem," *Harper's Weekly* 47 (August 15, 1903): 1324-1325.

[26]Rev. Atticus G. Haygood, *Our Brothers in Black*, cited by Kelley Miller, "The Attitude of the Intellectual Negro Toward Lynching," *Voice of the Negro* 2 (May 1905): 308; Thomas Dixon, Jr., *The Leopard's Spots: A Romance of the White Man's Burden* (A. Wessells, 1906 [c. 1902]), *The Clansman: An Historical Romance of the KuKlux Klan* (Doubleday, 1905), and *The Traitor: A Story of the Fall of the Invisible Empire* (Grossett and Dunlap, 1907); William B. Smith, *The Color Line* (1905; reprint ed., Negro Universities Press, 1969); Charles Carroll, *"The Negro a Beast" or, "In the Image of God"* (St. Louis: American Book and Bible House, 1900). See also Woodward, *Origins of the New South*, 352; Frazier, *Black Bourgeoisie*, 122-123; Maxwell Bloomfield, "Dixon's *The Leopard's Spots:* A Study in Popular Racism," *American Quarterly* 16 (Fall 1964): 387.

[27]Bloomfield, "Dixon's *The Leopard's Spots*," p. 392.

[28]Ibid., 399-400. Herbert Shapiro, "The Muckrakers and Negroes," *Phylon* 21 (Spring 1970): 76-88. See also Arthur and Lila Weinberg, eds., *The Muckrakers: The Era in Journalism that Moved America to Reform* (Capricorn Books, 1964).

[29]E. Franklin Frazier, "The Pathology of Race Prejudice," *Forum* 77 (June 1927): 856-862. Frazier speaks here in terms of "dissociation of consciousness" about attitudes toward the Negro.

[30]Walter Winston Kenilworth, "Negro Influence in American Life," *Forum* 46 (August 1911): 169-178. A list of supposed Negro racial characteristics may be found here.

[31]W. E. B. DuBois, *Darkwater: Voices from within the Veil* (1920; reprint ed., Schocken Books, 1969) 116, 95-96. See also, Ray Stannard Baker, *Following the Color Line: American Negro Citizenship in the Progressive Era* (1908; reprint ed., Harper Torchbooks, 1964) 117-118.

[32]William Dorsey Jelks, "The Acuteness of the Negro Question: A Suggested Remedy," *North American Review* 184 (February 15, 1907): 389-395.

[33]"The Science of Race Hatred," *Nation* 89 (July 8, 1909): 26-27. The article took cognizance of two recent offerings in other periodicals, the second suggesting amalgamation of the races.

[34]Charlotte Perkins Gilman, "A Suggestion on the Negro Problem," *AJS* 14 (July 1908): 78-85. The author of this article, it might be noted, was a leading feminist who published widely and was much in demand as a lecturer during the first two decades of this century.

[35]Albert E. Jenks, "The Legal Status of Negro-White Amalgamation in the United States," *AJS* 21 (March 1916): 666-678; Gilbert Thomas Stephenson, *Race Distinctions in American Law* (D. Appleton and Co., 1910), passim.

[36]Gossett, *Race*, 414.

[37]Fullinwider, *Mind and Mood of Black America*, 60-61; Goldman, *Rendevous with Destiny*, 97-98; Gossett, *Race*, 416, 418-424; Grant, "Social Gospel and Race," 27-28.

[38]Gossett, *Race*, 373-374; Newby, *Jim Crow's Defense*, 40-42.

[39]Otto Klineberg, "Tests of Negro Intelligence," Research memorandum, Carnegie-Myrdal Study, 6-7. Used in the preparation of Gunnar Myrdal, *American Dilemma*, 20th anniversary ed. (Harper & Row, 1962).

[40]See, for instance, Franz Boas, "The Problem of the American Negro," *Yale Review* 10 (January 1921): 384-395, and Fallacies of Racial Inferiority," *Current History and Forum* 25 (February 1927): 676-682. See also Gossett, *Race*, 418, 429-430. Gossett states that "the racists of the 1920's rightly recognized Boas as their chief antagonist . . . . It is possible that Boas did more to combat race prejudice than any other person in history." Ibid., 418.

[41]Fullinwider, *Mind and Mood of Black America* 101; Gossett, *Race*, 168-172; E. Franklin Frazier, "Sociological Theory and Race Relations," *ASR* 12 (June 1947): 269-270.

[42]Myrdal, *An American Dilemma*, 148; Gossett, *Race*, 424. Although now rather dated, some brief outlines of the history of the investigation of race and racial differences are: Charles S. Johnson and Horace M. Bond, "The Investigation of Racial Differences Prior to 1910," *JNE* 3 (July 1934): 328-339; E. B. Reuter, "Racial Theory," *AJS* 50 (May 1945): 452-461; Charles H. Wesley, "The Concept of Negro Inferiority in American Thought," *JNH* 25 (October 1940): 540-560.

[43]Racism and racial theorizing often met, of course, but only racism attempted value judgments. See Grant, "Social Gospel and Race," 4-5.

[44]John M. Mecklin, "The Philosophy of the Color Line," *AJS* 19 (November 1913): 343-357.

[45]Ray Stannard Baker, "Gathering Clouds Along the Color Line," *World's Work* 32 (May 1916): 232-236.

[46]Reported in *Crisis* 14 (May 1917): 25.

[47]Carl Sandburg, *The Chicago Race Riots, July, 1919* (1919; reprint ed., Harcourt, Brace and World, 1969) 9. This small volume is a pastiche of

Chicago's South Side, written first as a series of articles for the *Chicago Daily News* and published over a two-week period before the riots.

[48]See, for instance, William H. Baldwin, Jr., "Unconstitutional Segregation," *New Republic* 13 (January 19, 1918): 345-346. See also Franklin, *From Slavery to Freedom,* 447.

[49]Claude McKay, *Banjo, A Story Without a Plot* (1929; reprint ed., Harcourt Brace Jovanovich, 1970), 193-194.

[50]*Crisis* 18 (May 1919): 14.

[51]Walter Lippmann, in introduction to Sandburg, *Chicago Race Riots,* xix, xx.

[52]Herbert J. Seligman, "Race War?" *New Republic* 20 (August 13, 1919): 49. See also "Our Own Race War," *North American Review* 210 (October 1919): 436-438. For conditions after the war and the genesis of the Red Scare that so agitated the country, see almost any history of the period. Frederick Lewis Allen's little classic, *Only Yesterday: An Informal History of the 1920's* (1931; Perennial Library ed., Harper & Row, 1964), conveys some of the intense emotions loose in the land in these days. "Bolshevism" was seen everywhere and there was nothing worse than a red black. See, for instance, New York (State) Legislature (Lusk Committee Report), "Propaganda Among Negroes," in *Report of the Joint Legislative Committee Investigating Seditious Activities* (Albany: J. B. Lyon Co., 1920), pt. 1, vol. 2, 1476-1520.

[53]Emma Lou Thornbrough, "Segregation in Indiana During the Klan Era of the 1920's," *JAH* 47 (March 1961): 609. See also Franklin, *From Slavery to Freedom,* 479-480; Kenneth T. Jackson, *The Ku Klux Klan in the City, 1915-1930* (Oxford University Press, 1967), pt. 3.

[54]See "Johnstown's Flood of Negro Labor," *Literary Digest* 79 (October 6, 1923): 18, for a review of press reaction to Mayor Cauffiel's order. See also *Crisis* 27 (November 1923): 27; Roger B. Sherman, "Johnstown v. the Negro: Southern Migrants and the Exodus of 1923," *Pennsylvania History* 30 (October 1963): 454-464.

[55]Oswald Garrison Villard, "The Crumbling Color Line," *Harper's Magazine* 159 (July 1929): 156-157.

[56]Jay Saunders Redding, *On Being Negro in America* (1951; reprint ed., Bobbs-Merrill Co., 1962), 45-50.

[57]Melville J. Herskovits, "Race Relations," *AJS* 35 (May 1930): 1052-1062. For a medley of reaction, North and South, see *Crisis* 36 (September 1929): 298-299, 317-320.

[58]Gossett, *Race,* 390-398.

[59]It is difficult for today's generation to imagine the popularity of this program. Erik Barnouw writes in his history of radio broadcasting, that Amos 'n'

Andy "became, according to some estimates, the consuming delight of forty million people. It would influence dinner hours across the nation. It would involve the attention of Presidents. And it would pose a racial issue." Erik Barnouw, *A History of Broadcasting in the United States*, vol. 1: *A Tower of Babel* (Oxford University Press, 1966), 225. See also Allen, *Only Yesterday*, 293.

[60]Gilbert Osofsky, "Symbols of the Jazz Age: The New Negro and Harlem Discovered," *American Quarterly* 17 (Summer 1965): 234-235.

[61]H.L. Mencken, *American Mercury* 12 (October 1927): 159.

[62]Langston Hughes, *The Big Sea* (Hill and Wang, 1963), 228.

[63]Ibid., 247.

[64]Franklin, *From Slavery to Freedom*, 496; Ruth G. Bergman, "The Negro's Livelihood," *Survey* 65 (October 1930): 80-82; Charles S. Johnson, "Incidence upon the Negro," *AJS* 40 (May 1935): 737-745; "Negroes Out of Work," *Nation* 132 (April 22, 1931): 441-442; E. Franklin Frazier, "Some Effects of the Depression on the Negro in Northern Cities," *Science and Society* 2 (Fall 1938): 489-499.

[65]Sherwood Anderson, "Look Out, Brown Man!" *Nation* 131 (November 26, 1930): 580.

[66]Horace R. Cayton, "The Black Bugs," *Nation* 133 (September 9, 1931): 255-256. For "black bugs" read "red blacks."

[67]Fullinwider, *Mind and Mood of Black America*, 172, 173.

3

THE BLACK URBAN
NORTH, 1890-1930

Huh!de wurl' ain't flat
An' de wurl' ain't roun',
Jes' one long strip
Hangin' up an' down.
Since Norf is up,
An' Souf is down,
An' Hebben is up,
I'm upward boun'.[1]

I N T H E northern urban centers a color line has separated the Negro from the dominant white society since before the American Revolution. Racial thought in America, it has already been noted, was such that it hardly could have been otherwise. Since Jamestown, W. E. B. DuBois wrote in 1902, white men have entertained "the sincere and passionate belief that somewhere between men and cattle God created a *tertium quid*, and called it a Negro,—a clownish, simple creature, at times even lovable within its limitations, but . . . foreordained to walk within the Veil."[2] Yet it was not until American race relations dipped to an all-time low after the end of Reconstruction that modern black America came into existence. When white America launched its search for a new social order congruent with the emerging urban-industrial realities, it also launched modern black urban America in all of its complexities.

There was, of course, a great deal of variety among the black

urban communities. Each city had its individuality, its own counte-
nance. The larger centers whose black population grew so explosively in the early decades of the twentieth century especially possessed an individual flavor. The substantial number of foreign-born
blacks who had settled in New York by the early 1920s, for example,
helped make Harlem unique among the larger black population centers.[3]

Moreover, each Negro community related differently to the
dominant white community. Interracial harmony or dissonance in
the small city and in the booming black metropolis were played in
different keys. Even day-to-day existence differed. New York provided more diversified occupations than the steel manufacturing
cities of Pennsylvania or the automobile plants of Detroit and also a
greater gradation of skill levels. Where basic industries existed, Negroes usually worked in unintegrated gangs, as in the Pittsburgh
steel mills.[4] This last difference had some important effects when the
southern black migrant changed to city dweller. In 1925, James
Weldon Johnson noted: "A thousand Negroes from Mississippi put
to work as a gang in a Pittsburgh steel mill will for a long time
remain a thousand Negroes from Mississippi. Under the conditions
that prevail in New York they would all within six months become
New Yorkers."[5]

In the communities that mushroomed during the World War I
era and the 1920s the variations were great. The visage that Harlem
presented to the world in the 1920s, for instance, was something
quite different from that displayed to the world by New York's
turbulent San Juan Hill district two decades earlier. Black Chicago
was quite different at any time from the Negro communities in such
cities as Boston or Syracuse. But given these variations, it is the
shared characteristics that are striking and that permit one to regard
them in composite terms.

The most obvious of the shared characteristics is residential
segregation. Physically the black northern community for the most
part offered to the world a rather run-down face. But it was not
alone in this: so did those enclaves occupied by other minority
groups who were on their way to the famous American melting pot.
Throughout the period the northern Negro was forced into
congested and almost invariably segregated sections, blocks, alleys,
or groups of buildings that received little if any attention from the

city fathers when it came to services. "The Czar of all the Russias is not more absolute upon his own soil than the New York landlord in his dealings with colored tenants," wrote police reporter Jacob Riis in 1890. "Where he permits them to live, they go; where he shuts the door, stay out. By his grace they exist at all in certain localities; his ukase banishes them from others."[6] This was a facet of black life in the North that did not change much decade after decade. In Manhattan, for example, distinct Negro sections had existed since at least 1800. Not that residential segregation found any legal sanction in the North. The first concerted efforts along these lines can be dated to a Baltimore segregation ordinance of 1910. When such ordinances failed court tests, the use of private covenants restricting the sale of the covered property became popular across the North.[7]

Most ordinary black New Yorkers at the turn of the century resided in close quarters around Pennsylvania Station and in pockets along with the Irish in the San Juan Hill district. The Negro professional—the musicians, stage people, and the like—resided in a pocket on West Fifty-third Street. At the time, the San Juan Hill district, situated between Sixtieth and Sixty-fourth streets, enjoyed a reputation only slightly less unsavory than that of the neighboring Hell's Kitchen district to the south.[8]

One variation of the common model exhibited by New York City was the pattern of residential segregation found in Philadelphia and Washington, D.C. These cities had long had large black populations that provided services to the white community and who facilitated such service by living in close proximity to the families and districts they served. A highly scattered but segregated residential pattern was the result. By the turn of the century, former carriage houses in interior courts and narrow alley residences housed much of the black population. In this respect these cities resembled the urban South more than the urban North, a resemblance that would continue well into the twentieth century. The distinction or variation ends here, however. Physically the worst of these residences jammed into narrow courts, passageways, and minor streets rivaled the worst conditions found in the more famous New York slums described so vividly by Jacob Riis.[9]

Chicago displayed a variation in the pattern of residential segregation as well. A black belt across the South Side of the city—the district that would become Chicago's famous Bronzeville—was already emerging before the Civil War according to one historian of the black North.[10] Several other scattered enclaves still existed in 1900 to give a picture of a dispersal of Negroes throughout the city, but a black city-within-a-city was already emerging. By 1906 Chicago was termed the most segregated city in the North, with more than nine-tenths of the black population living on the South Side.[11]

Variations on the pattern of residential segregation were found everywhere. Toledo, for example, although it had a smaller black population than other industrial cities of its size in the late 1920s, had eight scattered Negro districts, each associated with an industrial area.[12] (The maps that are found in T.J. Woofter, Jr.'s *Negro Problems in Cities* [1928] graphically depict the variations.)[13] The exact pattern in each instance was determined by more than just ubiquitous racial discrimination, although, as Myrdal noted, lacking the South's laws and racial etiquette as a means of separation, "institutional segregation in the North often [had] only residential segregation to rest upon."[14] The distribution of businesses and manufacturing sections, the kinds of industry in the community, the distribution of the property that the Negro could afford to occupy, and the number of Negroes in the population played key roles.

Cities across the urban North took on a new look of sameness when the trickle of black migrants from the South became a flood in the second decade of this century. This was most obvious in New York and Chicago where the black cities of Harlem and Bronzeville exploded into being. One contemporary observer, the Reverend Rollin Hartt, noted: "Everywhere huge churches and synagogues surrendered by whites, ring with Negro 'amens.' Sometimes whole avenues of suburban mansions turn black. In Chicago, Washington Park becomes 'Booker T. Washington Park,' and the South State Street car line 'the African Central.'"[15]

Everywhere housing for the Negro became a critical problem, as an already limited number of housing units strained against the artificial limits imposed by residential separation. "[A] great dark tide from the South" washed upon the city, poet Langston Hughes wrote of the Cleveland of his youth, and "Sheds and garages and store fronts were turned into living quarters. As always, the white neighborhoods resented Negroes moving closer and closer—but when the whites did give way, they gave way at very profitable rentals."[16]

Everywhere residential segregation became more pronounced. Using ward and census tract data over a period of several decades, sociologists Karl and Alma Taeuber constructed indexes indicating the degree of black-white separation for ten northern cities. They found that the index of separation in Cleveland, for example, rose from 60.6 in 1910 to 70.1 in 1920 and to 85.0 in 1930. Other cities showed comparable changes: Buffalo had an index of 62.6 in 1910, 71.5 in 1920, and 80.5 in 1930; Chicago 66.8 in 1910, 75.7 in 1920, and 85.2 in 1930; and Syracuse, 64.0 in 1910, 65.2 in 1920, and 86.7 in 1930.[17]

Across the North black urban slums expanded—or rather, slums changed color from white to black. Where whites and blacks shared a residential district, it often became a wide open section of town that earned such appellations as "The Bad Lands," as in Columbus, Ohio.[18] In some cases the industrial North provided instant slums for black workers who were imported from the South. In his novel dealing with the Negro worker and the Great Migration, William Attaway describes the living conditions that greeted the workers brought north to labor in the Pennsylvania steel mills.[19] It is a striking narrative that finds vivid confirmation in an article by W. E. B. DuBois in 1923. "One has but to review the housing offered Negroes in the employ of the companies of the newest steel merger: well-bred pigs ought not to be housed as colored workers are housed in and around Coatesville, Pa., by the Midvale, Bethlehem and other steel companies."[20]

Obviously the black North was not one continuous slum. Jacob Riis noted in 1890, for example, that "there is no more clean and orderly community in New York than the new settlement of colored people that is growing up on the East Side from Yorkville to Harlem."[21] Certainly Harlem was far from a slum area as Negroes moved into building after building north of 130th Street in the early years of the twentieth century. Not alley dwellings but "new-law" apartment buildings greeted the Negro. "Elevator Apartments the Latest in Harlem," the *New York Age* noted in mid-1912. "Prospective Tenants Will Be Compelled to Give References Before Allowed to Occupy Apartments."[22] Harlem by the mid-1920s had become the

black capital of the nation, a king-size example of the many little social worlds that had come into being in the North.[23]

The black communities across the North are distinctly American subcommunities.[24] Harlem, for instance, is not, as anthropologist Melville Herskovits once argued, "to all intents and purposes an
American community peopled by individuals who have an additional
amount of pigmentation in their skins."[25] Nor is the American Negro, as Nathan Glazer and Daniel Moynihan more recently argue,
"only an American, and nothing else."[26] The shaping force of the
general American culture upon the black American minority is certainly apparent. What is overlooked in such assertions as those
above is the different nature of the influence when coupled with
American racism. The injection of ideas of black inferiority, for
example, mutates ordinary cultural influences into singularly powerful shaping forces that the black American must learn to cope with
from childhood. A cultural difference is created that has meaning in
the *conscious existence* of Negro Americans and that is internalized
early in life because of its very pervasiveness. In other words, being
black in America affects the very way one looks at reality. The black
American, as Robert Bone has observed, is forced to "structure his
life in terms of a culture to which he is denied full access. He is at
once a part of and apart from the wider community in which he
lives."[27]

To be black in America, Richard Wright says in one of his more
noted short stories, means to be apart, to think differently, to be of
another world.

> Saul Sanders was born black in a little Southern town, not
> many miles from Washington, the nation's capital, which
> means that he came into a world that was split in two, a white
> world and a black one, the white one being separated from the
> black by a million psychological miles. So, from the very
> beginning, Saul looked timidly out from his black world, saw
> the shadowy outline of a white world that was unreal to him
> and not his own.[28]

Saul was an American—but different. What separated him and
other black Americans from the larger society was the color line,

that ubiquitous yet strangely intangible line that gained so much of its definition during the last years of the nineteenth century. It is a castelike line, although the validity of calling it such has been periodically questioned. Here, borrowing from Adelaide Hill's 1952 study, "The Negro Upper Class in Boston," *caste* means simply "that group of persons historically deprived of social, political and economic equality by virtue of membership in a specific racial group, the basis for its recognition . . . [being] primarily pigmentation."[29]

The term *caste* was in literary use in this connotation before the Civil War.[30] It gained popular currency as a result of sociologist W. Lloyd Warner's pioneering studies of social class in America in the early twentieth century. Yet others soon argued that the term bred mere confusion with reference to race relations in America. Nothing was to be gained by trying to make race relations analogous to caste relations they said. Several of the better arguments offer that it is more profitable to see these as class exploitations rather than caste relations.[31] Yet a recent reexamination of the class structure in a community studied in one of the Warner-directed investigations of class in America in the 1930s showed again a dual social system, one on each side of a color line.[32] Certainly, observes psychologist Gordon Allport, "The Negro in America is socially a better example of caste than he is of race."[33] But perhaps today the use of the label *caste* is only a matter of "semantic preference." Nevertheless, it does usefully dramatize the "two-ness" of the American social structure.[34]

The intensity of the caste differentiations—the social and economic, the political and religious, the recreational and legal differentiations, to name a few—varied with time and place. The color line was wavy here and there, and where ill defined, its customs were not consistent.[35] But that a color line existed and that it affected their daily lives, all black Americans could attest to. Daily the color line served to focus the Afro-American's attention on—to make him more conscious of—the cultural *difference* the dominant society's attitudes created.[36]

It was just this consciousness of difference that went to work in the black urban centers to create the modern black America. Shut out of white American considerations by the turn to extreme racism the Negro American minority started more and more to "think black." Obviously the context here is relative. Thinking black did not suddenly happen on a particular date any more than extreme racism was inaugurated by white America along with President Hayes or adopted with the first defeat of presidential candidate William Jennings Bryan. Rather, both evolved to stand full upon the scene in the 1890s. The Negro in America, in the words of Charles S. Johnson, found "his relation to the American culture . . . conditioned vigorously by his historical role in it."[37]

Continually isolated, but now more rigorously than before, black America developed a "universe of discourse," as sociologist Samuel Strong puts it.[38] This communion served to define the Negro community to itself and make clearer its relationship with the white world across the color line. And this sense of communion, this consciousness of the cultural difference, grew within the Negro minority as their numbers grew within the northern urban centers. But obviously a community or subcommunity does not depend upon numbers. Nor does it have to be, as Milton Gordon asserts, "a place on the map of the city . . . . It is rather a social construct in the minds of the city's residents. But it is no less real for that."[39] Neither is the subcommunity some kind of an underworld. It is a very real world, as W. E. B. DuBois so poignantly observed:

> When a white person comes . . . to realize the disabilities under which a negro labors, . . . the question comes, How can they stand it? The answer is clear and peculiar: They do not stand it; they withdraw themselves as far as possible from it into a community of their own. They live and move in a community of their own kith and kin and shrink quickly and permanently from those rough edges where contact with the larger life of the city wounds and humiliates them . . . . Contact with the whites is practically confined to economic relationships, the streets, and street cars, with occasionally some intercourse at public amusements.[40]

White America, for its part, lumped all in the black community together into a single group. Myrdal notes in his famous study that "Southern whites . . . often refuse to recognize class differences in the Negro community and insist upon distinguishing only between 'bad niggers,' 'good niggers,' and 'uppity niggers,' and that they, until recently, have succeeded in retaining a legal and political system which corresponds most closely to this view."[41] The viewpoint was not peculiar to the South, however, but common in this period. Negroes in the upper ranks, it was noted by James Weldon Johnson in his famous novel *The Autobiography of an Ex-Coloured Man*, had good reason for maintaining social distance within the black community; they knew only too well that the "good-for-nothing darkies" end up representing the whole Negro race.[42] "The world classes them [the "upper class"] with the mass of their race," wrote DuBois in 1901, "and even in a city like Philadelphia makes but little allowance for their culture or means."[43]

Class divisions in the black community continued to respond to such white attitudes. Black America found that its social distinctions would persistently be shaped, as J. W. Johnson noted, "not so much in respect to themselves as in respect to their relations with the white."[44] That is, white perceptions of the Negro's role determined to a measurable degree the social divisions on the Negro's side of the color line. Hence, those with such visible connections to the sources of white power as governmental clerical positions would remain well situated in the black social hierarchy. The force with which one was thrust into the inferior world of blackness depended upon one's relationship with the larger society. Some, such as the established Negro tailor and the like, remained able to pass back and forth between their incongruent positions in the black and white communities without being too badly scarred by the racial imperatives of either. But for most, the black community was a complete world, and the role of being black assigned by the dominant culture was hardly questioned.

The class structure of the black urban community was a peculiar one, set apart as the community was by a color caste that automatically assigned inferior status to all who fell on the darker side. By the 1920s the broad lines were clearly imitations of the white class structure. But in the 1890s the makeup is rather difficult to define. What divisions did exist in these early years are tenuous and can perhaps best be illustrated by providing a general definition of social classes. They are, in Harold Hodges' useful definition, "the blended product of shared and analogous occupational orientations, educational backgrounds, economic wherewithal, and life experiences."[45] In other words, those factors that may be seen as contributing to a consensus—to a sort of common universe of discourse—are the best guidelines in identifying the class divisions.

Applying this definition, there seems to have been only a single social class in the typical black urban center of the North just prior to the turn of the century. For the most part, to apply the occupational orientations criteria, it was composed of domestics and service workers. It was topped, to consider one aspect of education, earnings, and experience, by only a small elite of "better quality" folk while at the very bottom was a yet smaller group of black outcasts, some living just marginally within the law. Thus, what gave shape to the social structure was the great bulk of rather ordinary people in the middle.

This large group—from 80 to 90 percent of the population—will here be referred to as the "respectables," a term that was of special significance on the black side of the color line. This group had its origins in pre-Civil War America, but, like much in the rest of American society in the turmoil that followed that war, it remained a vague and indefinite grouping of people and varied with time and place. But some generalizations can be made. The origin of the designation *respectable* has been lost, and the term is, obviously, a value-loaded one. Moreover, it has been used by writers defining the Negro social class structure in a number of ways. For instance W.E.B. DuBois used it as a designation for the tiny black aristocracy in his study *The Philadelphia Negro*, while at the same time making respectability a virtue of the better-off working class.[46] Sociologist E. Franklin Frazier saw the changing measures of respectability as delimiting the old elite from the new elite that grew up after the turn of the century.[47] Others saw *respectable* as meaning different things at different social levels within the community.[48]

This last way of looking at respectability (that the term meant different things at various levels) helps to explain much of the rancor between the ordinary Negro mass and the small elite group. The old Negro elite of Boston, Philadelphia, and Washington, D.C., for example, were obsessed with all that the term conveyed at their level: manners, success, "good breeding." In fact to them respectable meant not just proper conduct, but exemplary conduct, superior manners. If their respectability only had been equal to that of their white neighbors, they knew they would not have been considered "respectable"—as circular as the logic may sound.[49]

This superrespectability is somewhat different from the respectability that the large middle group used as a measure. The appellation was not worn as a mantle here but was rather an everyday kind of thing; it was a tacit acknowledgment that a person and his neighbors were doing the best they could in spite of the odds and in spite of individual lapses and shortcomings. For the large middle group it just meant earning a living in an acceptable and more-or-less steady manner, accompanied by an appropriate life-style and public conduct. In this sense it describes the majority of the Chicago Negro community by the time of the first World's Fair in 1893, for instance. Chicago's Bronzeville at that time, according to sociologists St. Clair Drake and Horace Cayton, was composed of a mass of respectables capped by a small class of "refined" people, both groups looking down upon the undisciplined "riff-raff."[50]

Such attitudes continued to be important throughout the period. Richard Wright's Bigger Thomas, a character who in many ways epitomizes all of the worst imaginable qualities in the white stereotypes of the Negro, came from a respectable black home. It was one room and it was rat infested, but it was respectable.[51] The very fact of ubiquitous residential segregation made the criterion of respectability all the more important. As the black North grew, all became more closely jammed together. Most were poor and black: in many cases, respectability was the only differentiating factor within the Negro community.[52]

The term thus has a potent descriptive value, and because the social structure of the black community at this time so little resembled that of the white as it is usually described, the conventional nomenclature (upper, middle, lower class) cannot really be used with as much meaning—not for another decade or so at any rate.

Literature confirms the threefold division sketched to this point as well as providing the generalized guidelines that show membership in one group or another.[53] In his *Autobiography of an Ex-Coloured Man*, James Weldon Johnson saw the outlines of this lopsided structure. The smallest group he defined in this novel set in the

1896-1903 period corresponds to the outcast riff-raff mentioned. It can be pictured as resting at the nether end of a social class continuum. Johnson depicted the riff-raff as displaying a propensity to strike back quickly and violently when the white man's discriminations chafed through their customary indifference.[54]

The largest group Johnson identified extends across the whole middle of the continuum and corresponds to that mass of ordinary black folk that have here been termed the respectables. As domestics and providers of personal services they were in close and continuous physical contact with the white world. Because of this close contact, Johnson said, the group sometimes acted as a buffer between the two worlds.[55]

At the upper end of the social class continuum rested the small group of local elites. They were the businessmen and professionals, the educated, the owners of small service businesses (garages, caterers, and so on). These, said Johnson, were the furtherest removed from the white dominant society that surrounded the whole community, and they had the least contact with it. What is more, since they did not fit into the white conception of the proper role for a Negro, they were scornfully dismissed by whites as "Cullud Sassiety."[56]

Some in this latter group, the old elite or refined class, were related to old white aristocratic families. Others claimed such white lineage. They set themselves apart from the black community and looked forward to acceptance in the larger society—an aspiration that earned them the derisive label of "blue veins" within the black community. "The original Blue Veins," the respected early Negro novelist Charles Chesnutt wrote, "were a little society of colored persons organized in a certain Northern city shortly after the [Civil] war. Its purpose was to establish and maintain correct social standards among people whose social condition presented almost unlimited room for improvement."[57] "I have no race prejudice," says a character in one of Chesnutt's most noted short stories, " . . . but we people of mixed blood are ground between the upper and the nether millstones. Our fate lies between absorption by the white race and extinction in the black. The one doesn't want us yet, but may take us in time. The other would welcome us, but it would be for us a backward step."[58]

Leadership in blue vein circles did not necessarily depend upon light skin color, but it was a measure to be considered along with irreproachable manners, neat somber dress, and impeccable morals.[59] These were for the most part the older settlers in the northern cities; they were, for instance, the "O.P.'s," the Old Philadelphians. "Colored Philadelphia," novelist Jessie Fauset observed in 1924, " . . . is organized as definitely as, and even a little more carefully than, Philadelphia white society. One wasn't 'in' in those old days unless one were first, 'an old citizen,' and, second, unless one were eminently respectable,—almost it might be said God-fearing."[60]

The class structure described here pretty well fits the small northern city as well as the large. In his autobiography, George Schuyler uses essentially these same criteria to describe the class lines of Syracuse, New York, which had a black community of fewer than a thousand at the turn of the century. He, too, notes respectability as a measure.[61] The same makeup was noted by W.E.B. DuBois in a series of articles in the *New York Times* in late 1901, although he depicted four classes stretched along the continuum.[62] The middle group described here he divided into two groups, again on the basis of respectability: the "hard-working, good-natured, . . . honest and faithful, of fair and rapidly improving morals" and the "good-natured but unreliable workman, . . . and in general people poor but not criminal nor grossly immoral." In Philadelphia, he said, these collectively made up some 82 percent of the Negro population. The group at the lower end of the continuum DuBois termed the "submerged Tenth," though with more poetic than arithmetic accuracy, noting that they made up some 6 percent of the black population of that city. The remaining 12 percent (by DuBois's calculations) constituted "an aristocracy of wealth and education."[63] In other articles of the series he painted similar pictures of Boston and New York City.

Black insistence upon respectability as a measure certainly reflects the sharp impact that white attitudes had on values in the Negro community. But by the end of the last decade of the nineteenth century, the old elite was noticeably losing its superior position to a middle class that was being fostered by changes taking place on the white side of the color line. Further, an indication that

respectability as a criterion now declined somewhat points to the reorientation of values that was taking place in black America at the
end of the nineteenth century—to the "turning inward," as it has
been termed here. [64] By itself, of course, even given the import of the
many different connotations of the term along the social class continuum, such a subjective designation of class as respectable would
not be a very effective way of determining class membership. But
stratification within the black community also was in large part
dependent upon occupation, a very functional type of index that
tended to be closely related to respectability. [65] W. E. B. DuBois
neatly packaged this index in several studies made about the turn of
the century.

DuBois, according to Norval Glenn's most useful compilation
of data from a number of studies, essentially assigned upper occupational prestige to any person "not engaged in menial services."
"Teachers, physicians, barbers, tailors, carpenters, shoemakers,
waiters [in white restaurants], ministers, blacksmiths, [and] postal
employees" all fell into this category according to DuBois's 1902
study of Negroes in Athens, Georgia. [66] In the northern centers similar pursuits also were considered to be in the "upper" category, although the spread of occupations was not quite so broad as in the
South. [67] Just how high or how low the individual ranked, of course,
depended upon the status ascribed by the black community to a
given occupation. In general the ranking favored the professions and
white-collar occupations that displayed a good measure of stability
and economic security. A postal service employee thus ranked near
the top of the scale, job stability and income security even providing
an edge over the educational requirements of the professions. [68] In
fact, the visible connection of an occupation with white authority—
as in the case of postal clerks and the like—almost certainly ensured
high ascribed status to an occupation.

A more vivid picture of the black northern community—especially of the respectables—is perhaps conveyed by turning to the
numbers involved in some of the occupations where Negroes found
employment. Massachusetts in 1890 had a black labor force of just
over eleven thousand. More than 65 percent were engaged in domestic and personal service occupations, while slightly less than 2 percent were in the professional services category. New York State's

black labor force was 37,036 compared to Pennsylvania's 53,238. In New York about 69 percent (25,596) were in the domestic and personal service category with just about the same percentage being so classified in Pennsylvania. Only 706 and 781, respectively, or less than 2 percent, were in the professional service category in the two states.[69]

Looking at individual cities the numbers are even more striking. In 1890, 78 percent of the employed black women in Boston were either servants or laundresses; in Philadelphia 84 percent were so engaged; in Chicago, 77 percent; in Washington, D.C., 85 percent; and in New York City, 88 percent.[70] A decade later, some 40 percent of white working women in New York City were engaged in domestic and personal service, while some 90 percent of working Negro women were so employed. "Unlike the foreigner, the Negro woman finds larger opportunity and comes in greater numbers than the men," wrote one observer in 1911. "Their range of work is narrow, but within it they can command double the wages they receive at home, and if they are possessed of average ability, they are seldom long out of work."[71] The same was true for the male Negro worker, although the combined percentages of the laborers and servants categories do not run as high.[72]

The groupings "Professional Services" and "Domestic and Personal Services" used by the Bureau of the Census are rather unrefined, but they serve quite well here to emphasize the lopsided nature of the Negro class structure. The professional service category, by 1900 census criteria, included actors, showmen and musicians, architects, doctors, lawyers, teachers, and engineers.[73] Taking New York City as the example, over 60 percent (440 out of 729) of the males in this category were actors and musicians. About 53 percent of the females were so classified. Ninety-six females of the 281 in this category, or about 35 percent, were teachers.

The domestic and personal service category included bootblacks and laborers, housekeepers and laundresses, waiters and waitresses, midwives and nurses, and watchmen, policemen, and firemen. But this spread of occupations is deceiving, as the figures above, when analyzed, indicate. Again using New York City in 1900 as the example, over half of the males in the domestic and service category were servants and waiters (11,843 out of 20,395), and over one quarter were laborers. Less than 1 percent were classified as watchmen, policemen, and firemen, which were rather high prestige occupations in the Negro community in that each exhibited stability and income security, entailed "clean" work, and had a visible connection with authority. [74]

Of the females in the domestic and personal service category, almost 93 percent were servants, waitresses, and laundresses. "Seventy-four per cent of the working negro population [in New York City] are common laborers and servants," DuBois noted in 1901. "The work of the negroes was least remunerative," he went on, "they receiving a third less per week than the other nationalities."[75] If there was an exception to this general pattern of occupation and stratification, it was in Boston; there, DuBois said, only 60 percent "are servants and ordinary laborers—less than half of the men, and three-fourths of the working women."[76]

Similar figures may be demonstrated for other cities and the same generalizations applied. What is implicit in such figures is that by far the larger percentage of blacks in the northern cities lived in poverty or on its edge. Even those working in manufacturing and the retail trades were, for the most part, assigned to porter's tasks and the like and not to the higher paid jobs. Of a small New Jersey city it was noted in 1903 that the Negro "may drive a garbage wagon, coal cart, grocery wagon or hack or, if he is fortunate, get a place as a private coachman. He may become a day laborer or do cleaning and white-washing or be a house servant, but he may not enter a trade or compete in any skilled labor with the white man."[77] Nevertheless all of these occupations were considered respectable; they varied only in status (prestige) within the black community, depending upon the criteria outlined.

Obviously a job ceiling existed. Custom had for years insured that the Negro did not compete openly in the job market. Rather, he was restricted to occupations deemed appropriate for a black. The job ceiling varied with time and place simply because there were never enough blacks to entirely fill up the bottom tier of least desirable occupations. Some whites continued to find themselves in competition with blacks at the mudsill. Only in the role of Pullman porter did the color line and the job ceiling clearly coincide. [78]

There is a significance in these data that needs to be reiterated, however. It should again be noted that by far the larger portion of the black northern community was employed in positions relating directly to the white portion of the population. In effect the Negro community was being structured by its relationship to the white community. One of the most striking examples of such white lever-age on the black community is the excess of females in cities where there were no great concentrations of heavy industry, the reverse being the case where heavy industrial labor demands existed. DuBois, for example, pointed to the excess of women over men in Philadelphia and New York City—six to five and five to four, respec-tively—and said the situation was created by the demand for housemaids.[79]

The relationship between the black and white communities of the urban North obviously was affected by the number of Negroes in the North. A northward migration was already underway in the late nineteenth century. But more than this, the migration was a city-ward movement, a demographic change that was going on in the South as well.[80] The total Negro urban population increase is marked: in 1890 only 19.8 percent lived in the city; in 1900, 22.7 percent; and in 1910, 27.4 percent.[81] The proportion of Negroes in the population of northern cities during these years of urban growth remained relatively constant, however. Negroes comprised 1.3 per-cent of the total urban population of New York State in 1890, 1.5 percent in 1900, and 1.6 percent in 1910. In Illinois, Negroes com-prised 2.0 percent of the total population in 1890, 2.3 percent in 1900, and 2.5 percent in 1910.[82] In this sense the Negro did not be-come much more "visible" in the overall community in this earlier period in spite of his increased numbers. But obviously the increases were sufficient to create tensions when, as a general rule, residential segregation in the northern cities caused the black districts to bulge noticeably and then spill over the de facto "fall lines" that existed in all communities. Take Boston as an example. In 1885, there were 9,481 Negroes in the metropolitan area, up only some 200 from a decade earlier. In 1895, the black population was 16,307; in 1905, 21,234; in 1910, 23,115. By 1910 there were already a dozen cities in the country with more than 40,000 Negro residents, the largest being in the North.[83] Thus do the great black ghettos of cities like New York and Chicago date from the middle of the first decade of the twentieth century.

As insignificant as it was in comparison to later movements, this internal migration caught the national eye quite early. One study of 1897 challenged the comfortable white idea that the southern Negro would continue a supposed drift to the Southwest as he was crowded out by foreign migrants following the southward movement of industry into the border states and beyond.[84] Booker T. Washington emphasized that the Negro was better off in the South where there were better opportunities in a better moral atmosphere than the North could possibly provide.[85] "In spite of all talk of exodus, the Negro's home is permanently in the South," he often repeated, "for, coming to the bread and meat side of the question, the white man needs the Negro, and the Negro needs the white."[86]

The white South also commented—and complained. A letter in *Harper's Weekly* shortly after the turn of the century pointed to two themes that in a few years would often be reiterated: "The Southern people are stirred up because they are losing that part of the negro population that would be most useful if it stayed; and the North will sooner or later wake up to the fact that it is soon going to experience the pleasure of trying to keep two races content within its own limits."[87] These new residents could not fit in, it was offered. Primarily farmers, they could not make a go of it in the city. These facts, said *Harper's* in 1906, account for "the recent shocking revelations of crimes committed by negroes against white women in the city of New York."[88]

The overall picture of the black northern community from 1890 to about 1910, then, is one in which the class structure was largely dependent upon occupation and occupationally related features. If those at the bottom of the black social structure, the undisciplined, unchurched, uneduated riff-raff are disregarded (as the skid row inhabitant and those outside the law are disregarded in an analysis of social stratification), the picture is one of a single class of poor and barely prosperous black Americans struggling to make ends meet— just as a smaller portion, though a good majority in the white community was similarly struggling. These generally undereducated, church-going, hard-working respectables, so defined, gave form to

the entire black urban community, while at the same time they owed
their existence to the needs of the dominant white society. Paradoxically, the white society as a whole took their presence so much for
granted during most of these years that their very existence was for
the most part ignored. Social invisibility would in fact continue to af-
flict the Negro in America even when his physical presence was
noted.[89]

From the lopsided social structure of the last decade of the
nineteenth century and the first of the twentieth, there emerged by
about 1920 a three-strata social framework that was a distorted facsimile of that of the dominant white society. A middle class evolved
at various rates in the northern urban centers, in other words. As it
rose the social class hierarchy in the black community was re-
ordered, bringing about a fall in relative status for many. By the
1920s the black class pyramid supported small but identifiable middle and upper classes. The latter were made even more noticeable, in
contrast, by a continued northward-cityward migration from the
South that expanded the massive lower-class portion of the pyramid
upon which they rested.

The changing class structure in the black urban North was the
product of at least three interrelated factors, as has already been
suggested. Changing patterns of race relations had been brought
about by what has been termed a search for order in a dynamic
young nation searching for maturity and fulfillment of its destiny.
The industrialized and urbanizing nation had to have new social
imperatives. This was accompanied by a turning inward of the black
community, a giving up of the hopes that the generation after the
Civil War had held. And accompanying this changing mood was an
increasing flow of black Americans to the southern but especially the
northern cities.

Migration from the South had long been urged. From Reconstruction days onward black militants saw it as a most meaningful
form of protest. Such a stance was taken by Bishop Henry McNeal
Turner of the African Methodist Episcopal church, for example.
Turner, a Civil War chaplain and member of the Georgia state legislature for a short while, outspokenly advocated migration to Africa
as a solution to the black man's troubles in white America.[90] Still,
the significance of black northward movement before the so-called

Great Migration of the World War I period is often overlooked. Even as early as 1910 the old slave states were "whiter" than they had been a decade earlier, with the exception of Arkansas.[91]

Yet up to 1910 northward migration was still a trickle, relatively speaking, and such a trickle does not seem of too much moment. One authority suggests that the Negro, still suffering from a low morale in the South, was "held by the terror" and the caste conditions existing there.[92] Whatever bound blacks to the South, they could certainly expect to face prejudice in the North and were as well held at arm's length by their northern cousins and the European immigrants who shared their mudsill role. The northern job market was expanding and foreign immigrants were struggling into jobs, but for the rural southern black all was uncertainty.

"The uncertainty," W. E. B. DuBois noted in 1917, "was increased by a persistent Southern . . . propaganda in the North decrying [the nature of] Negro labor, and in the South by alleging that the Negro could not get work in the North."[93] Coupled with this, he went on, was the fact that "northern Negroes were bidding for higher places in the industrial machinery and gradually getting them. They feared that wholesale Southern migration would arouse prejudice and dispossess them."[94] Their fears were not groundless, of course. The old settler in the northern cities did find his position altered by the influx of migrants. William Pickens, an early NAACP official, wrote in 1924 that the northern urban resident

> began to be unlawfully segregated,—barred from eating and drinking places, theatres, parks, beaches, and other public resorts. In Dayton, Ohio,—which has a street named in honor of its great Negro poet, Dunbar,—its colored people before the migration could go unquestioned into any place of amusement and be served to any usual public accommodation. But when five Negroes came instead of one. . . .[95]

But the pull of wider opportunities in the North was certainly working, regardless of a chilly welcome from some, and the city exercised its magnetism on black youth as well as on white. It was the young men and women, less bound by old imperatives of interracial etiquette, who were already swelling the Negro districts of the industrial cities of the North.[96]

The push of southern conditions exercised considerable influence as well. This is a continuous theme in the period. One Negro newspaper noted in 1898: "The Wilmington, N.C. *Messenger* says nearly 1,400 colored people have left that city since the riot there. There is nothing startling in the announcement."[97] The suggestion was repeatedly made in these early years that the migration would abate if black southern farmers were given security in their lives and property and such fundamentals as education for their children.[98]

Once the Jim Crow system was firmly established, migration was again urged upon the southern Negro as a potent form of protest against southern conditions. The northern Negro press took up this cry and, pointing to growing opportunities in the North, urged Negroes to give up their southern burdens. Their influence was striking.[99] "Unrest Is Due to Oppression," read the lead of a *New York Age* article. "Negroes Demand Square Deal; Revolt Throughout the South."[100] The *Chicago Defender* was perhaps most noted for its appeals, as reflected in the following verse of folk blues.

> *I'm gonna leave this morning if I have to ride the rods.*
> *Got a mind for to ramble, a mind for to leave this town.*
> *Michigan water tastes like cherry wine.*
> *There's a great big headline in the* Chicago Defender *news,*
> *Says my gal down South got the up-country blues.*[101]

As a result of such propaganda, some southern localities tried to control the distribution of black newspapers. The move was necessary, quotes Detweiler in his study of the Negro press, "to keep the 'nigger from getting beside himself, and to keep him in his place.'"[102]

By the time of World War I conditions in the South found premier listing as a cause of the migration. "Lynchings, burnings, persecutions are the main reason why colored folk have been flocking to New York, where a 'nigger slaughter' is not so frequent an occurrence," wrote one observer in *Harper's*.[103] In a verse of his "Bound No'th Blues," Langston Hughes captures the sentiment.

> *Goin' down de road, Lord,*
> *Goin' down de road.*
>
>   . . .

Road, road, road, O!
On de no'thern road.
These Mississippi towns ain't
Fit for a hoppin' toad.[104]

The migration by the time the United States entered World War I had the decided overtones of a protest movement. Regardless of the improved economic opportunities being offered, going north still required making a big move. It was a deliberate act, a flight from the Negro's home. There were no leaders in this hegira, one commentator noted, although he exaggerated when he added, "For the first time in history the negro had taken his affairs into his own hands."[105] The Kansas Exodus of 1879 and the all-Negro towns established mostly in the South and West in the late nineteenth century particularly belie the claim. "Migration to northern cities amounted to a second emancipation of the plantation Negro," wrote E. Franklin Frazier. "It meant the break down of all the traditional and customary modes of behavior, the throwing off of the forms of accommodation to the white man's world in the South."[106]

The push of conditions in the South was potent then, but scholars largely agree that, even in the violent 1890s, it did not exercise as much influence as the pull of wider opportunities, especially economic opportunities, in the North. This was even more true after 1915 when northern industry was struggling to meet the increased demands of a European war at the same time that its foreign migrant labor supply was largely cut off.[107] In part the migration can thus be characterized as a natural response to changes in the fortunes of the nation's industries.[108]

Northern industries sent south for labor. Agents spread across the Black Belt with tickets for railroad transportation and money in their pockets. When the departures were not so large as to hurt the local labor supply, the southern town crowed "good riddance." "The dispersion of the Negroes in the North has been a great service to the South," said the Knoxville, Tennessee, *Sentinel*. "It has taught the North some of the meaning of the race problem and has made the North more tolerant."[109] Some wished the black migrant luck. The South really had his best interests at heart, one well-wisher said, and he had had it pretty good, all things considered. Now, what with the boll weevil and all, perhaps the North could reap some benefits, while at the same time draining off the excess black labor from the South.[110] In the 1920s James Weldon Johnson, then executive secretary of the NAACP, recalled the early war years.

> I was in Jacksonville, Fla., for a while . . . , and I sat one day and watched the stream of migrants passing to take the train. For hours they passed steadily, carrying flimsy suit cases, new and shiny, rusty old ones, bursting at the seams, boxes and bundles and impedimenta of all sorts, including banjos, guitars, birds in cages and what not . . . . The first wave of the great exodus of Negroes from the South was on.[111]

But the exodus soon got out of hand. The South began to use every pretext to stem the loss of its labor supply. Labor agents were generally harassed and often subjected to special licensing fees, a favorite method in the Deep South. In one case the fees were placed at a phenomenal $25,000. Still the agents continued to operate, and the movement went on.[112]

It is perhaps here that southern social conditions played their most prominent role in urging the Negro north. In some Black Belt areas, the exodus was likened to a mass strike by black plantation workers. Word of mouth, letters from those who had already gone to the "promised land," the northern Negro press—even the reactions of the southern white press—all spread the word. In many cases the persuasions of labor recruiters were hardly needed.[113]

The wages offered in the North seemed wonderful to the poor southern black whose usual wage did not top $1.25 a day. Even the thirty or forty cents an hour offered by the lower-paying jobs looked tremendous to the southern agricultural laborer who earned ten or fifteen cents an hour at the best of times. Moreover, being "paid in cold cash by the week or month instead of in store credit once a year," as Louise Kennedy notes in her study of Negro migration, made these wages seem "fabulous sums promising speedy wealth and success."[114] Few thought of the increased cost of living that went with the better wages, and even if they had, the increase in real wages was still marked for many.[115]

In some of the industrial centers the Negro labor force grew explosively. For example, the Negro population of Akron increased

749 percent between 1910 and 1920; that of Detroit, 611 percent; that of Cleveland, 307 percent. Except for New York City and Buffalo, New York State had few cities that offered the kind of job opportunities that attracted the Negro. Buffalo's black population increased 154 percent between 1910 and 1920, while New York City's grew some 66 percent. Farther west, Columbus, Ohio, served as a dispersal point to such industrial centers as Pittsburgh, Youngstown, Detroit, and Chicago.[116] Chicago, one of the main terminal points of the migrants, saw its black population leap to 109,000 in 1920, up from 44,000 in 1910 and 30,000 in 1900.[117]

For the most part, the black population concentrated in ten industrial areas in the North between 1910 and 1920. Almost 75 percent of the Negroes in the North lived in these industrial regions, more than half being concentrated in the Chicago, Philadelphia, and New York districts.[118] As a section, the North in 1920 had 14.1 percent of the total U.S. Negro population, up from 10 percent in 1900.[119]

By far the greater portion of the new northerners had a hard time getting started; they ended up swelling the mass situated at the nether end of the black social structure. Most, armed with only the cultural equipment of the rural South, were unprepared to cope with urban life when they arrived—a fact black accommodationist leaders had been pointing to for years.[120] It was difficult making a living, and it was easy to get discouraged. Langston Hughes caught well the resulting sentiment in his "Evenin' Air Blue":

> *Folks, I come up North*
> *Cause they told me de North was fine.*
> *I come up North*
> *Cause they told me de North was fine.*
> *Been up here six months—*
> *I'm about to lose my mind.*[121]

For the most part the migrants stuck it out, though. Southern propaganda tried to lure the Negro back "home," but the postwar years became violent ones that more than canceled out any positive effect the propaganda might have had. "85% of Migrants Are Sticking to Jobs up North," one paper announced in reporting the results of an Associated Negro Press survey in mid-1923.[122] As bad as conditions admittedly were for many, as hard as most had to work just to make ends meet, the general consensus still seemed to be that it was better than going back "home."[123] Sadie, Thomas Campbell's fictional character, had been scraping in the South and had had to scrape since she arrived in Newark, but "she commiserated the 'po' coons back home . . . . Ain't got sense enough ter leave.' She congratulated her visitors, including herself, on being free, 'up-an'-comin',' 'livin' North.' "[124] It was hard and they were homesick sometimes, but they would only go back, in the biting words of some telling doggerel:

> *When lions eat grass like oxen*
> *And an angleworm swallows a whale,*
> *And a terrapin knits a woolen sock,*
> *And a hare is outrun by a snail.*
>
> . . .
>
> *When ideas grow on trees,*
> *And wool on cast-iron rams,*
> *I then may return to the South,*
> *But I'll travel then in a box.*[125]

It can hardly be doubted that the influx of black Americans into the cities, North and South, altered the entire character of race relations in the nation. Considered by some to be the most significant event in black American history since emancipation, the migration may have, as some suggest, changed a rural Negro peasantry into an urban proletariat in a little over a generation.[126] "A new type of Negro is evolving," wrote Charles S. Johnson in the mid 1920s, "—a city Negro . . . . In ten years [since 1915], Negroes have been actually transplanted from one culture to another . . . Whether apparent or not, the newcomers are forced to reorganize their lives, to enter a new status and adjust to it that eager restlessness which prompted them to leave home."[127] The migrant "underwent a mental transition" when he was absorbed into a Harlem or a Bonzeville, Robert Brisbane agreed a generation later in his study, "The Rise of Protest Movements Among Negroes." "His racial attitude was swiftly hammered into conformity with a new pattern."[128] "My

God! Must be a million niggers in Chicago," muses Ed in Alden
Bland's novel, *Behold a Cry*. " . . . Sure can tell they just got here
all right. Funny, wasn't so long ago I felt dressed up in them
starched jumpers. It's that scared, lost look they got. . . . Like they
out of place and know it."[129]

It was a swift and difficult adjustment that had to be made. Mr.
Simple, Langston Hughes's noted character, would say to a recent
arrival:

> "Set down and I will tell you about Harlem, Minnie, so you
> will be clear in mind. In fact, I will tell you about the North.
> Down South you're swimming in a river that's running to the
> sea where you might drown but, at least, you're swimming with
> the current. Up North we are swimming the other way, against
> the current, trying to reach dry land. I been here twenty years,
> Minnie, and I'm still in the water, if you get what I mean."[130]

The weight of their numbers, however, probably had less to do
with directly changing the Negro social structure in the northern
urban centers than events on the white side of the color line.

In the dominant culture, as has been noted and emphasized because of the implications it held for black America, part of the
motive force behind the emergence of the new middle class was the
need to define the white social structure in a way that was congruent
with the social imperatives of an industrialized-urbanized society. A
social system that had its parameters set in Horatio Alger's America
was not able to cope with the bureaucratic needs of a complex urban
society. White society of the time was in fact in some ways quite
similar to the black. The traditional three-class structure usually
depicted has a tendency to disintegrate if examined closely, as
Robert Wiebe notes. The white middle class seems to meld all too
easily with the lower class into a single mass not unlike that of the
black respectables.[131]

It was from this single mass that the new white middle class
emerged—a new group of professionals and business specialists that
fulfilled the bureaucratic needs of urban-industrial development.
Prestige in this new group was more a matter of skill and talent than

of wealth and ethnic background. These changes in the larger society—changes in business organization and methods, as well as technological changes in manufacturing—when coupled with a growing racial antipathy, forced concomitant changes in the black community.[132]

Each Negro community had had its small number of black professionals and small entrepreneurs from before the turn of the century. They ranged in social standing from the upper reaches of the so-called respectable grouping into the small, closed group of older elites. Though considered the well to do of the black community, they did not have very large incomes. "Remembering the high cost of living," Mary Ovington noted, "and the exorbitant rental paid by black men, we can see that, gauging by the white man's standard, the Negro with his two or three or four thousand dollars a year is poor."[133] Their existence—and, in fact, a good deal of their prestige—depended upon white patronage, not black.[134] The black class structure, to emphasize the point again, was ordered by white needs and white ideas of the proper role of the Negro.

By 1920 this changed in a measurable degree as a growing proportion of Negro enterprises served Negro needs. Many of the small black entrepreneurs who had wholly depended upon white trade simply went out of business.[135] The change took place at different rates in the various urban centers, but by 1920 a fairly large Negro business community existed that provided the backbone of a recognizable Negro middle class and of a newly rising social elite. The professionals and business people increasingly replaced many of the old elite at the top of the social structure, especially those whose status had rested upon personal service. "The Negro doctors, dentists, lawyers, and businessmen, who could not boast of white ancestors or did not know their white ancestors," E. Franklin Frazier wrote, "were becoming the leaders of Negro 'society.'"[136] In Washington, D.C., those holding official positions still headed the social roster as they had earlier, and everywhere civil service occupations still ranked high because of their security. Some of the old elite maintained their position, but more experienced a downward shift in their relative status. Class relationships within the Negro community came, as a result, to resemble more closely those of the dominant society.

Contemporaries often misread this change and frequently complained that the Negro was losing out in the occupations he had formerly monopolized. Lack of efficiency on the part of the Negro was the explanation often offered.[137] But as socialist reformer Mary White Ovington noted, the Negro had never been numerous enough in the northern cities to have monopolized any occupation, let alone all those claimed—barbering, bootblack stands, waiters, janitorial services, and catering businesses. Numerically small, the Negro labor force continued to occupy the unenviable position of being easily replaced.[138] Perhaps the view persisted because the Negro failed to see the shifting occupational lines in the white community. Whites were moving into occupations that had formerly been considered Negro occupations. His concern was certainly well placed, though. The jobs to which he had been restricted were those that meant food for his family, shoes for his children, a dress for his wife.[139] So, too, did the view persist that skilled black artisans among the migrants could not find openings in their trades but were forced to do menial labor. Zeddy in Claude McKay's *Home to Harlem* put it succinctly:

"Scab job or open shop or union am all the same jobs to me. White mens don't want niggers in them unions, nohow. Ain't you a good carpenter? And ain't I a good blacksmith? But kain we get a look-in on our trade heah in this white man's city? Ain't white mens done scabbed niggers outa all the jobs they useter hold down heah in this city? Waiter, bootblack, and barber shop?"[140]

Yet by far the majority of the migrants were unskilled laborers, and "Negro" jobs were those positions not being filled at the time by native whites or white immigrants.

At the turn of the century some Negro leaders dreamed of black capitalism and large-scale industry. But, as Frazier has noted, the ever-increasing strength of the Negro businessman in the black community was largely a myth.[141] By 1914 there were 40,000 Negro business enterprises according to the Negro Business League, double the number existing in 1900.[142] Obviously the number of Negro enterprises in any given city was very small. For instance, there were eight

Afro-American enterprises in Paterson, New Jersey, providing services for a population of 1,182. In Buffalo, New York, there were
thirty in a population of 1,698. [143] From 1900 to the start of the Great
Migration, there came to be some 500 Negro enterprises in Chicago.
Most were small personal-service businesses providing to the black
community those kinds of services the white community refused to
provide: barber shops, beauty shops, undertakers, and the like. The
city-dwelling black was still dependent upon the white community to
supply the everyday needs of life. [144] By way of example, in a call for
race solidarity an advertisement placed by a Negro life insurance
company noted that when white owners of ghetto stores had closed
during the bloody Chicago riot of 1919, black residents were left
without even the bare essentials. [145]

Significantly, however, while small businesses were multiply-
ing, the occupational base of the whole black community was broad-
ening. The number of professionals grew. More importantly, each
decade after the turn of the century, but especially the war years,
saw increasing numbers of sales and clerk positions, and in the number of skilled workers, foremen, semiskilled operatives, transportation workers, and the like. Historian Harold Faulkner writes:

> In 1900, agriculture and domestic and personal service, tradi-
> tional Negro work, occupied 86.7 per cent of those gainfully
> employed; by 1920, the percentage of Negroes engaged in these
> two occupations had declined to 67.06. By 1920, about
> 1,506,000, 31.2 percent of those gainfully employed, were
> engaged in manufacturing, trade and transportation. [146]

White-collar workers were 3.6 percent of the Negro labor force
in 1920 as compared to 3.0 in 1910. Skilled blue-collar workers rose
to 3.0 percent of the force, while semiskilled workers and operatives
rose to 7.3 percent. The number of laborers and service workers rose
slightly, but there was a significant drop in the percentage involved
in farm work: 46.6 percent, down from 50.4 percent in 1910. [147]

But even as the new middle class grew and the occupational
base broadened to encompass more fields, the menial job was still
the only occupational opening for the ordinary Negro. [148] An article
in the *Southern Workman* said that domestic service was almost the

"birthright" of the black women; thus she should be efficient.[149] To this end the YWCA offered courses of instruction in laundress, housemaid, lady's maid, and waitress work to, as an advertisement in a Negro magazine put it, "young women over fifteen years of age, of good moral character."[150] In Pittsburgh in 1911, it was asserted that only three Negro women held fairly responsible positions in white businesses.[151] The Negro fire company of Columbus, Ohio, organized in 1880 came to an abrupt end in 1913 when the department was motorized and the black firemen were replaced by whites.[152]

Before the European war broke out in 1914 the white immigrant had been displacing the Negro in the better domestic service positions. The white view remained "Negroes are servants; servants are Negroes," in W. E. B. DuBois's words, but by 1920 the majority of the domestic and service workers had fallen in relative status.[153] Some of this group—the Pullman porters, resort hotel waiters who moved with the seasons, a few of the old elites in personal service—maintained a relatively high status position (the "upper servants" as DuBois termed them). As far as the Negro community was concerned, they became part of the developing black middle class.[154] The great mass of Negroes in the community, though, lost in relative status. The loss may not have been always realized and the reasons for this state of affairs may not have been of continuous conscious concern for the majority of the black city dwellers, but it certainly did not escape them. They understood the situation in just the manner W. E. B. DuBois described it, even if they would not have been able to express it in the same way. The social system, DuBois said, was the product of "the 'manure' theory of social organization": "We believe that at the bottom of organized human life there are necessary duties and services which no real human being ought to be compelled to do. We push below this mudsill the derelicts and half-men."[155]

The perceptive Rudolph Fisher, in his novel *The Walls of Jericho*, concurred. A central character attending a large social function "picked out two or three strangers, [and] conjectured about their occupations. This lopsided one was undoubtedly a waiter, that plump cocoa one a porter, the bald, custard one whose cheeks had been left in the oven a trifle too long a—Well, what the hell else were boogies but waiters and porters?[156]

By the 1920s, then, the black class pyramid was a distorted image of the white, resting upon a massive lower class, which was continually expanded by migration from the South. Urged on by the same forces that motivated the earlier waves of migrants, but especially the continued labor needs of the North and the resulting economic opportunities, the population pressure these new migrants created was marked. "In Pittsburgh," the National Urban League periodical *Opportunity* declared, "Negro home seekers have been forced to retreat to the uninhabitable cliffs isolated from the city's gas and water supply."[157] In Newark, New Jersey, Thomas Campbell wrote in his novel, *Black Sadie*, that migrants "came to roaring, squalid Orange Street and entered a vast ramshackle tenement. The tottering structure was fairly bursting with darkies. They crowded every nook and cranny. They overflowed on landings and stairs. They spilled themselves and their belongings profusely into the street. Men, women, babies, garbage."[158] By 1930, 20.3 percent of black America lived in the North, a striking demonstration of the numbers that continued to move northward in the 1920s.[159]

A brief examination of some of the numbers involved displays just how askew the Negro social structure was by the fourth decade of the twentieth century. Staid old Boston saw an increase of some 4,000 black Americans between 1920 and 1930, bringing its Negro population to 20,574. The surrounding metropolitan districts remained about the same. New York City's Negro population stood at 327,706, up some 175,000 over 1920. Most blacks found their way to Manhattan, its black population alone accounting for 115,000 of the increase. In the Empire State, the only other city showing a really marked increase continued to be Buffalo, up to 13,563 in 1930 from 4,511 in 1920, a 200 percent increase. Other cities showing marked increases over the decade were Chicago, up 113.7 percent to 233,903; Philadelphia, up 63.6 percent to 219,599; Detroit, up 194 percent to 120,066; Cleveland, up 108.7 percent to 71,899; Newark, up 129 percent to 38,880; and Dayton, up 89.2 percent to 17,077.[160]

By categorizing the employed Negro males of New York, Chicago, Philadelphia, Cleveland, and Cincinnati as either middle class or lower class on the basis of occupation alone, E. Franklin Frazier found that in 1920 just about 90 percent still fell into the lower class but that the middle class was growing. Of the employed males in New York in 1920, 11.4 percent could be classified as middle class as could 10.4 percent in Chicago, 7.9 percent in Philadelphia, and 5.8 percent in Cleveland. Cincinnati, with only 5.5 percent falling into the middle-class category, was really more on a par with New Orleans where only 4.7 percent could be placed in the middle class. In 1930, the percentages falling into the middle class category were: Chicago, 12.9 percent; New York, 13.4 percent; Cincinnati, 6.5 percent; Cleveland, 8.5 percent.[161]

The numbers do not tell the whole story, but they provide a striking backdrop. The human details can be gleaned from such sources as the New York City survey of Negro women in industry in that city. Reporting on this survey the *New York Age* noted that most of the subjects were employed in the flower and feather trade, the millinery industries and the like, and in button factories and the candy industry.[162] Almost all were engaged in unskilled labor and earned two to five dollars less a week than whites doing the same work.[163] One finds a similar story in Chicago, Detroit, and other cities.[164] Noting the prevalence of the idea that blacks for some reason should be paid less than whites for the same work, and that this was actually influencing governmental agencies, George Haynes, Director of Negro Economics in the Department of Labor wrote: "It would seem that the Negro is expected to produce from his dark skin some sort of alchemy which will transmute smaller pay than white workers receive into equal standards of food, shelter and clothing."[165] The want ads read: "Wanted: Factory helpers; experienced only; white $24.00, colored $20.00. Apply . . ."[166] And even where the Negro was paid the same wages as the white, he in turn paid the higher rents and food prices that go hand in hand with residential segregation.[167]

In short, it was costly to be black in white America in more ways than one. It is a brutal truth that the essentials always eat up a disproportionate share of the poor man's income. Nowhere was this more apparent than in the black northern community. Rent took a larger share of the Negro's wages than the white worker's, while at the same time he was often paid a lower wage than the white for the same work. "Most pertinent to the Negro newcomer," Mary Ovington suggested in 1910, "is not where he will live nor how he will live, but whether he will be able to live in New York at all, whether he can meet the landlord's agent the day he comes to the door."[168] When the average worker's earnings at the time was only about twenty-two dollars a week and job security for the easy to replace never very sure, getting ahead was a pretty nebulous proposition.[169]

There were, in sum, certain ubiquitous and enduring facets to black life in the North that permit one to put together a composite portrait that is recognizable as one and as many Americans at the same time.[170] Especially apparent in the picture's background are segregation and the job ceiling. In a sense the height of the job ceiling might be used as a barometer of the economic climate of the nation in that the Negro was the last hired and first fired. Langston Hughes did not recall much of a slump after World War I. The newspapers in the early 1920s carried numerous help-wanted ads, he wrote in his autobiography:

> I bought the papers and began to answer ads regarding jobs I thought I could handle—office boy, clerk, waiter, bus boy, and other simple occupations. Nine times out of ten—*ten* times out of ten, to be truthful—the employer would look at me, shake his head and say, with an air of amazement: "But I didn't advertise for a colored boy."[171]

It is this background of sameness that makes the changes wrought during these years stand out so clearly. The Negro class structure that emerged was, in E. Franklin Frazier's words, "the result of a slow and difficult occupation differentiation of the Negro population."[172] It is important to note again, however, that the subjective measures of class membership cannot be disregarded in favor of the more objective occupational yardstick; occupations simply did not carry the same class connotations in the black world as in the white. A social worker could qualify as a "society" leader, other things being equal, just as easily as the minister, lawyer, or businessman. In some instances so might one in domestic service still qualify even in the 1920s.[173] Just who got pushed up and who got pushed down was not entirely settled even by the 1930s, and, as one contemporary observer wrote then, "the sheep are [still] found rubbing noses with the goats" in black society. "The goat just happens to be the big ram's father or brother or some other close relative."[174]

That such wavy class lines existed helps to explain the white inability to see, or to admit to, class distinctions in the black world.
"Just because we're colored they think we got to be equal," were frequent words of complaint according to one commentator on Negro
society.[175] It also helps to explain the black American's continued
tendency to claim that class distinctions were barely present if they
existed at all. As one of Rudolph Fisher's characters insisted: "But I
always say the top ain' but a little way from the bottom—can't be,
'tain' been risin' long enough. And ain' none of us so much better'n
the rest of us that we can afford to get uppity 'bout it."[176]

The indefinite class lines also help to explain the tension that
continued to exist between the top and bottom rungs of the social
class ladder and the quizzical, skeptical look on the face in the common portrait. The great mass of ordinary Negroes, in ways that will
be elaborated later, tended to be distrustful of the rising new middle
class just as they had been of the older elite. Historian Rayford
Logan writes:

> The lower classes resent being used as a stepping stone to help
> the lawyer or doctor or teacher to remove himself from their
> intellectual society, and economic orbit; the upper classes con-
> demn the lower for "making it hard for us." The professional
> class approach the masses with the typical twentieth century
> "uplift" psychosis; the masses have the perfectly natural re-
> action of suspecting ulterior motives on the part of their self-
> professed friends.[177]

When the Great Depression hit, class distinctions became even
less clear as some who had climbed a peg or two were rudely shoved
back down to the bottom. One authority noted that the class
pyramid came to resemble a steeple in the 1930s.[178] Yet it would
continue to evolve toward the white model more and more as time
went on, even though the class lines would remain far from clearly
defined even in the 1940s. Paradoxically, the increasing resemblance
of the black structure to that of the dominant society allowed more
and more blacks to avoid contact with the white world.[179]

To the casual observer it would seem that such persistent reminders of inferiority as having one "nigger day" a year in the city's

parks, as in Cincinnati, would make any semblance of an orderly existence in the black subcommunity impossible.[180] Certainly such reminders placed monumental stresses on many facets of just getting along from day to day and help explain those little lines of stress and anxiousness that are so visible in the picture. But the black American subcommunity provided shelter from the worst of these. Black America had long since learned how to live with its blackness.

NOTES

[1] From "Northboun'" by Lucy Ariel Williams, in *Opportunity* 4 (June 1926): 184.

[2] W.E.B. DuBois, "Of the Training of Black Men," *Atlantic Monthly* 90 (September 1902): 289.

[3] W. A. Domingo, "Gift of the Black Tropics," in Alain Locke, ed., *The New Negro* (1925; reprint ed., Arno Press, 1968): 342.

[4] C.S. Johnson, "New Frontage on American Life," in ibid., 289; J.W. Johnson, "Harlem: The Culture Capital," in ibid., 310.

[5] Johnson, "Harlem: The Culture Capital," 310.

[6] Jacob A. Riis, *How the Other Half Lives* (1890; reprint ed; Hill and Wang, 1957), 110. Much in the following pastiche draws upon such studies as Gilbert Osofsky's *Harlem: The Making of a Ghetto* (Harper & Row, 1963); Allan H. Spear's *Black Chicago: The Making of a Negro Ghetto, 1890-1920* (University of Chicago Press, 1967); and Constance McLaughlin Green's *The Secret City: A History of Race Relations in the Nation's Capital* (Princeton University Press, 1967), as well as on numerous novels and short stories.

One also finds numerous "The Negro in ———" articles in the periodical literature of the times. The sameness that is found in these is striking. An elitist flavor is apparent in most. For example, one article on housing in New York concludes that "the fact that there is no good and no bad Negro section . . . constitutes the worst evil of the existing state of affairs." Mary Rankin Cranston, "The Housing of the Negro in New York City," *Southern Workman* 31 (June 1902): 332. One wonders if much concern would have been exhibited had a "good" section existed. Some other articles of this nature spanning the period being considered are: Alice M. Bacon, "A Negro District in New Haven," *Southern Workman* 36 (July 1907): 378-382; Lillian Brandt, "The Negroes of St. Louis," *American Statistical Association* 8 (March 1903): 203-268; Nahum Daniel Brascher, "Cleveland —A Representative American City," *Voice of the Negro* 2 (August 1905): 532-536; Frank W. Quillan, "The Negro in Cincinnati," *Independent* 68 (February 24, 1910): 399-403; and John Marshall Ragland, "The Negro in Detroit," *Southern Workman* 52 (November 1923): 533-542.

[7] Gilbert T. Stephenson, "The Segregation of the White and Negro Races in Cities," *South Atlantic Quarterly* 13 (January 1914): 1-18; Gunnar Myrdal, *An American Dilemma,* 20th anniversary ed. (Harper & Row, 1962), 623-624.

[8] George Edmund Haynes, *The Negro at Work in New York City: A Study in Economic Progress* (1912; reprint ed., Arno Press, 1968), 48; Osofsky, *Harlem,* 12-16; James Weldon Johnson, *Black Manhattan* (1930; reprint

ed., Atheneum, 1969), 58-59, 147; Mary White Ovington, *The Walls Came Tumbling Down* (1947; reprint ed., Schocken Books, 1970), 35.

⁹ The alley and interior court pattern continued in both Philadelphia and Washington even after the World War I era. Washington did not see a centralized Negro district develop even after the promising Alley Dwelling Act of 1934 was passed to cope with the worst of these slums. The pattern in Philadelphia resolved down to three fairly distinct areas of black residential expansion by 1930, areas in which the population was shifting from predominantly white to predominantly black. See Green, *Secret City*, 127, 175, 233; W.E. Burghardt DuBois, *The Philadelphia Negro: A Social Study* (1899; reprint ed., Schocken Books, 1967), 303-309; Clara Alberta Hardin, "A Study of the Negroes of Philadelphia" (Ph.D. diss., Bryn Mawr, 1943), 73; Edith Elmer Wood, "The Negro Alleys of Washington," *Southern Workman* 43 (June 1914): 350-358. For an early discussion of the "nucleus" housing pattern, as W.E.B. DuBois termed the "alley" scheme, see his "The Problem of Housing the Negro: The Southern City Negro of the Lower Class," *Southern Workman* 30 (1901): 688-693.

¹⁰ Spear, *Black Chicago*, 11-12.

¹¹ Ibid., 12-27; St. Clair Drake and Horace R. Cayton, *Black Metropolis* (1945; revised ed., Harper Torchbook Edition, 1962), 175-177; Richard R. Wright, Jr., "The Negro in Chicago," *Southern Workman* 35 (October 1906): 557.

¹² "A Study of the Negro Families in the Pinewood Avenue District of Toledo, Ohio," *Opportunity* 7 (August 1929): 243.

¹³ T.J. Woofter, Jr., and Associates, *Negro Problems in Cities* (1928; reprint ed., College Park, Maryland: McGrath Publishing Co., 1969), 40-67. See also Myrdal, *American Dilemma*, appendix 7.

¹⁴ Myrdal, *American Dilemma*, 618.

¹⁵ Rollin Lynde Hartt, "When the Negro Comes North," *World's Work* 48 (May 1924): 86. See also *World's Work* 48 (June 1924): 184-192, and (July 1924): 318-323. Residential segregation of the type represented by the growth of the black city within a city in Chicago and New York in the first two decades of this century, as compared to the alley-type enclaves in the South, is thus a special measure of the importance of residential separation to the Jim Crow scheme in the North.

¹⁶ Langston Hughes, *The Big Sea* (1940; reprint ed., Hill and Wang, 1963), 27.

¹⁷ Karl and Alma Taeuber, *Negroes in Cities* (Chicago: Aldine Publishing Co., 1965), 54 (table 10).

¹⁸ Richard C. Minor, "The Negro in Columbus, Ohio" (Ph.D. diss., Ohio State University, 1937), 116-119.

¹⁹ William Attaway, *Blood on the Forge* (1941; reprint ed., Collier Books, 1970), pt. 3.

[20]W.E.B. DuBois, "The Segregated Negro World," *World Tomorrow* 6 (May 1923): 136. One firsthand narrative of the life-style and living conditions of the black migrant in the iron and steel areas is W.F. Young, "The First Hundred Negro Workers," *Opportunity* 2 (January 1924): 15-19. For a contemporary description of the migrant camp set up by the Pennsylvania Railroad that in the months following July 1, 1916, alone brought north 12,000 black workers, see John T. Emlen, "Negro Immigration in Philadelphia," *Southern Workman* 46 (October 1917): 555-557.

[21]Riis, *How the Other Half Lives*, 112.

[22]*New York Age*, June 22, 1912.

[23]E. Franklin Frazier, "The Negro Community; A Cultural Phenomenon," *Social Forces* 7 (March 1929): 415-420; J.W. Johnson, "Harlem: The Culture Capital," in Locke, ed., *The New Negro*, 301; Claude McKay, *A Long Way from Home* (1937; reprint ed., Harcourt, Brace and World, 1970), 49; George Samuel Schuyler, *Black and Conservative: The Autobiography of George S. Schuyler* (New Rochelle, New York: Arlington House, 1966), 97; Alain Locke, "Harlem," *Survey Graphic* 53 (March 1, 1925): 629-630. The best descriptions of the evolution of these black metropolises are Osofsky's *Harlem*, Seth M. Scheiner's *Negro Mecca: A History of the Negro in New York City, 1865-1920* (New York University Press, 1965), Spear's *Black Chicago*, and Drake and Cayton's *Black Metropolis. The Negro in New York: An Informal Social History*, ed. Roi Ottley and William J. Weatherby (Praeger Publishers, 1969), which was prepared from the manuscripts of the Federal Writers Project found in the Schomburg Collection of the New York Public Library, captures the tone being striven for here.

[24]Milton M. Gordon, *Assimilation in Americal Life* (Oxford University Press, 1964), provides lucid discussion and good bibliographical entry into such concepts as subcommunity, marginality, and class. The concept of a "culture of poverty" that cuts across racial and ethnic lines is a comfortable and attractive one. It certainly eliminates many of the fundamental problems facing the white liberal concerned about the obvious inequities in modern American life. Oscar Lewis recognized this in his exposition on the subculture of poverty in *La Vida: A Puerto Rican Family in the Culture of Poverty—San Juan and New York* (Random House, 1966), xlii-lii. Lewis hinted that the applicability of the concept might be locked out in this case by the castelike lines of racial discrimination in America and the peculiar relationship the black world has with the white. For instance, as a Negro moves out of the culture of poverty on the black side of the color line, he moves into a subculture that has white, not black, values. Also see Christopher Lasch, *The Agony of the American Left* (Vintage Books, 1969), 124-126, which asserts the validity of the concept and the shallowness of the

black protest against it, and Michael Harrington's extended discussion in the appendix to his *The Other America* (Penguin Books, 1963), 171-186.

[25] Melville J. Herskovits, *The American Negro: A Study in Racial Crossing* (1928; reprint ed., Indiana University Press, 1964), 57. Elsewhere Herskovits stated: "What there is today in Harlem distinct from the white culture which surrounds it, is . . . merely a remnant from the peasant days in the South. Of the African culture, not a trace." Herskovits, "The Negro's Americanism," in Locke, ed., *The New Negro*, 359. Later, However, Herskovits reversed his stand. See Myrdal, *American Dilemma*, 930.

The controversy over the existence of survival of African cultural traits in the Negro American culture and whether such survivals, given they exist, are the added ingredients that make *Negro* American institutions is not being considered here. At best this is a moot point not likely to be resolved one way or the other. See St. Clair Drake, "Hide My Face? On Pan-Africanism and Negritude," in Herbert Hill, ed., *Soon, One Morning* (Alfred A. Knopf, 1963), 78-105; Romeo B. Garrett, "African Survivals in American Culture," *JNH* 51 (October 1966): 239-245.

[26] Nathan Glazer and Daniel Patrick Moynihan, *Beyond the Melting Pot: The Negroes, Puerto Ricans, Jews, Italians, and Irish of New York City* (Cambridge, Massachusetts: The M.I.T. Press, 1963), 53.

[27] Robert Bone, *The Negro Novel in America* (rev. ed., New Haven: Yale University Press, 1965), 3. See also Harrington, *Other America*, 23-24, chap. 4, passim, and Clemont E. Vontress, "The Negro Personality Reconsidered," *JNE*, 35 (Summer 1966): 210-217.

The statements quoted above are quite explicit and have not been wrenched out of context. Yet Herskovits and Glazer and Moynihan all acknowledge that being black in white America has sociological and psychological implications. Herskovits, for example, said, "The fact that he is a Negro is something which figures in his life every hour of the day, something he is never allowed to forget" (*The American Negro*, 58). It would seem that these statements—and they are not unique, of course—nicely highlight the consistency of the liberal white's viewpoint over quite an extended period of time. Concerned over the depressing nature of race relations in the nation, they emphasized the Negro's Americanism by making him a Nordic with a dark skin. See Myrdal, *American Dilemma*, 930; Andrew Billingsley, *Black Families in White America* (Englewood Cliffs, New Jersey: Prentice-Hall, 1968), 37; M. Gordon, *Assimilation in American Life*, 14, 77n.27; Thomas F. Pettigrew, "Negro American Personality: Why Isn't More Known," *Journal of Social Issues*, 20 (April 1964): 14-15; John J. Appel, "American Negro and Immigrant Experience: Similarities and Differences," *American Quarterly* 18 (Spring 1966):

95-103; Scheiner, *Negro Mecca*, 86; Alma F. and Carl E. Taeuber, "The Negro as an Immigrant Group; Recent Trends in Racial and Ethnic Segregation in Chicago," *AJS* 69 (January 1964): 374-382.

[28]Richard Wright, "The Man Who Killed a Shadow," in his *Eight Men* (1961; reprint ed., Pyramid Books, 1969), 157.

[29]Adelaide C. Hill, "The Negro Upper Class in Boston—Its Development and Present Social Structure" (Ph.D. diss., Radcliffe College, 1952), 1n.3. See also Bone, *Negro Novel in America,* 16.

[30]Myrdal, *American Dilemma,* 667.

[31]W. Lloyd Warner, "American Caste and Class," *AJS* 42 (September 1936): 234-237; Oliver C. Cox, "The Modern Caste School of Race Relations," *Social Forces* 21 (December 1942): 218-226; Cox, "Class and Caste: A Definition and a Distinction," *JNE* 13 (Spring 1944): 139-149; and Cox, "Race and Caste: A Distinction," *AJS* 50 (March 1945): 360-368; Maxwell R. Brooks, "American Class and Caste: An Appraisal," *Social Forces* 25 (December 1946): 207-211; Myrdal, *American Dilemma,* 667-669; E. Franklin Frazier, "Sociological Theory and Race Relations," *ASR* 12 (June 1947): 265-271, and "Race Contacts and the Social Structure," 3.

[32]Jerry W. Robinson, Jr., and James D. Preston, "Class and Caste in 'Old City,' *Phylon* 31 (Fall 1970): 244-255. See also Jay Reigle Williams, "Social Stratification and the Negro American: An Exploration of Some Problems in Social Class Measurement" (Ph.D. diss., Duke University, 1968), 2-9.

[33]Gordon W. Allport, *The Nature of Prejudice*, abridged edition (Doubleday Anchor Books, 1958) 304.

[34]Robinson and Preston, "Class and Caste in 'Old City,' " 245.

[35]Of the period, satirist George S. Schuyler writes: "Years later when I traveled intensively in the South I found in going from place to place that differences in race relations were so great that one could not generalize about the area nor even about the same state because local customs so varied, as did the people." *Black and Conservative*, 52.

[36]Allison Davis, "Caste, Economy, and Violence," *AJS* 51 (July 1953): 7-15; see also M. F. Ashley Montague, "The Nature of Race Relations," *Social Forces* 25 (March 1947): 336-342.

[37]Charles S. Johnson, "The Education of the Negro Child," *ASR* 1 (April 1936): 264.

[38]Samuel Strong, "Negro-White Relations as Reflected in Social Types," *AJS* 56 (July 1946):23. See also Robert Ernst, "Negro Concepts of Americanism," *JNH* 39 (July 1954): 213-214.

[39]Gordon, *Assimilation in American Life*, 163. "The counterpart to white solidarity on the Negro side of the caste gulf," Myrdal notes, "is the 'protective community.' " *American Dilemma*, 680.

[40]W.E.B. DuBois, "The Black North," *New York Times*, November 24, 1901.

[41]Myrdall, *American Dilemma*, 693.

[42]James Weldon Johnson, *Autobiography of an Ex-Coloured Man* (1912; reprint ed., Hill and Wang, 1960) 155-156. This novel, it may be noted, has been termed "the first of the 'passing' novels, the first treatment of the Black Bohemia of New York, and the first novel attempting to give a cross section of Negro life." Sterling A. Brown, Arthur P. Davis, and Ulysses Lee, eds., *The Negro Caravan: Writings by American Negroes* (The Dryden Press, 1941), 168.

[43]W. E. B. DuBois, "The Black North," *New York Times*, December 1, 1901.

[44]Johnson, *Autobiography of an Ex-Coloured Man*, 76.

[45]Harold M. Hodges, *Social Stratification: Class in America* (Cambridge, Massachusetts: Schenkman Publishing Co., 1964), 13.

[46]Dubois, *The Philadelphia Negro*, 310-311.

[47]E. Franklin Frazier, *Black Bourgeoisie* (The Free Press, 1957), 109 and note 21.

[48]See, for instance, Drake and Cayton, *Black Metropolis*, 48.

[49]An excerpt from Dorothy West's *The Living Is Easy*, found in Hill, ed., *Soon, One Morning*, 481-502, provides a picture of these different connotations in a short span. The story is set in Boston in the World War I period.

[50]Drake and Cayton, *Black Metropolis*, 48. See also "Negro Class Distinctions," *Southern Workman* 28 (October 1899): 372.

[51]See Richard Wright, *Native Son* (1940; reprint ed., Signet Books, 1964) 7-10.

[52]See, for example, Mary White Ovington, "The Negro Home in New York," *Charities* 15 (October 7, 1905): 25-30; see also Williams, "Social Stratification and the Negro American," 23-27.

[53]The groups outlined were identified by white authors as well. See, for instance, Sterling A. Brown, "Negro Characters as Seen by White Authors," *JNE* 2 (April 1933): 179. The ordinary white did not make class distinctions, however, and, as noted, tended to lump all blacks together regardless of black delineations.

[54]Johnson, *Autobiography of an Ex-Coloured Man*, 76-78. This latter phenomenon has often been noted. As pointed out earlier (in n. 50 to chap. 1 above), the amount of anti-Negro news coverage (as a measure of inter-

racial relations) can be correlated to the percentage of blacks in the community engaged in domestic and personal service work and the percentage employed in areas that place the Negro in direct competition with whites. The first is an acceptable role for the Negro as far as the white is concerned, the second is not. See, for instance, E. B. Reuter, "Why the Presence of the Negro Constitutes a Problem in the American Social Order," *JNE* 8 (July 1939): 291-298.

[55]Johnson, *Autobiography of an Ex-Coloured Man*, 78-79.

[56]Ibid., 79-82. See also Frazier, *Black Bourgeoisie*, 23-41.

[57]Charles W. Chestnutt, "The Wife of His Youth," in *The Wife of His Youth and Other Stories of the Color Line* (1899; reprint ed., University of Michigan Press, 1968) 1.

[58]Ibid., 7.

[59]Ibid., 4. See also George W. Harris, "Boston Colored People," *Colored American Magazine* 14 (January 1908): 28-31.

[60]Jessie R. Fauset, *There Is Confusion* (Boni and Liverright, 1924), 31. See also Jessie R. Fauset, *The Chinaberry Tree: A Novel of American Life* (Frederick A. Stokes Co., 1931), 23-24; Bone, *Negro Novel in America*, 102; Frazier, "The Negro Community," 418; Schuyler, *Black and Conservative*, 3-4; Chesnutt, "Her Virginia Mammy," in *The Wife of His Youth*, 38.

[61]Schuyler, *Black and Conservative*, 25-26.

[62]W. E. B. DuBois, "The Black North, A Social Study," *New York Times* November 17, 24, December 1, 8, 20, 15, 1901.

[63]Ibid., December 1, 1901.

[64]Donald L. Noel, "Correlates of Anti-White Prejudice" (Ph.D. diss. Cornell University, 1961), 103-104.

[65]Occupation is, it has been noted, "perhaps the best single index of social class position." Robert M. Frumkin, "Race, Occupation, and Social Class in New York," *JNE* 27 (Winter 1958): 62. See also Alvin Boskoff, "Negro Class Structure and Technicways," *Social Forces* 29 (December 1950): 124-125. For a discussion of occupation as an index of class, see Milton M. Gordon, *Social Class in American Sociology* (McGraw-Hill Book Co., 1963), 151-161.

[66]Noval D. Glenn, "Negro Prestige Criteria: A Case Study in the Bases of Prestige," *AJS* 68 (November 1963): 654 (table 5).

[67]John Daniels, *In Freedom's Birthplace: A Study of the Boston Negroes* (1914; reprint ed., Johnson Reprint Corp., 1968) 191; August Meier, *Negro Thought in America, 1880-1915: Racial Ideologies in the Age of Booker T. Washington* (University of Michigan Press, 1966), 151.

[68]See, for instance, Hill, "The Negro Upper Class in Boston," 90-91. Glenn notes that in sixteen studies of black stratification, education, oc-

cupation, income, and respectability were the most frequently used measures of prestige. Glenn, "Negro Prestige Criteria," 646 (table 2).

[69]Henry Gannett, *Occupations of the Negroes* (Baltimore: The Trustees [of the John F. Slater Fund], 1895), 9-10 (table). The study provides a digest of the 1890 census data. A direct comparison is difficult to make, but gross figures may provide some insights. The 1890 census data reflect that for the nation as a whole, 3.72 percent of the persons involved in "professional services" were "colored," while 67.86 percent were native white of native parentage. Only 16.34 percent were native whites of foreign parentage, and 12.08 percent were foreign-born whites. U.S., Department of the Interior, Census Office, *Population of the United States at the Eleventh Census: 1890*, pt. II (Washington: GPO, 1897), cxvii.

[70]Kelly Miller, "The City Negro," *Southern Workman* 31 (June 1902): 342-343. New York City data from Haynes, *Negro at Work in New York City*, 72 (table XVI). In each case the data were extracted from the 1890 census.

[71]Mary White Ovington, *Half a Man: The Status of the Negro in New York* (1911; reprint ed., Schocken Books, 1969) 146, 147.

[72]For example, 48 percent in Boston and 50 percent in Philadelphia. Haynes, *Negro at Work in New York City*, 72.

[73]Unless otherwise noted, all data were compiled from U.S., Department of Commerce and Labor, *Twelfth Census of the United States, 1900: Special Reports: Occupations at the Twelfth Census* (Washington: GPO, 1904), table 43.

[74]Williams, "Social Stratification and the Negro American," 12-27.

[75]DuBois, "The Black North," *New York Times*, November 17, 1901, Drake and Cayton, *Black Metropolis,* chap. 9, provide a detailed analysis of the occupational picture in Chicago from 1890 to 1930. In a series of figures, they compare the distribution of jobs in that city between native whites, foreign-born whites, and Negroes. In 1890, for example, Negroes held less than 1 percent of the jobs in Chicago that were classified as "clean" work, 1 percent of those classified as manual labor, but 11 percent of those in the servant category. (The "clean" work category encompassed 31 percent of the available jobs in 1890, manual labor 57 percent, and the servant category only 12 percent.) Four decades later the percentages in these categories were 2 percent, 9 percent, and 34 percent, respectively. Ibid., 225 (figure 14).

[76]Dubois, "The Black North," *New York Times*, December 8, 1901. Although DuBois points to a normal sex distribution among the Negro population of Boston about 1900 and to the fact that only 62 percent of the 12,000 population were employed (indicating a more *normal* home and

family life), the structure is not really too different. The "job ceiling" for Negroes was perhaps a little higher and the white community perhaps a little less overtly prejudiced, but as Daniels indicates in *In Freedom's Birthplace,* 118-119, this was changing.

[77]Caroline B. Chapin, "Settlement Work Among Colored People," *Annals* 21 (March 1903): 337. See also Ovington, "Negro Home in New York," 25.

[78]Drake and Cayton, *Black Metropolis,* 112, 224-232, 233ff; Kelly Miller, "The Negro as a Workingman," *American Mercury* 6 (November 1925): 310-311; Myrdal, *American Dilemma,* 291-296, and appendix 6.

[79]DuBois, "The Black North," *New York Times,* November 17, 1901. See also Lilian Brandt, "The Make-up of the Negro City Groups," *Charities* 15 (October 7, 1905): 7-11.

[80]Haynes, *Negro at Work in New York City,* 14-18, 23.

[81]U.S., Bureau of the Census, *Negro Population in the United States, 1790-1915* (1918; reprint ed., Arno Press, 1968) 92 (table 9); U.S., Bureau of the Census, *Historical Statistics of the United States, Colonial Times to 1957* (Washington: GPO, 1960), 46-47 (Series C 25-73); Marion Hayes, "A Century of Change: Negroes in the U.S. Economy, 1860-1960," *Monthly Labor Review* 8 (December 1962): 1361-1362; Dean Dutcher, *The Negro in Modern Industrial Society: An Analysis of Changes in the Occupations of Negro Workers, 1910-1920* (Lancaster, Pennsylvania: Ph.D. diss. Columbia University, 1931), 23n.6; Preston Valien, "General Demographic Characteristics of the Negro Population in the United States," *JNE* 32 (Fall 1963): 329-336; Brandt, "Make-up of Negro City Groups," 7-8.

[82]*Negro Population in the United States,* 92 (table 9).

[83]Daniels, *In Freedom's Birthplace,* 139; *Crisis* 4 (September 1912): 217-218; Taeuber and Taeuber, *Negroes in Cities,* 25.

[84]Frederick J. Brown, *The Northward Movement of the Colored Population: A Statistical Study* (Baltimore: Cushing and Co., c. 1897), 41.

[85]Booker T. Washington, "The Case of the Negro," *Atlantic Monthly* 84 (November 1899): 577-587.

[86]Victoria Earle Mathews, comp. *Black-Belt Diamonds: Gems from the Speeches, Addresses, and Talks to Students of Booker T. Washington* (1898; reprint ed., Negro Universities Press, 1969) 19.

[87]Albert Bushnell Hart (letter to the editor, signed), "Where Negroes May Not Come," *Harper's Weekly* 47 (December 5, 1903): 1950.

[88]"The Negro at the North," *Harper's Weekly* 50 (March 31, 1906): 436.

[89]Ralph Ellison, *Invisible Man* (Modern Library, 1952), powerfully relates this facet of being black in white America.

[90]Edwin S. Redkey, *Black Exodus: Black Nationalist and Back-to-Africa Movements, 1890-1910* (New Haven: Yale University Press, 1969), chap. 2.

See also Meier, *Negro Thought in America*, 9-10; Drake and Cayton, *Black Metropolis*, 53; W. E. B. DuBois, "The Passing of 'Jim Crow,' " *Independent* 91 (July 14, 1917): 54; William O. Scroggs, "Interstate Migration of Negro Population," *Journal of Political Economy* 25 (December 1917): 1038-1040; Guy B. Johnson, "The Negro Migration and Its Consequences," *Journal of Social Forces* 2 (March 1924): 404.

⁹¹Scroggs, "Interstate Migration of Negro Population," 1039.

⁹²Arnold Rose, *The Negro's Morale:Group Identification and Protest* (University of Minnesota Press, 1949), 37. DuBois, pointing to the youthful makeup of the Negro population in New York City, offered that it was explained by the pressure of violence in the South pushing the Negro North. "The Black North," *New York Times,* November 17, 1901.

⁹³DuBois, "The Passing of 'Jim Crow,' " 54.

⁹⁴Ibid. See also, W. L. Fleming, "Pap Singleton, The Moses of the Colored Exodus," *AJS* 15 (July 1909): 66.

⁹⁵William Pickens, "Migration to Fuller Life," *Forum* 72 (November 1924): 603. See also Taeuber and Taeuber, *Negroes in Cities*, 126-127; Drake and Cayton, *Black Metropolis*, 73-76; Gilbert Osofsky, "Race Riot, 1900: A Study of Ethnic Violence," *JNE* 32 (Winter 1963): 17.

⁹⁶Paul U. Kellogg, "The Negro Pioneers," in Locke, ed., *The New Negro*, 273; Taeuber and Taeuber, *Negroes in Cities*, 12-13. See also Benjamin Young, "The Boll Weevil Starts North—A Story," *Opportunity* 4 (February 1926): 42-43, 53. Young's story deals with the older migrants and sees them as the ones pushed out by economic causes. They cannot really be thought of as having followed the younger migrants north, he implies, for not all of these made it all the way. Many dropped out along the way; others went back to the farm in disillusionment.

⁹⁷Salt Lake City *Broad Ax*, December 13, 1898.

⁹⁸"Causes and Remedies for the Negro's Flocking to the Cities," *Voice of the Negro* 1 (May 1904): 209-210; Mathews, comp. *Black-Belt Diamonds*, 8.

⁹⁹Frazier, *Black Bourgeoisie*, 147; Arna Bontemps and Jack Conroy, *Anyplace But Here* (Hill and Wang, 1966; originally published as *They Seek a City,* 1945), chap. 11; Carl Sandburg, *The Chicago Race Riots, July 1919* (1919; reprint ed., Harcourt, Brace and World, 1969), 60-61; Drake and Cayton, *Black Metropolis,* 59-60; Edward Margolies in introduction to Attaway, *Blood on the Forge,* xi; *Crisis* 12 (October 1916): 270, and 13 (January 1917): 115; Frederick G. Detweiler, *The Negro Press in the United States* (1922; reprint ed., College Park, Maryland: McGrath Publishing Co., 1968), 72; Hartt, "When the Negro Comes North," 83-89. Hartt suggests that the motives of the Negro press for their campaigns urging migration might well have included revenge. That is, heavy migration would visit

economic havoc on the South. The migrants themselves also held this attitude, he reported. Ibid., 84-86. The *Pittsburgh Courier*, August 11, 1923, with obvious pleasure, carried a story that the exodus would cost Georgia $27 million in 1923 in lost labor, vacant farms, and so forth. "The destruction caused by this quiet migration is described as no less striking than the destruction caused by Sherman's army."

[100]*New York Age*, February 15, 1917.

[101]Quoted in Harry L. Jones, "An Essay on the Blues," *CLA Journal* 13 (September 1969): 65. See here especially Bontemps and Conroy, *Anyplace But Here*, chap 11..

[102]Detweiler, *Negro Press in the United States*, 1. The influence of the Negro press is also well demonstrated in Emmet Scott, comp. "Letters of Negro Migrants of 1916-18," *JNH* 4 (July 1919): 290-340.

[103]Konrad Bercovici, "The Black Blocks of Manhattan," *Harper's Magazine* 149 (October 1924): 613. See also "The Negro Migrations—A Symposium," *Forum* 72 (December 1924): 855-856; *Pittsburgh Courier*, July 21, 1923; Hartt, "When the Negro Comes North," 85; Robert W. Bagnall, "The Labor Problem and Negro Migration," *Southern Workman* 49 (November 1920): 518-523; "The Negro Migration," *Opportunity* 1 (August 1923): 254-255; Sandburg, *Chicago Race Riots*, 15-16, 31-32.

[104]From Langston Hughes, "Bound No'th Blues," in *Selected Poems of Langston Hughes* (Alfred A. Knopf, 1959), 174.

[105]Rollin Hartt, quoted in Harold A. Farrell, "Theme and Variation: A Critical Evaluation of the Negro Novel, 1919-1947" (Ph.D. diss., Ohio State University, 1949), 181. See also Emmet Jay Scott, *Negro Migration During the War* (1920; reprint ed., Arno Press, 1969) 13; Ray S. Baker, "The Negro Goes North," *World's Work* 34 (July 1917): 319.

[106]E. Franklin Frazier, "Certain Aspects of Conflict in the Negro Family," *Social Forces* 10 (October 1931): 77. See also Rose, *The Negro's Morale*, 38; Locke, *The New Negro*, 6; Dutcher, *Negro in Modern Industrial Society*, 27; Carter G. Woodson, *A Century of Negro Migration* (1918; reprint ed., Russell and Russell, 1969), 168-169; Ray Stannard Baker, *Following the Color Line* (1908; reprint ed., Harper Torchbooks, 1964), 133.

[107]Scroggs, "Interstate Migration of Negro Population," 1041; Otis D. and Beverly Duncan, *The Negro Population of Chicago: A Study of Residential Succession* (University of Chicago Press, 1957), 6-7; Harold U. Faulkner, *The Decline of Laissez Faire, 1897-1917* (Harper & Row, Torchbooks, 1968), 99-100; Scheiner, *Negro Mecca*, 10, 11; John Hope Franklin, *From Slavery to Freedom* 3rd ed., (1966; reprint ed., Vintage Books, 1969), 471-472; Baker, "The Negro Goes North," 315; Charles S. Johnson, "How Much Is the Migration a Flight from Persecution?" *Oppor-*

tunity 1 (September 1923): 272-274; Charles S. Johnson, "The Negro Migration: An Economic Interpretation," *Modern Quarterly,* 3 (July 1924-1925): 314-326; Hayes, "Century of Change," 1360; Scott, *Negro Migration During the War,* 6; Louise Venable Kennedy, *The Negro Peasant Turns Cityward: Effects of Recent Migration to Northern Centers* (Columbia University Press, 1930), 42. None, of course, dismissed the efficaciousness of social conditions as a cause, and most strived to construct a medley of causes. See Myrdal, *American Dilemma,* chap. 8.

[108]Charles S. Johnson, "American Migrant: The Negro," in *Proceedings of the National Conference of Social Work, 1927* (University of Chicago Press, 1927), 554; U.S., Department of Labor, Division of Negro Economics, *The Negro at Work During the World War and During Reconstruction* (Washington: GPO, 1921), 10.

[109]Quoted in *Crisis* 2 (June 1911): 56. See also Blanton Fortson, "Northward to Extinction," *Forum* 72 (November 1924): 596.

[110]Kingsley Moses, "The Negro Comes North," *Forum* 58 (August 1917): 181-190.

[111]J. W. Johnson, "Harlem: The Culture Capital," in Locke, ed., *The New Negro,* 305.

[112]Scott, *Negro Migration During the War,* 72-85; Leo Ailunas, "Statutory Means of Impeding Emigration of the Negro," *JNH* 22 (April 1937): 148-162; Hartt, "When the Negro Comes North," 84.

[113]T. J. Woofter, Jr., "The Negro on a Strike," *Social Forces* 2 (November 1923): 84; Frazier, "The Negro Community," 419: Lyonel C. Florant, "Negro Internal Migration," *ASR* 7 (December 1942): 788-791. See also "'Cruiter" [a one act play] by John Mathews, in Alain Locke and Montgomery Gregorys, eds., *Plays of Negro Life* (Harper, 1927), 187-204.

[114]Kennedy, *Negro Peasant Turns Cityward,* 44.

[115]Ibid., 44, 95-100; See also Scott, *Negro Migration During the War,* 17; "Southern Negroes Moving North," *World's Work* 34 (June 1917): 135.

[116]Eugene Kinckle Jones, "Negro Migration in New York State," *Opportunity* 4 (January 1926): 8; Minor, "The Negro in Columbus," 17. Eight cities in the North saw increases of between 50 and 100 percent. Eric D. Walrond, "Negro Exodus from the South," *Current History and Forum* 18 (September 1923): 942.

[117]Duncan and Duncan, *Negro Population of Chicago,* 21, 25 (table 2).

[118]Monroe N. Work, "The Race Problem in Cross Section: The Negro in 1923," *Social Forces* 2 (January 1924): 246. The Negro population of the ten districts was almost 1.2 million; almost 500,000 were concentrated in the New York-Philadelphia districts.

[119]U.S., Bureau of the Census, *Negroes in the United States, 1920-32* (1935; reprint ed., Arno Press, 1969) 7.

[120]See, for example, "Migration Cityward," *Southern Workman* 31 (March 1902): 131; Miller, "The City Negro," *Southern Workman* (April 1902): 217-218.

[121]From "Evenin' Air Blues," by Langston Hughes, in James A. Emanuel and Theodore L. Gross, eds., *Dark Symphony* (Free Press, 1968), 207-208.

[122]*Pittsburgh Courier*, June 23, 1923. See also Robert T. Kerlin, *Voice of the Negro: 1919* (1920; reprint ed., Arno Press, 1968), 132-135; "The South Calling Negroes Back," *Literary Digest* 54 (June 23, 1917): 1914.

[123]Hartt, "When the Negro Comes North," *World's Work* 48 (June 1924): 186; George E. Haynes, "Negro Migration: Its Effect on Family and Community Life in the North," *Opportunity* 2 (September 1924): 273; Rudolph Fisher, "The Promised Land," *Atlantic Monthly* 139 (January 1927): 37-45; Alden Bland, *Behold a Cry* (Charles Scribners, 1947), passim.

[124]Thomas Bowyer Campbell, *Black Sadie* (Boston: Houghton Mifflin Co., 1928), 65.

[125]From "When I Return to the Southland It Will Be," by Sparrell Scott, quoted in Bontemps and Conroy, *Anyplace But Here*, 171-172.

[126]Frazier, "Race Contacts and the Social Structure," 2; Bone, *Negro Novel in America*, 53.

[127]C. S. Johnson, "The New Frontage on American Life," in Locke, *The New Negro*, 285.

[128]Robert H. Brisbane, Jr., "The Rise of Protest Movements Among Negroes Since 1900" (Ph.D. diss., Harvard University, 1949), 50.

[129]Bland, *Behold a Cry*, 3.

[130]Langston Hughes, *The Best of Simple* (Hill and Wang, 1961), 207.

[131]Robert Wiebe, *The Search for Order* (Hill and Wang, 1967), 13-14.

[132]Ibid., 112-113; August Meier, "Negro Class Structure and Ideology in the Age of Booker T. Washington," *Phylon* 23 (Fall 1962): 259.

[133]Ovington, *Half a Man*, 178.

[134]Meier, "Negro Class Structure and Ideology," 259; August Meier and David Lewis, "History of the Negro Upper Class in Atlanta, Georgia, 1890-1958," *JNE* 28 (Spring 1959): 128.

[135]Ibid.; Meier, "Negro Class Structure and Ideology," 259; Boskoff, "Negro Class Structure and Technicways," 130; Frazier, *Black Bourgeoisie*, 51-52.

[136]Frazier, *Black Bourgeoisie*, 165.

[137]Samuel R. Scottron, "The Industrial and Professional Pursuits of Colored People in Old New York," *Colored American Magazine* 13 (October 1907): 265-267; Ovington, *Half a Man*, 77-78; "Negro Waiters Are Losing Out, but Why?" *New York Age*, April 6, 1911; William Hannibal Thomas, *The American Negro; What He Was, What He Is, and What He May*

Become: A Critical and Practical Discussion (Macmillan Co., 1901), 67-69; Hardin, "A Study of the Negroes of Philadelphia," 26.

[138]Ovington, *Half a Man*, 78; "The Superfluous Negro," *New Republic* 7 (June 24, 1916): 187-188. In the labor-scarce war years his relative position improved, of course. He remained in a most vulnerable position, however, even if the war years had been an especially prosperous time for him. He simply did not have in his power the economic means of negating the color line. Dutcher, *Negro in Modern Industrial Society*, 34-35; Robert C. Weaver, "Negro Labor Since 1929," *JNH* 35 (January 1950): 20-21.

[139]Ulyssess S. Poston, "The Negro Awakening," *Current History and Forum* 19 (December 1923): 473.

[140]Claude McKay, *Home to Harlem* (Harper and Brothers, 1928), 48.

[141]Frazier, *Black Bourgeoisie*, 42, 51-52, chap. 2. Articles extolling the expansion of Negro business were common in the *Colored American Magazine*, probably because of Booker Washington's connection with it. Its stories of individual successes are not too impressive, however, when the actual capital involved is noted. See, for instance, a report of the Negro Business League praising growth between 1900 and 1924 in "The Growth of Negro Business," *Literary Digest* 83 (October 25, 1924): 62. Nor would the picture of black business change much in the next two generations. An article entitled, "The Birth Pangs of Black Capitalism," *Time*, October 18, 1968, 98, reported that "though Negroes constitute 12% of the U. S. population, they own scarcely 1% of the country's 5,000,000 private business firms. One out of every 40 white Americans is a proprietor, but only one Negro in 1,000 is."

[142] Meier, "Negro Class Structure and Ideology," 259-260. It is Meier's thesis that these businessmen were a new group of men, men in whom "the philosophy of racial progress through economic solidarity, or the formation of what DuBois called a group economy, and the philosophy of Booker T. Washington found their greatest support." Ibid., 260. The numbers supposedly involved in business must be addressed with caution. The Negro Business League tended to be rather all inclusive, Frazier notes, and it counted even newsboys as businessmen. Frazier, *Black Bourgeoisie*, 132. In 1899, a survey conducted under DuBois's direction showed only 1,906 Negro businessmen and only 218 in the North. W. E. B. DuBois, ed., "The Negro in Business," in *The Atlanta University Publications* (1899; reprint ed., Arno Press, 1968).

[143]Richard R. Wright, Jr., "The Economic Conditions of Negroes in the North," *Southern Workman* 38 (January 1909): 39-40.

[144]Frazier, *Black Bourgeoisie*, 51-52.

[145]*Chicago Defender*, September 20, 1919.

[146]Faulkner, *Decline of Laissez Faire,* 100-101. See also Hayes, "A Century of Change," 1362-1363; Haynes, *Negro at Work in New York City,* 70, 77; Walrond, "The Negro Exodus from the South," 942-944.

[147]Billingsley, *Black Families in White America,* 85 (table 5).

[148]Ovington, *Half a Man,* 93, 100-101; C. S. Johnson, "New Frontage on American Life," in Locke, ed., *New Negro,* 283.

[149]Fannie Barrier Williams, "The Problem of Employment for Negro Women," *Southern Workman* 32 (September 1903): 432.

[150]*Colored American Magazine* 7 (April 1907): advertising section.

[151]*New York Age,* August 24, 1911.

[152]Minor, "Negro in Columbus," 179.

[153]W. E. B. DuBois, *Darkwater* (1920; reprint ed., Schocken Books, 1969), 115 (emphasis removed).

[154]Ibid., 115-116. This point highlights some of the problems that arise in attempting to define the class structure of the Negro community. In this connection, see also Myrdal, *American Dilemma* 1386n.32; Elaine Ogden McNiel and Horace R. Cayton, "Research on the Urban Negro," *AJS* 47 (September 1941): 176-183.

[155]DuBois, *Darkwater,* 120.

[156]Rudolph Fisher, *The Walls of Jericho* (1928; reprint ed., Arno Press, 1969) 265.

[157]*Opportunity* 1 (October 1923): 290.

[158]Campbell, *Black Sadie,* 64.

[159]Bureau of Census, *Negroes in the United States, 1920-32,* 7. Natural increase cannot be ignored in these numbers, but it should be noted that one result of the cityward movement was a declining birth rate. The death rate also dropped during these years, although it remained about twenty years behind the white death rate. Migration from the South must thus be credited with the dramatic increase of the northern black urban population. See Kennedy, *Negro Peasant Turns Cityward,* 170-171; E. Franklin Frazier, *The Negro in the United States,* 2d ed. (Macmillan, 1957), 577-578.

[160]Bureau of Census, *Negroes in the United States, 1920-32,* 55-66 (tables 1, 11).

[161]E. Franklin Frazier, *The Negro Family in the United States* (University of Chicago Press, 1939), 422-425. Frazier's categories were as follows: middle class: professional, public service, trade, and clerical; lower class: skilled, semi-skilled, domestic service, and laborers. This again points out the difficulty of trying to structure the Negro community of this time along neat class lines. Frazier, for instance, would place all those engaged in domestic work in the lower class regardless of higher status assigned by other criteria. See also Frazier, "Occupational Classes Among Negroes in Cities," *AJS* 35 (March 1930): 718-738.

[162]"Complete Survey of Race Women in Local Industries," *New York Age*, March 22, 1919.

[163]Ibid. The average salary for Negro women at the time was between eight and twelve dollars a week. A survey of conditions in 1921 showed just about the same situation existing; most black women were still being employed in either domestic and personal service, manufacturing and mechanical industries (tobacco, clothing, food processing, and other small manufactures), or in agriculture. Elizabeth Ross Haynes, "Two Million Negro Women at Work," *Southern Workman* 52 (February 1922): 64-72.

[164]U.S., Department of Labor, Women's Bureau, *Negro Women in Industry* (Washington: GPO, 1922), passim; U.S., Department of Labor, Women's Bureau, *Negro Women in Industry in 15 States* (Washington: GPO, 1929), passim.

[165]George E. Haynes, "Effect of War Conditions on Negro Labor," *Proceedings, Academy of Political Science* 8 (February 1919): 303.

[166]Quoted in *Opportunity* 4 (February 1926): 68.

[167]See, for instance, Kerlin, *Voice of the Negro*, 54-56. *The Pittsburgh Courier* noted in 1919 that "even in the most prosperous parts of the North it [Negro income] probably averages less than $1,600 a year . . . , [and] it would probably be very difficult to muster more than 25,000 Negroes who average more than $1,600 a year." "Let's Quit Pretending?" *Pittsburgh Courier*, November 30, 1919. See also Sterling D. Spero and Abram L. Harris, *The Black Worker* (1931; reprint ed., Atheneum, 1968) 174-177.

[168]Ovington, *Half a Man*, 50.

[169](New York) Urban League, "Twenty-Four Hundred Negro Families in Harlem: an Interpretation of the Living Conditions of Small Wage Earners," typescript, Urban League Papers, file box A-21, Library of Congress. Everywhere a substantial portion of the black population opened up their homes to lodgers to help make ends meet. As early as 1915, 32 percent of New York's Harlemites were lodgers. (National) Urban League, *Housing Conditions Among Negroes in Harlem, New York City* (Poole Press Association, printers, 1915), 20. The ubiquitous lodger is a facet of black urban life that has been often noted. See, for example, Woofter, *Negro Problems in Cities*, 86-88; Osofsky, *Harlem*, 138; Spear, *Black Chicago*, 149-150; Haynes, *Negro at Work in New York City*, 65, 145; Fisher, "The Promised Land," 38-45.

[170]See, for instance, Gilbert Osofsky, "The Enduring Ghetto," *JAH* 55 (September 1968): 243-255.

[171]Langston Hughes, *The Big Sea* (Hill and Wang, 1963), 85-86.

[172]Frazier, *Black Bourgeoisie*, 26.

[173]Frazier, "Certain Aspects of Conflict in the Negro Family," 79; and "Race Contacts and the Social Structure," 9.

[174]Eugene Gordon, "Negro Society," *Scribner's Magazine* 88 (August 1930): 135.

[175]Ibid., 135-136.

[176]Fisher, *The Walls of Jericho*, 165.

[177]Rayford W. Logan, "The Hiatus—A Great Negro Middle Class," *Southern Workman* 58 (December 1929): 531. See also James T. Laing, "Social Status Among Migrant Negroes," *Social Forces* 16 (May 1938): 562-568.

[178]Allison Davis, "The Socialization of the American Negro Child and Adolescent," *JNE* 8 (July 1939): 264.

[179]Frazier, *Black Bourgeoisie*, 24-25; Wilson Record, "Social Stratification and Intellectual Roles in the Negro Community," *British Journal of Sociology* 8 (September 1957): 235-255.

[180]Frank W. Quillan, "The Negro in Cincinnati," *Independent* 68 (February 24, 1910): 400.

4

THE NEW
BLACK AMERICAN

We have to-morrow
Bright before us
Like a flame
Yesterday, a night-gone thing
A sun-down name
And dawn to-day
Broad arch above the road we came,
We march. [1]

THE GROWTH of racial consciousness, marked since the 1890s, created modern black America. Obviously black America had a racial identity before then; racial consciousness was probably present from the founding of the continental colonies, and certainly it was much influenced by the nature of American slavery. [2] There is no doubt that the "old settlers" in the northern communities possessed such an awareness before the Civil War. [3] And certainly the old Negro elite, feeling themselves apart from the ordinary black mass, held some such identification—one based upon free status before the war, pride in blood relationship to leading white families, "political" connections to the seats of power in the form of clerkships, and so forth. By the 1890s, however, this sense of group belonging was being frustrated by changes on both sides of the color line, and it had reached low ebb. [4]

Thrust from his tenuous toehold in the mainstream of America by political, social, and economic proscriptions, the black American

flopped about "like a fish caught in a net," as Lerone Bennett, Jr.,
aptly put it.[5] The old elite continued for some time to see themselves
as being more class akin to their counterparts in the dominant culture—an attitude that was perpetuated in the nascent middle class
of the decade. They hoped to make some sort of an adjustment with
the white view that saw the black community as an undifferentiated
unity. But the ordinary black respectable was closer to the reality of
racist America. By the 1890s the urban Negro especially had given
up, at last, the hopes of the Reconstruction period, hopes that black
Americans had previously rather naively accepted. Instead they accepted the realities manifest in white America's turn to extreme
racism.[6]

Enforced social distance made blacks accept such conditions,
but it also gave a new dimension to their sense of racial being—a
feeling of "peoplehood," a "we-group" sense of identity. These
shorthand expressions of racial consciousness refer to what sociologist Milton Gordon terms "participational identification," a sense of
identity distinct from the "historical identification" that precedes
it.[7] Black urban America began to interpret its experiences more
and more in terms of blackness. More and more the Negro identified
himself now as a special kind of American. At bottom he saw his
position was to be continually defined by his special relationship to
the dominant white society.[8] Something of this, albeit a negative
aspect, may be seen in such remarks of the time as: " 'Well, this is a
white man's country,' or 'well, you must remember you are
colored.' "[9]

That the ordinary Afro-American was turning inward toward a
sense of peoplehood by the mid-1890s at the latest may not be un-
questionably demonstrated, to be sure, but the available evidence is
convincing. Some authorities tie the growth of this sentiment, which
is confidently asserted to have existed in the 1920s, to the Great
Migration and World War I.[10] Making northern city dwellers out of
an ever-increasing number of black southern migrants undoubtedly
strengthened the sentiment and speeded up the process and thus accounts for its increased perceptibility by 1919. But, as mentioned
earlier, the significance of the migration prior to that time is often
overlooked. Furthermore, the turn to a new sense of racial consciousness might better be seen as a reaction to the cresting of white
racial consciousness in the 1890s. In this sense the rise of black

racial consciousness was an entirely rational response to the reordering of the white social community underway at the time. White
America had embarked on a search for order that in one of its facets
sought to further exclude black Americans from the mainstream of
American life. Black America, with the northern urban dweller in
the van, also had embarked on a search for order, but its search
moved from the premise that the American culture had to be interpreted in terms of blackness.[11]

W. E. B. DuBois, noting the discontent among black Philadelphians in the 1890s, pointed to the new orientation in that community. The younger generation of respectables, he said, was addressing the continued color discrimination that so obviously made
them a special kind of American from a different perspective.[12] A
black commentator in 1899 made the discontent explicit in an article
in the national magazine *Forum*. All of the suggested solutions to
the race problem in America—education, industrial usefulness and
property acquisition, religion—are useless in and of themselves,
W. H. Councill asserted. "Whether North, South, East or West be
his ambition, his aspirations are chained to a stake, are circum-
scribed by Anglo-Saxon prejudice and might: his movements are circular." Only when black Americans become a people, this critic
went on, will they be able to attack the chain.[13]

Just as Sutton Grigg's 1889 novel, *Imperium in Imperio*, had
pointed to the arrival of a "new Negro" on the scene, such comments
foreshadowed the protest of the first decade of the new century that
culminated in the abortive Niagara Movement and the founding of
the NAACP.[14] Walled in by white racism, "the American Negro
began to reject the idea of the world's belonging to white people
only, and to think of himself, in concert, as a potential force in the
organization of society," as Saunders Redding writes in his introduction to a 1961 edition of DuBois's famous *Souls of Black Folk*.[15]

But can the fact that some highly articulate blacks saw new strident criticism boiling up from among the black mass be pointed to
as indicating a sense of racial being had come into existence there?
One might instead point to the highly vocal Bishop Henry Turner of
the African Methodist Episcopal church and his call for emigration
to Africa.[16] It is the widening challenge to the white status quo, however, that indicates that the sense of peoplehood was percolating upward in the black community. Even the conservative *Colored Amer-*

ican Magazine, whose pages were much devoted to praising the rising new black middle class, found room for comment. In a 1905 editorial it charged that "half of the population of the South has Negro blood in its veins. The South has produced no man of genius of whom it has been said, and it is much believed, and perhaps can be proved, that he was of mixed origins."[17] Later, in response to a statement by President Eliot of Harvard that he would "advocate separation" if the number of Negro students warranted it, an editorial asserted that it was not because of any "desire to associate with whites that we decry this American habit of 'Jim Crowing' us, but because of the disadvantages following it."[18] The same issue remarked, "The American white man's tolerance may need educating and preparation for the new Negro, for if we shall have a new Negro we must also have a new white man."[19]

There were few that continued to hope for a new white man, of course. Rather than waiting for him, blacks consolidated their own communities. This is clear from the "completeness" of such black communities in the larger northern cities by 1910. By that time, Mary Ovington noted, the sense of community had developed to the point where everyday matters were not only being interpreted from a position of blackness, but positions of contending opinion on things economic, social, and political had evolved in these communities.[20]

The sense of racial consciousness that had developed becomes clearer, if still inferential, in the charges issued by black periodicals to the Negro community. "The Negro . . . is chiefly tolerated because of his usefulness as a laborer and producer," asserted the *Colored American Magazine*.[21] In 1909 the *Broad Ax* stated flatly, "The quicker the Negro learns that he is an unimportant and insignificant factor politically as far as the achievement of any substantial results for the race is concerned, . . . the better it will be for him."[22] How can the average Negro be expected to see much purpose in educating his children, stormed this black newspaper, when he knows they will not be able to use it? The solution lay within the black community: "We have been whining and complaining for so long until even those who were our friends have grown tired and threadbare of us."[23]

The enhanced sense of racial consciousness obviously was in many ways the product of the shift in the social structure of black

America already described. But it was also fostered by such agencies as the Negro Business League whose membership had a vested interest in seeing the development of a strong sense of racial solidarity. The league, founded by Booker T. Washington in 1900, had the long-range objectives of bringing Negro Americans together along practical lines and reducing prejudice. At the same time, and more immediately, the heightening of racial consciousness was of definite advantage to this segment of the "disadvantaged." Some businessmen gained at least partial monopolies within the black community. They were subject to most of the same disabilities afflicting the ordinary Negro, but these very disabilities worked to safeguard their positions within the black community.[24] If white prejudice forced the Negro to turn to black businessmen and professionals, so much the better as far as black entrepreneurs and professionals were concerned.

Fostering race pride was simply good business for some. More and more the Negro undertaker now served only the black community. The same was true for the Negro tailor, barber, caterer, physician, and so on as the early decades of the century passed. In the mid-1920s, W. E. B. DuBois observed in the influential *American Mercury*:

> Remember that the advance of the black American in the past twenty-five years has been, despite himself and unnoted by his friends, mainly along separate lines. There has been increasing separation, with separate institutions, a larger group economy by which colored people serve themselves through their own stores, insurance societies and professional services, a tremendous and sometimes an almost fanatic increase in race pride. White people do not sense this. They see increasing race segregation and they are content and happy. The Negro too is content and happy. He is beating the white folks at their own game. He is gaining power. Larger and larger numbers are escaping all contact with the whites.[25]

Campaigns to "buy black" excited and fed upon the growing sense of peoplehood in the community.[26] Negro newspapers argued the need for cooperation: "Organization for Race Good" read one

New York Age headline in 1916.[27] Articles such as this conveyed the sense of shifting values. The black Horatio Alger tenet of individual worth and reward, they intimate, must be subordinated to that of solidarity at all levels. At the same time, though, they could not disguise entirely that solidarity among the mass of ordinary blacks would assist the rising middle class to approximate more closely white middle class life-style—a fact that the ordinary Negro resented.

The Negro History Movement that grew up during the period also fostered and fed the Negro's sense of peoplehood. It too was nourished by "the blatant Caucasian racialist with his theories and assumptions of race superiority . . . ," the first curator of the New York Public Library's Negro Division, Arthur Schomburg, wrote. It "bred his Ethiopian counterpart . . . who . . . tried to prove half of the world's geniuses to have been Negroes and to trace the pedigree of nineteenth century Americans from the Queen of Sheba."[28] Many have noted this propensity for racial propaganda within the Negro History movement. Arnold Rose pointed out, for instance, that "although the movement consciously tends to build race pride, it may also cause Negroes unconsciously to recognize that group pride is built partly on delusion, and therefore may result in a devaluation of themselves for being forced to resort to self-deception."[29]

If in its propaganda aspect the movement generated some rather fantastic claims, in its true historical aspect, as embodied in the Association for the Study of Afro-American Life and History founded in 1915 by historian Carter G. Woodson, the movement provided the Negro community with a scholarly vehicle for protest.[30] Scholarly appeals to a sense of historical identification did not particularly reach those at or near the bottom of the black social structure, however. But conveying similar messages were appeals, commercial in large part to be sure, such as that of the Douglas Specialties Company of Chicago. "RACE PRIDE—WHAT DO YOU TEACH YOUR BOY OR GIRL?" ran their advertisement for pictures of racial heroes. "Do you only hold up examples of deeds of great white people—or do you tell of the wonderful accomplishments of your own racial heroes."[31]

So racial consciousness long antedated the Great War and the special havoc its aftermath visited upon the black urban community, though these events are often pointed to as the real source. Undoubtedly, nevertheless, the war helped accelerate the established trend. The Afro-American's participation in the war demonstrated to him that, however much separated, he was also thoroughly involved in the American society. He learned too the benefits of coordinated action.[32] Much of the cooperation in the black community was still spontaneous or ad hoc in nature. For example, black police had traditionally patrolled the Jewish business section of Philadelphia's black district. When they were removed at the request of the local businessmen's association, a sudden and effective boycott brought about their return. The local businessmen denied bringing their removal about and even pretended not to belong to the business association.[33] In one of Rudolph Fisher's best short stories, the Italian owner of a fruit store in Harlem is wise in the ways of that Negro Mecca. "Patronage had a queer way of shifting itself in Harlem," he thought. "You lost your temper and let slip a single *'nègre!'* A week later you sold your business."[34]

The hopes raised by the very real advances made by many northern blacks during the war period dissolved in the postwar wave of violence that swept through the cities. In compensation for the expectations that lay broken in the rubble of the riots of the Red Summer of 1919, racial consciousness soared.[35] The *New York Age* observed in early 1919 that "there is nothing that commands the admiration and respect of the white world like a man who fights back, and the harder he fights, the more admiration and respect it accords him. Some day the Negro in this country is going to realize that fact."[36]

Comments such as this were not atypical. "Playing the Monkey," the *Chicago Defender* captioned an editorial that asked, "How long will we be harnessed to the chattel ideas of our forefathers?"[37] A New York paper observed, "If the 10,000,000 or more Negroes in the U.S. worried wisely over their future, it would give the white people of this country so much to worry about that they would be glad to give the Negroes what they are entitled to."[38] "Much is said of the 'new Negro,'" declared the *Chicago Defender* in an editorial early in 1920, but "we haven't such a critter[:] just the same old tinted individual roused into self-consciousness, awakened to his own possibilities, with stiffened backbone, with . . . new hopes for the future."[39] The Reverend Rollin Hartt wrote: "'When we get possession of Africa,' a negro said to me in Harlem the other day, 'we are going to build a civilization so splendid that white women will blacken their faces and frizz their hair.'"[40] "Wishbone," "Jawbone," and "Funny-bone" Negroes are out, said a 1921 editorial in the Richmond *St. Luke's Herald.* "Backbone Negroes" are in.[41] Another editorial charged:

> NO NATION has contributed so much to this so-called color tide as America. Here color is a dementia . . . . FOR MUCH OF THIS AMERICAN SPIRIT toward us we do not hold ourselves blameless. We permitted them to enslave us for more than two centuries. We freely confess our shame for this much of our history.[42]

It is evident, of course, that many elements had to coalesce to bring about the heightened sense of community so apparent in black urban America at this time, elements that had been building tension into the community. The reordering of the black social structure may be pointed to again in this context. Even the change urbanization brought to the Negro's religious organizations contributed. In a short story set in the period immediately following the war, the perceptive Langston Hughes, taking advantage of white stereotypes, wrote:

> As long as they were singing and praying, they forgot about the troubles of this world. In a frenzy of rhythm and religion, they laid their cross at the feet of Jesus.
> Poor over-worked Jesus! Somehow since the War, he hadn't borne that cross so well. Too heavy, it's too heavy! Lately, Negroes seem to sense that it's not Jesus' cross, anyhow, it's their own.[43]

Critic Edward Margolies notes that many of these tensions may best be seen as orginating in the "racial tensions [that] flared as labor unions which were often racially exclusionist to begin with, confronted rural Negroes who traditionally and psychologically owed their loyalties more to individuals than to groups."[44] The drama of the development of group consciousness over individual loyalties is to be found in such conflicts. Alden Bland's protagonist in *Behold a Cry* was caught in the flareup in Chicago after the war.

> "You know, it didn't make no difference to me at first, union or no union. But I found out one thing from this riot. They pounded it in my head. White folks really hate us! You can't trust them no more than you can a snake. I wouldn't belong to nothing they belong to!"
>
> He passed his tongue over the sharp edges of his teeth [broken when mobbed by whites].
>
> "Niggers got to stick together more . . . Got to lean on one another. To hell with them crackers!"[45]

Do such comments and observations actually demonstrate a rising racial consciousness? It might be argued that they were little more than reflections of a not very surprising instability and anxiety created by rapid social change and wartime tensions. But the changes were too massive to be explained by such an argument. Black Americans now had more than three decades of experience with the growing white racism. The conciliatory philosophy of Booker Washington had been demonstrated a failure innumerable times at the local level as well as on the national scene. Organized protest at the national level had existed for a decade in the form of the NAACP, although it had yet to reach down to the ordinary Negro's level. Then at the end of the war came the rise of Marcus Garvey and his Universal Negro Improvement Association (UNIA), which can be seen only as a mass Negro movement whose every tenet reflected racial consciousness.

The UNIA was an international pan-African organization, but it was in the United States that it enjoyed its largest successes.[46] At its peak the UNIA boasted of black-owned enterprises organized under its Negro Factories Corporation and a steamship company appropriately named the Black Star Line. It had a military-like African Legion and white-clad Black Cross nurses, and it sponsored its own religious institution, the African Orthodox church. Exactly how many adherents the movement attracted—militant, active and vocal, concurring but passive, silent but hopeful—will never be re-

solved to everyone's satisfaction. Garvey's following has been estimated to have numbered anywhere from a few thousand to several
million. In 1928 Garvey himself claimed UNIA membership was
eleven million.[47] But numbers, while important, are not able to relate the most important aspects of Garvey's colorful career and its
impact upon the maturing sense of community in the North.

Marcus Garvey, a West Indian-born Negro, was a racial Zionist
who came to the United States in 1916 and who accepted at face
value the ever-present white expressions of prejudice—as did the
ordinary black American. He turned these expressions of inferiority
back upon the white world: they were indicative of the real position
of the black man in the West in general and in the United States in
particular. Offering a doctrine of blackness—black was good, white
was evil—Garvey appealed to both black and white prejudices. If
miscegenation was a horror to the whites, so too was it a horror to
blacks. He called for racial purity and economic self-sufficiency, two
things white America had consistently denied. He made eloquent
appeals to the past glories of the black race, stealing weapons from
the middle-class Negro History Movement in doing so.[48] Let blackness be your glory, not your burden, Garvey told ordinary black
Americans. And he enumerated black individual rights—something
the ordinary Negro could not safely do from his position of
weakness. Blackness was something to be displayed; it was a
virtue.[49]

No words could have been more welcome to the ears of people
whose anticipations had been so efficiently and thoroughly deflated.
Just the existence of the UNIA gave the individual Afro-American
measurably better stature in his own eyes, even though whites did
not take Garveyism very seriously. To himself the Afro-American
became a "fellow man of the Negro race."[50] Even after the trappings
of Garveyism have been discounted—and one observer noted that
Garvey's tinsel and ritual was "infinitely less absurd than that of the
Ku Klux Klan and . . . neither secret nor sinister"—the
movement, it must be acknowledged, imbued ordinary black Americans with a massive dose of self-esteem.[51] "The movement," Ira
DeA. Reid later wrote,

> was the first that was able to break through nationality lines,
> the first that broke the crust of middle class leadership among

Negroes, the first to create pride in a slowly changing aspect of
Negro life—color. Garvey was berated, despised, arrested and
extradited [deported]. He was the voice for thousands of Negroes who had never left the south, [and] for thousands of
others who had found recent haven in Northern communities
. . . . Garvey failed in his Back-to-Africa movement, but he
aroused and organized the Negro community in the United
States as it had not been organized before.[52]

Resting upon a solid base of mass support, Garveyism played
an important role as a Negro protest organization during the first
half of the 1920s. Not even the black middle class had anticipated
how strong the attraction of Garvey's propaganda would be to those
at the bottom.[53] It was the ordinary Negro—the old respectables,
now the lower class in black America—that Garvey was talking to,
and their support issued forth from all over America. "I am for
Marcus Garvey," read a postcard to the NAACP from Ketchikan,
Alaska. "I have read the Magazine and Leading Corlord Papper and
Marus Garvey has done more than any Negrow of day . . . put to
Lime Light of the colord race."[54]

By the early 1920s white America had to take some notice. The
comfortable white illusion of a unity in blackness—"of the Negro as
an undifferentiated caste"—was revealed to those who chose to
see.[55]

Garvey's influence began to decline about 1923 as a result of
internal struggles within his organization, continual money troubles,
and external attack. The UNIA rapidly disintegrated as a mass
organization in the United States, and by the time Garvey was de-
ported in 1927, the movement had lost much of its vitality.[56] In the
long history of black nationalism, however, it marked a real beginning. "Garveyism," asserts one recent scholar of the movement,
"was the first serious challenge to white hegemony."[57] ". . . By and
large it can be said that the one distinctive and coherent ideology
which has taken root among Africans and lower class Negro movements in this century has been the various brands of the Garvey
philosophy."[58]

But for the immediate period the movement became bankrupt
and was unable to fulfill its promise. "Garveyism failed," writes
historian E. David Cronon, "largely because it was unable to come

up with a suitable alternative to the unsatisfactory conditions of American life as they affected the Negro."[59] This may be correct, but the movement portended of things to come, for Garvey's mass following brought focus to the deep unrest existing among ordinary Negroes and reflected their anxiety about their future in white America. The editors of *World's Work* do not go too far out of bounds perhaps in claiming in late 1920 that Garveyism was "the best point at which to study what is going on inside the heads of the ten million colored people in the United States."[60]

Unfortunately, how the great mass of black Americans may actually have felt about Garvey himself will probably remain obscure. "A weaver of dreams," wrote Claude McKay of Garvey, "he translated into a fantastic pattern of reality the gaudy strands of the vicarious desires of the submerged members of the Negro race."[61] A close white observer, Rollin Hartt, wrote:

> It is not easy to determine what negroes in general think of Garvey. One gets such responses as, "He is very idealistic," "He builds his mountains too high," or, "I think he's going to waste all that money. What does a colored man know about running steamship lines [referring to Garvey's ill-fated business venture, the Black Star Line]?" But you notice that invariably the reply is preceded by a moment or two of hesitation and you wonder if perhaps the negro is not giving you the answer he imagines you would like to hear. At all events, every American negro seems to know about Garvey, and when Garveyites held high carnival in Madison Square Garden one night last summer [the first convention of the UNIA in August 1920] the building was thronged to capacity with an all-black audience.[62]

Garvey might have been, as some observers believe, of greater significance to the mass at the bottom of the black caste had he approached the situation differently—if, for instance, he had recognized the deep American identity of the ordinary Negro. Rudolph Fisher captures this element in a short story written in the mid-1920s.

"Africa, . . . dat de only chance. Teng mo' years, mahn, dis Harl'm be jes' like downg Georgia. Dis a white mahn's country!"

"Back to Africa!" snorted Payner. "Go on back b'ys. Me—I doan give a dahm f' all de Garveys an' all de Black Star liners in Hell. I stay right here!"

"You t'ink only for you'self," charged Chester. "You t'ink about you' race an' you see I am right. Garvey is de Moses of his people!"

"Maybeso. But I be dahm' if Moses git any my money. Back to Africa! How de hell I'm goin' back where I never been?"[63]

Claude McKay's Banjo exclaimed, "Marcus Garvey was one nigger who had a chance to make his and hulp other folks make it, and he took it and landed himself in prison. That theah Garvey had a white man's chance and he done nigger it away . . . . Garvey wasn't worth no more than the good boot in his bahind that he done got."[64]

Could something like Garveyism have taken place earlier in America? Was the racial consciousness upon which the movement fed intense enough? Probably not. It was not until after the turn of the century that the ordinary black American so consistently interpreted his experiences in terms of blackness. It was not until this time that the black American consistently separated the fact of being Negro from the role white America had assigned to the Negro. The 1920s for Negro America was a period of high morale.[65] "Hitherto," said the articulate Alain Locke, "it must be admitted that American Negroes have been a race more in name that in fact, or to be exact, more in sentiment than in experience. The chief bond between them has been that of a common condition rather than a common consciousness; a problem in common rather than a life in common."[66]

Direction for this spirit of blackness was what was lacking. It was at this point that Garveyism entered black American life.[67] Garvey's praise of things black brought only fleeting harmony to the lower levels of black society, however, but it left a residue. "Black Is a Beautiful Color," read the lead of an article in the *Pittsburgh*

Courier. "The new glory of black is the growing success of the Negro."[68] Black dolls used to be rare but were now quite acceptable in
the black community, noted a black editor, now that white was no
longer the only standard.[69]

At the same time that racism continued to demonstrate to many
the correctness of Garvey's assertion that black Americans had no
future in their own country, white America ironically "discovered"
the Negro—or rather, the "New Negro." Each generation since the
Civil War had had its New Negro, and each New Negro had in some
way challenged the accepted pattern of interracial relations. None,
however, attracted the attention of white America so much as the
New Negro of the Harlem Renaissance.[70] Garveyism was at bottom
an expression of nationalism on the part of lower-class black urban
America. The Renaissance was at bottom an expression of cultural
nationalism on the part of middle-class, intellectual black urban
America. The former found its support within the black community
alone, the latter in the white community as well as in black intellectual circles. Both, obviously, registered the heightened racial consciousness of the time.

The black author of the Harlem Renaissance gained a good
deal of notice in the 1920s, although he was destined to find little
place in American literary history.[71] But much of the recognition
came about in a secondhand manner, as the result of the attention
paid to black subjects by white authors and white patrons. Black
Americans and the problem of being black in a white society were
used by the white as a means of criticizing the "American way of
life" and the "return to normalcy" that had followed the war. They
found in black America none of the superficialities that had cor-
rupted white America.[72]

As white artists exploited black subject matter—Eugene
O'Neil, Sherwood Anderson, and Carl Van Vechten, to mention but
three—black artists found opportunity opening up to them. Once
discovered, Negro art and artists suddenly were in vogue. And in
black America a controversy immediately erupted. Some argued, as
did George Schuyler, that as "the Aframerican is merely a lamp-
blacked Anglo-Saxon," the whole idea of "negro" art in America
was "hokum."[73] Others argued that because the Negro's art stemmed from his peculiar nature and experiences, it was the key to
interracial understanding.

The black artist was placed in an odd position. In the South he was ignored, and when he came North, the South was unaware of any loss. In the North, the white intellectual often lent a hand but then overvalued his output just because he was black. It was a strange Alice-in-Wonderland society.[74]

Many of the participants were at a loss to explain the movement as anything but a fad, as an "epidemic of Negroism," as author Rudolph Fisher put it. Perhaps the white world had finally tuned in the black wavelength, he said, and was now responding to the same basic human drives as the Negro had always been able to in his world. Whites invaded Harlem, but the only lasting effect was that some of the famous old Negro cabarets—the clubs where such entertainers as Ethel Waters gained their early fame—began to cater to whites and to exclude Negroes. There could not be much depth in such manifestations of interracial understanding.[75]

Langston Hughes also thought the movement hollow—but a lot of fun while it lasted. When it ended, when white folks found it hard going when the depression began, he said, they had no time or money for Negro "art."[76] In one of his short stories he ridicules the idea that the "Problem of Problems" would fall before the onslaught of art. A character challenges:

"And as for the cultured Negroes who were always saying art would break down color lines, art could save the race and prevent lynchings! Bunk!" . . . "My ma and pa were both artists when it came to music, and the white folks ran them out of town for being dressed up in Alabama. And look at the Jews! Every other artist in the world's a Jew, and still folks hate them."[77]

Claude McKay noted in his autobiography that the number of black artists who saw the Harlem Renaissance as a means of entry into white upper-class society was surprising to him. "I don't think that it ever occurred to them that perhaps such white individuals were searching for a social and artistic significance in Negro art which they could not find in their own society."[78] McKay questioned the ability of the Renaissance artists who held such attitudes to identify with the ordinary black and the brutal realities of the ordinary

Negro's world. He included in his skepticism the orginator of the phrase "Negro Renaissance," Alain Locke.[79]

But the major artists of the New Negro movement of the 1920s portrayed black life as they found it. Their criticisms of black life revealed the foibles of the black world to the white, breaking the dictate that they be hidden from the dominant society. Wallace Thurman's *The Blacker the Berry* . . . (1929), to cite but one example, nicely highlights this.[80] The black Renaissance artist also opened to white eyes the ordinary Negro's attitudes and opinions of the white world and the racism that was directed at him. If he too seemed preoccupied with race, it was because white men had made it *the* issue. Their "racism" was not necessarily antiwhite; but being black in a white world made other frames of reference less immediate in that white racism so much shaped the bounds of the black world.[81]

As a vehicle of interracial understanding, then, it seems that the awakening should have been suspect from the beginning.[82] To the ordinary Negro, who was the subject of much of the literary work the era produced, the whole New Negro movement was remote. The idea that art would break down the walls of discrimination that surrounded him was an idea that he would not have understood.[83]

The ordinary black American was concerned with one facet of the New Negro, however, for it brought up again a perennial problem: what should this special kind of American call himself? Much discussed again in the 1960s, the problem of a "name to go by" took on special significance during this period of a rising sense of peoplehood. Underlying the objection to the name "Negro" was the heritage of racial slavery. "Truly, you must now know that the word Negro in America means something not racial or biological, but something purely social, something made in the United States," wrote Richard Wright in the 1950s. "The Negro could not take his eyes off the auction block."[84] It was already an old controversy at the beginning of the twentieth century, then.[85] Defenders of the white-assigned name usually had the better part of the argument, however, over those who suggested such substitutes as "Coloureds, Coloured People, Coloured Americans, People of Colour, Ethiopians, Racemen, Negro-Saxons, African Americans, Africo-Americans, Afro-Americans, Aframericans," and "Ethican," a contraction of *Eth*iopian and Ameri*can*.[86] The wrangling was, of course, compli-

cated by the ambiguity of legal definition of just who was a "Negro."
How tangled was the issue is shown by a 1910 Louisiana Supreme
Court decision that held "that while every Negro is a person of color,
not every person of color is a Negro, and that persons of less than full
African descent are not Negroes."[87]
The debate seems to have waned somewhat during the second
decade of the twentieth century, only to wax hot again at the end of
World War I. But again the defenders of the name had the better
part of the argument. The jousting hardly contributed to the battle
for civil rights, said journalist and author J. A. Rogers.[88] An editorial in *Opportunity* suggesting the subject be dropped concluded with
the proverb, "Never disclose the source of mortification or of joy if
you wish the one to cease, the other to endure."[89] In an open letter,
W. E. B. DuBois, who had seen his campaign to capitalize "Negro"
almost to victory by this time, charged that the name was really im-
material, for changing the name would do nothing toward changing
the attitudes toward its bearers.[90] To some, in short, being black in
America included even a hateful label, but the growing sense of peoplehood helped to dilute the hurt it conveyed.

Black America as a whole continued to assimilate a sense of
peoplehood throughout the 1920s. Given free rein to develop at the
bottom of the black caste, the subculture had matured, was accepted, provided a viable plan for living, and possessed sufficient
strength to survive even the disruptive Great Depression. Already
assigned to the very bottom of the American social and economic
hierarchies, the Negro was the hardest hit by the economic collapse
that saw so many hopes smashed. It pinched out those few expectations that had been nurtured by the apparent betterment of the Negro's economic position in the 1920s. Because of his position of
weakness, the black American was forced to mark time during the
1930s. But that the new racial consciousness attained survived the
hard times—that thinking in terms of blackness had become the
usual mode of addressing the reality of being black in white America
—is apparent in the events of the early 1940s. The "eruption from
the bottom" early in World War II made it known that black America could not again be disappointed in its expectations.[91]

NOTES

[1]"Youth," by Langston Hughes, in Alain Locke, ed., *The New Negro* (1925; reprint ed., Arno Press, 1968), 142.

[2]Contrast here Winthrop D. Jordan, *White over Black* (Baltimore: Penguin Books, 1969), ch. 2, with Oscar Handlin, *Race and Nationality in American Life* (Doubleday, Anchor Books, 1957), chap. 1.

[3]Leon F. Litwack, *North of Slavery* (University of Chicago Press, 1961), passim.

[4]Arnold Rose, *The Negro's Morale* (University of Minnesota Press, 1949), 30.

[5]Lerone Bennett, Jr., *Before the Mayflower: A History of the Negro in America,* rev. ed. (Baltimore: Penguin Books, 1966), 236.

[6]Rose, *Negro's Morale*, 3; John S. Lash, "Race Consciousness of the American Negro Author: Toward a Reexamination of an Orthodox Critical Concept," *Social Forces* 28 (1949-1950): 29-30.

[7]Milton Gordon, *Assimilation in American Life* (Oxford University Press, 164), 53 (emphasis removed). See also Edward Sayler, "Negro Minority Group Strategy as a Social Movement" (Ph.D. diss., University of Ohio, 1948), 53; Lash, "Race Consciousness of the American Negro Author," 26; W. O. Brown, "The Nature of Race Consciousness," *Social Forces* 10 (October 1931): 90-91; Rose, *Negro's Morale*, 178; Cyril Robert Friedman, "Attitudes Toward Protest Strategy and Participation in Protest Groups Among Negro Americans" (Ph.D. diss., University of Connecticut, 1967), 35.

[8]Lash, "Race Consciousness of the American Negro Author," 26; Gordon, *Assimilation in American Life*, 23-30; Sayler, "Minority Group Strategy," 163-164; Monroe Work, "The Race Problem in Cross Section," *Journal of Social Forces* 2 (January 1924): 248.

[9]Noted in J. A. Rogers, *From "Superman" to Man* (Privately printed, New York, 1965; first copyright, 1917), 75. Rogers was a prolific author and journalist for the *Pittsburgh Courier*.

[10]See, for example, E. Franklin Frazier, "Ethnic and Minority Groups in Wartime, with Special Reference to the Negro," *AJS* 48 (November 1942): 375; Locke ed., *The New Negro*, 7; Herbert J. Seligman, "Democracy and Jim-Crowism," *New Republic* 20 (September 3, 1919): 151-152; George E. Haynes, "The Effect of War Conditions on Negro Labor," *Proceedings, Academy of Political Science* 8 (February 1919): 299-312.

[11]A present-day corollary of this point was emphasized recently by historian Oscar Handlin. "It is the ultimate illogic of integration to deny the

separateness of the Negro and therefore to inhibit him from creating the communal institutions which can help cope with his problems . . . To confuse segregation, the function of which is to establish Negro inferiority, with the awareness of separate identity, the function of which is to generate the power of voluntary action, hopelessly confuses the struggle for equality." Oscar Handlin, "The Goals of Integration," *Daedalus* 95 (Winter 1966): 284. See also, Lash, "Race Consciousness of the American Negro Author," 29-30; Jack Abramowitz, "Accommodation and Militancy in Negro Life, 1876-1916" (Ph.D. diss. Columbia University, 1950), 94.

[12]W. E. B. DuBois, *The Philadelphia Negro* (1899; reprint ed., Schocken Books, 1967), 136-139; see also Constance McLaughlin Green, *The Secret City: A History of Race Relations in the Nation's Capital* (University of Princeton Press, 1967), 176-177; Richard Wright, *White Man, Listen!* (Doubleday and Co., 1957), 122-125.

[13]W. H. Councill, "The Future of the Negro," *Forum* 27 (July 1899): 576.

[14]Harold A. Farrell, "Theme and Variation: A Critical Evaluation of the Negro Novel, 1919-1947" (Ph.D. diss. Ohio State University, 1949), 18.

[15]W. E. Burghardt DuBois, *The Souls of Black Folk* (1903; reprint ed., Fawcett Publications, 1965) ix.

[16]Edwin S. Redkey, *Black Exodus: Black Nationalist and Back-to-Africa Movements, 1890-1910* (New Haven: Yale University Press, 1969), chaps. 2, 8.

[17]*Colored American Magazine* 9 (August 1905): 407.

[18]Ibid. 12 (May 1907): 331.

[19]Ibid., 328.

[20]Mary White Ovington, *Half a Man* (1911; reprint ed., Schocken Books, 1969), 182-183.

[21]*Colored American Magazine* 12 (May 1907): 328.

[22]Chicago *Broad Ax*, April 24, 1909.

[23]Ibid., August 21, 1909.

[24]Rose, *Negro's Morale*, 67. See also J. Saunders Redding, *On Being Negro in America* (1951; reprint ed., Indianapolis: Bobbs-Merrill Co., 1962), 94-97; E. Franklin Frazier, "Human, All Too Human," *Survey Graphic* 36 (January 1947): 74-75, 99-100; E. Franklin Frazier, *Black Bourgeoisie* (Free Press, 1957), 139-140; Gunnar Myrdal, *An American Dilemma*, 20th anniversary ed. (Harper & Row, 1962), 800-805.

[25]W. E. B. DuBois, "The Dilemma of the Negro," *American Mercury* 3 (October 1924): 185. Noting that Negroes are often caught in the trap of fostering segregation through race pride, he asserted: "The point you must remember is this: the demands of democracy and the demands of group advancement cannot always be reconciled. The race pride of the Negroes is not

an antidote to the race pride of white people; it is simply the other side of a hateful thing." Ibid., 181. See also J. Milton Sampson, "Race Consciousness and Race Relations," *Opportunity* 1 (May 1923): 13-18.

[26]Some excellent examples of this kind of appeal may be found on the front pages of the *New York Age* for February and March 1914. Economic nationalism, while not new to the period, did not bloom until the turn-of-the-century period brought the changing social orientation of the white community.

[27]*New York Age*, October 5, 1916.

[28]Arthur A. Schomburg, "The Negro Digs Up His Past," in Locke, ed., *The New Negro*, 236.

[29]Rose, *Negro's Morale*, 92-93. See also August Meier, *Negro Thought in America, 1880-1915: Racial Ideologies in the Age of Booker T. Washington* (University of Michigan Press, 1966), 261-262.

[30]Myrdal, *American Dilemma*, 751-752; Meier, *Negro Thought in America*, 262-264.

[31]*Chicago Defender*, July 5, 1919. The pictures offered were of such men as Booker T. Washington, Frederick Douglass, Toussaint L'Ouverture. The development of a striking paradox in black American life is mirrored in this kind of advertisement. Developing racial consciousness, even granting that it evolved in reaction to white racial consciousness, placed the Negro's arguments for equality in a peculiar light. That is, the holding up of racial heroes implicitly acknowledged the importance of race, that it was somehow bound up in individual accomplishment. Then, to go hunting far afield for racial heroes—to look to Toussaint L'Ouverture, Alexander Dumas, and others from entirely *different* cultures—made this acknowledgment almost explicit. See Rose, *Negro's Morale*, 92. For a contemporary attack on the idea of "Negritude" expressed in such assertions of racial pride, see Ralph Ellison's comments in "A Very Stern Discipline," *Harper's Magazine* 234 (March 1967): 93-94. It is a "blood theory" that is the obverse of white racism, Ellison charges.

[32]See, for example, "What the War Did," *New York Age*, January 4, 1919.

[33]Ibid., July 13, 1916.

[34]Rudolph Fisher, "The City of Refuge," *Atlantic Monthly* 135 (February 1925): 184.

[35]See chap. 5. See also Redding, *On Being Negro in America*, 20-21.

[36]*New York Age*, March 22, 1919.

[37]*Chicago Defender*, July 12, 1919.

[38]*New York Age*, February 15, 1919.

[39]*Chicago Defender*, January 3, 1920.

[40]Rollin Hartt, " 'I'd Like to Show You Harlem,' " *Independent* 105 (April 21, 1921): 334.

[41]Quoted in Frederick G. Detweiler, *The Negro Press in the United States* (1922; reprint ed., College Park, Maryland: McGrath Publishing Co., 1968), 108.

[42]*Chicago Defender*, May 22, 1920. The editorial was attacking Lathrop Stoddard's recently published *The Rising Tide of Color Against White World Supremacy* (1920).

[43]Langston Hughes, "Father and Sons," in *The Ways of White Folks* (Alfred A. Knopf, 1963), 223.

[44]Edward Margolies, in introduction to William Attaway, *Blood on the Forge* (1941; reprint ed., Collier Books, 1970), xi-xii.

[45]Alden Bland, *Behold a Cry* (Charles Scribner's Sons, 1947), 98-99.

[46]For a brief statement of Garvey's international influence, see Hollis R. Lynch's introduction to Amy Jacques-Garvey, ed., *Philosophies and Opinions of Marcus Garvey* (1923, 1925; reprint ed., Atheneum, 1969).

[47]See Myrdal, *American Dilemma*, 748; Roi Ottley and William J. Weatherby, eds., *The Negro in New York: An Informal Social History* (Praeger Publishers, 1969), 209, 211; Shirley Willson Strickland, "A Functional Analysis of the Garvey Movement" (Ph.D. diss. University of North Carolina, 1956), 144-146. E. David Cronon, *Black Moses: The Story of Marcus Garvey and the Universal Negro Improvement Association* (University of Wisconsin Press, 1955), is still the most readable work on Garvey available. More recent works are Theodore G. Vincent, *Black Power and the Garvey Movement* (Berkeley, California: The Ramparts Press, 1971), and Elton C. Fax, *Garvey: The Story of a Pioneer Black Nationalist* (Dodd, Mead and Co., 1972). Vincent sees his work as a corrective to such "integrationist" interpretations of Garvey as Cronon's.

[48]Myrdal, *American Dilemma*, 750-751. See also Strickland, "Functional Analysis of the Garvey Movement," 151.

[49]Strickland, "Functional Analysis of the Garvey Movement," 181-182; Myrdal, *American Dilemma*, 746-747; Cronon, *Black Moses*, 172-177. See also Birgit Aron, "The Garvey Movement: Shadow and Substance," *Phylon* 8 (Fourth Quarter 1947): 337-343.

[50]Strickland, "Functional Analysis of the Garvey Movement," 152. One finds pretty much of a consensus among contemporary observers that Garvey possessed an uncanny understanding of being black in a white society and was able to exploit this understanding to make the movement the greatest expression of black consciousness the world has yet seen. See by way of further example: A. F. Elmes, "Garvey and Garveyism: An Estimate," *Opportunity* 3 (May 1925): 139-141; E. Franklin Frazier, "The

Garvey Movement," *Opportunity* 4 (November 1926): 346-348; Rollin L. Hartt, "The Negro Moses, and His Campaign to Lead the Black Millions into Their Promised Land," *Independent* 105 (February 26, 1921): 205-206, 218-219; Charles S. Johnson, "After Garvey—What?" *Opportunity* 1 (August 1923): 231-233. Even the sharp-tongued George S. Schuyler offered some left-handed recognition of this in his, "A Tribute to Caesar," *Messenger* 6 (July 1924): 225-226, 231.

[51]William Pickens, "Africa for the Africans—The Garvey Movement," *Nation* 113 (December 28, 1921): 751. See also Benjamin Brawley, "The Negro Literary Renaissance," *Southern Workman* 56 (April 1927): 177; Earl E. Thorpe, "Africa in the Thought of Negro Americans," *Negro History Bulletin* 23 (October 1959): 9.

[52]Ira DeA. Reid, "A Critical Summary: The Negro on the Home Front in World Wars I and II," *JNE* 12 (Summer 1943): 516.

[53]Redding, *On Being Negro in America*, 38-39.

[54]Charles W. Beasley, Ketchikan, Alaska, January 11, 1921, to NAACP, New York City, NAACP MSS, File Box C-304, Library of Congress. (No change made in original spelling.)

[55]Redding, *On Being Negro in America*, 39-40. See also Cronon, *Black Moses*, 223. For a medley of white press comment on Garvey when he was near the peak of his power, see *Crisis* 24 (October 1922): 273-274. DuBois, editor of *Crisis*, had long been at odds with Garvey and his philosophy. The medley is thus more revealing than DuBois intended, at least in retrospect.

[56]There was no sudden demise of the UNIA, as witnessed by the continued existence of branches in various cities. It is alive today. See Lathan Starling Sr. and Donald Franklin, "The Life and Works of Marcus Garvey," *Negro History Bulletin* 26 (October 1962): 36-38. The authors are members of the organization. See also Aron, "The Garvey Movement," 339.

Strickland argues that the Garvey movement was not killed but rather committed suicide by faults within its structure that necessarily brought its own downfall. "A Functional Analysis of the Garvey Movement," 232ff.

[57]Bernard Magubane, "The American Negro's Conception of Africa: A Study in the Ideology of Pride and Prejudice" (Ph.D. diss., University of California, Los Angeles, 1967), 217.

[58]Ibid., 231.

[59]Cronon, *Black Moses*, 224.

[60]Editor's note prefixed to Truman H. Talley, "Marcus Garvey—The Negro Moses?" *World's Work* 41 (December 1920): 153. The article is one of the most laudatory turned up in pursuit of this subject.

[61]Claude McKay, *Harlem: Negro Metropolis* (Dutton, 1940), 143.

[62] Hartt, "The Negro Moses," 218.

[63]Rudolph Fisher, "Ringtail," *Atlantic Monthly* 135 (May 1925): 657.

[64]Claude McKay, *Banjo, A Story Without a Plot* (1929; reprint ed., Harcourt Brace Jovanovich, Inc. 1970), 76.

[65]Rose, *The Negro's Morale*, 5, 40. V. F. Calverton, "The New Negro," *Current History and Forum* 23 (February 1926): 695.

[66]Locke, ed., *The New Negro*, 7.

[67]Robert Hughes Brisbane, Jr., "Some New Light on the Garvey Movement," *JNH* 36 (January 1951): 55.

[68]*Pittsburgh Courier*, January 31, 1925.

[69]Ibid., January 15, 1927.

[70]The best expression of the meaning of the Renaissance is still the introductory essay by Locke in *The New Negro*, 3-16. The forces involved in the genesis of the Renaissance, say the editors of a recent anthology, were "the defeat of Booker T. Washington's conciliatory position; the formulation of the NAACP; the World War; the migration of the Southern Negro to Northern Cities; and the Garvey movement." James A. Emanuel and Theodore L. Gross, eds., *Dark Symphony: Negro Literature in America* (Free Press, 1968), 65. See also Brawley, "The Negro Literary Renaissance," 177-184. Nathan Irvin Huggins's insightful *Harlem Renaissance* (Oxford University Press, 1971) should not be overlooked in any examination of the Harlem Renaissance.

[71]Abraham Chapman, "The Harlem Renaissance in Literary History," *CLA Journal* 11 (September 1967): 38-58.

[72]Gilbert Osofsky, "Symbols of the Jazz Age: The New Negro and Harlem Discovered," *American Quarterly* 17 (Summer 1965): 234.

[73]George S. Schuyler, "The Negro Art Hokum," *Nation* 122 (June 16, 1926): 662-663. See also Gustavus Adolphus Stewart, "The New Negro Hokum," *Social Forces* 6 (September 1927): 438-445.

[74]L. M. Hussey, "Aframerican, North and South," *American Mercury* 7 (February 1926): 196-200. See also Frank Luther Mott, "The Harlem Poets," *The Midland* 13 (January 1927): 121-128.

[75]Rudolph Fisher, "The Caucasian Storms Harlem," *American Mercury* 11 (August 1927): 393-398.

[76]Langston Hughes, *The Big Sea* (1940; reprint ed., Hill and Wang, 1963), 228, 247.

[77]Hughes, "The Blues I'm Playing," in *The Ways of White Folks*, 110. For an exposition of the idea that the creation of a favorable picture of the black man would dilute white prejudices and his stance of superiority, see James Weldon Johnson, "Race Prejudice and the Negro Artist," *Harper's* 157 (November 1928): 769-776. See also Arna Bontemps, "The Two Harlems," *American Scholar* 14 (Spring 1945): 167-173.

[78]Claude McKay, *A Long Way from Home* (1937; reprint ed., Harcourt, Brace and World, 1970), 321.

[79]Ibid., 312.

[80]James Weldon Johnson, "The Dilemma of the Negro Author," *American Mercury* 15 (December 1928): 480; Nick Aaron Ford, "The Negro Author's Use of Propaganda in Imaginative Literature," (Ph.D. diss., University of Iowa, 1946), 119; Emanuel and Gross, eds., *Dark Symphony*, 68.

[81]Recognition of just how often whiteness intruded upon black existence and the black's consciousness of his own existence is an often noted facet of this. Speaking through Ray, his protagonist, Harlem Renaissance author Wallace Thurman asserted: "I'm sick of discussing the Negro problem, of having it thrust at me from every conversational nook and cranny. I'm sick of whites who think I can't talk about anything else, and of Negroes who think I shouldn't talk about anything else." (*Infants of the Spring* [The Macaulay Co., 1932], 214). In his autobiography, poet Claude McKay concurred, noting that not even sympathetic whites "can feel fully the corroding bitterness of color discrimination," and for this reason he would refuse their company oftentimes. (*A Long Way from Home*, 735).

[82]Osofsky, "Symbols of the Jazz Age," 234.

[83]Nor did many critics. See, for instance, W. E. B. Du Bois, "Criteria of Negro Art," *Crisis* 32 (October 1926): 290, 294, 296-297.

[84]Wright, *White Man, Listen!* 119. See also "The Word 'Negro,' " *Negro Heritage* 1 (1961): 2; Abdul Hakimu Ibn Alkalimat (Gerald McWorter), "The Ideology of Black Social Science," *The Black Scholar* 1 (December 1969): 31; Oscar R. Williams, "Afro-American or Negro?" *Negro History Bulletin* 32 (March 1969): 18; John A. Morsell, "Negro, Black, or Afro-American?" *Negro History Bulletin* 32 (February 1969): 11 (reprinted from the *New York Times*, July 20, 1968).

[85]See by way of example Fannie Barrier Williams, "Do We Need Another Name?" *Southern Workman* 33 (January 1904): 33-36; J. W. E. Bowen, "Who Are We? Africans, Afro-Americans, Colored People, Negroes or American Negroes?" *Voice of the Negro* 3 (January 1906): 31-36; T. Thomas Fortune, "Who Are We? Afro-Americans, Colored People, or Negroes?" *Voice of the Negro* 3 (March 1906): 194-198.

[86]Cited in Harold R. Issacs, "Blackness and Whiteness: A Name to Go By," *Encounter* 21 (August 1963): 8, and Bertram Wilbur Doyle, "Racial Traits of the Negro as Negroes Assign Them to Themselves" (Master's thesis, University of Chicago, 1924), 116.

[87]Reported in *New York Age*, May 5, 1910. It might be noted that the founder and editor of the *Chicago Defender*, Robert S. Abbott, insisted that *race* be used in all stories instead of Negro. St. Clair Drake and Horace R. Cayton, *Black Metropolis* (Harper Torchbooks, 1962), 400.

⁸⁸J. A. Rogers, "What Are We, Negroes or Americans?" *Messenger* 8 (August 1926): 237-238, 255.

⁸⁹"On the Meaning of Names," *Opportunity* 4 (September 1926): 271.

⁹⁰W. E. B. DuBois, "The Name 'Negro,' " *Crisis* 35 (March 1928): 96. H. L. Mencken, "Designations for Colored Folk," *American Speech* 19 (October 1944): 161-174, provides a highly readable summary of the controversy and the campaign to capitalize "Negro," to that time.

⁹¹Richard M. Dalfiume, "The 'Forgotten Years' of the Negro Revolution," *JAH* 55 (June 1968): 90-91.

5

BLACK ON WHITE

The white man is a tiger at my throat
Drinking my blood as my life ebbs away,
And muttering that his terrible striped coat
Is freedom's and portends the Light of Day.
Oh white man, you may suck up all my blood,
And throw my carcass into potter's field,
But never will I say with you that mud
Is bread for Negroes! Never will I yield.[1]

THE MANNER in which the American Negro perceived his
world and the white world about him from 1890 to 1930 was dependent upon a number of factors, but the primary interests that described an axis across all black life were those bound up in interracial relations. Class, community, age, education, and individual
experiences all modified the press of Negro-white relations in everyday life, it is true, yet no black was able to escape entirely its
burden.[2] This is not to say that many of the black American's everyday life experiences were not in many ways the same as those of
whites of generally the same circumstances. It was rare, however,
that being black in white America did not intrude into the course of
day-to-day life. The color line was ever present—although not necessarily ever conscious—for the black community. Even breaks in the
color line reminded him of his blackness and inferior position, as
when it was announced in mid-1915 that "the game of 'Hit the Nigger,' which has been popular at summer amusement resorts, has
been forbidden in New York by the state legislature."[3] "I seldom live
through a whole day without being reminded that I am a Negro,"
writes critic Nick Aaron Ford of his experiences. "I do not seek the

reminder: it is thrust upon me. I am reminded of it at filling sta-
tions, in stores, in hospitals, in banks, in post offices, in theaters,
and even in churches."[4]

Although white racism determined initial social position and
justified all manner of subsequent discriminations, "Being a Negro
in America" became, as aptly expressed by one social psychologist,
"less of a racial identity than a necessity to adopt a subordinate
social role."[5] A consequence, as James Weldon Johnson wrote in his
noted *Autobiography of An Ex-Coloured Man*, was that the Negro
was "forced to take his outlook on all things, not from the view-point
of a citizen, or a man, or even a human being, but from the viewpoint of a *coloured* man.[6]

It was underscored in the preceding chapter that being black in
white America was to be a special kind of American. Yet it cannot
be overemphasized that black life *was not barren* and that the separate community into which the Negro was thrust constituted a
viable setting capable of providing sense and direction to black existence. There is, to quote the distinguished novelist Ralph Ellison
(somewhat out of context) a "complexity of circumstances which go
to make up the Negro experience."[7] Lutie, the protagonist of Ann
Petry's novel, *The Street,*

> never felt really human until she reached Harlem and thus got
> away from the hostility in the eyes of the white women who
> stared at her on the downtown streets and in the subway. . . .
>   These other folks feel the same way, she thought—that once
> they are freed from the contempt in the eyes of the downtown
> world, they instantly become individuals. Up here they are no
> longer creatures labeled simply "colored" and therefore all
> alike.[8]

An appreciation of the black's attitudes toward the white world
about him rests, in short, upon the recognition of just how often
whiteness intruded upon black existence—and upon the black's consciousness of his own existence. W. E. B. DuBois wrote in his 1940
autobiography, *Dusk of Dawn*, "I was not an American; I was not a
man; I was by long education and continual compulsion and daily

reminded, a colored man in a white world; and that world often existed primarily, so far as I was concerned, to see with sleepless vigilance that I was kept within bounds."[9]

Most northern Negroes lived with this reality. Most had their own personal "Miss Cramp," a cutting caricature of white America created by Rudolph Fisher. "Negroes to her," he wrote, "had been rather ugly but serviceable fixtures, devices that happened to be alive, dull instruments of drudgery, so observed, so accepted, so used, and so forgotten. . . . Negroes she had always accepted with horses, mules, and motors, and though they had brushed her shoulder, they had never actually entered her head."[10] Wrote poet Countee Cullen:

> She even thinks that up in heaven
> Her class lies late and snores,
> While poor black cherubs rise at seven
> To do celestial chores.[11]

George the porter or Snowball the shoeshine boy knew they were effectively invisible. The full impact of this social invisibleness—of existing in the eyes of the majority as a problem rather than as an individual—is difficult to convey. Lutie, in the above quotation, felt the relief of becoming an individual again when she came home to Harlem.[12] Ralph Ellison explicitly explores this theme in his noted first novel and captures the force with which this invisibleness hammered at Negro life. "Like the bodiless heads you see sometimes in circus sideshows, it is as though I have been surrounded by mirrors of hard, distorting glass. When they approach me they see only my surroundings, themselves, or figments of their imagination—indeed, everything and anything except me."[13] To Richard Wright's Bigger Thomas

and his kind [,] white people were not really people; they were a sort of great natural force, like a stormy sky looming overhead, or like a deep swirling river stretching suddenly at one's feet in the dark. As long as he and his black folks did not go beyond certain limits, there was no need to fear that white force. But whether they feared it or not, each and every day of their lives they lived with it; even when words did not sound its name, they acknowledged its reality. As long as they lived here in this prescribed corner of the city, they paid mute tribute to it.[14]

The northern white did not "see" the Negro even when he looked past the curtain of invisibleness. What he saw was a mask. The "wearing of the mask" is perhaps one of the most unique and ubiquitous facets in the life experiences of the black American who learned early to hide his true feeling toward whites. It was a necessity, W. E. B. DuBois wrote in 1920, when life is spent "looking for insults or hiding from them—shrinking (instinctively and despite desperate bolsterings of courage) from blows that are not always but ever; not each day, but each week, each month, each year."[15] Rejected, threatened, told in no uncertain terms they were not part of their own land, black Americans lived apart, physically and consciously.[16]

The better economic means of the well-to-do urban Negro provided him a measurable degree of isolation from rude white contact. He was even able to keep his children from suffering too harshly from contact with the white world.[17] This type of isolation was possible for some in the newly forming middle class as well, especially if their livelihood was taken entirely from within the Negro community. But for ordinary blacks this manner of withdrawal was impossible. Their means of livelihood placed them in direct and continuous contact with the white world. They made the best use of the "mask"—and many continue to do so. "It is precisely those silent people whom white people see everyday of their lives . . . ," said James Baldwin recently to a white audience, who "will tell you it's raining if that is what you want to hear, and they will tell you the sun is shining if that is what you want to hear. They really hate you— really hate you because in their eyes (and they're right) you stand between them and life."[18]

Born out of slavery, the mask provided a measure of self-defense. In the words of an old Negro folksong:

Me and my captain don't agree,
But he don't know, 'cause he don't ask me;

He don't know, He don't know my mind,
when he sees me laughing
Just laughing to keep from crying.
                        . . .

Got one mind for white folks to see,
"Nother for what I know is me;
He don't know, He don't know my mind,
when he sees me laughing
Just laughing to keep from crying.[19]

The ever-present possibility of conflict made the mask a necessary part of the Negro's relationship with the white. Said poet Paul
Laurence Dunbar:

We wear the mask that grins and lies,
It hides our cheeks and shades our eyes, —
This debt we pay to human guile:
With torn and bleeding hearts we smile,
And mouth with myriad subtleties.

Why should the world be overwise,
In counting all our tears and sighs?
Nay, let them only see us while
We wear the mask.

We smile, but, O great Christ, our cries
To thee from tortured souls arise.
We sing, but oh the clay is vile
Beneath our feet, and long the mile;
But let the world dream otherwise,
We wear the mask.[20]

Few whites were able to penetrate the mask; in fact, few even in
more recent times have been aware of its existence. Cutting across
black class lines, the need to play a role in interracial contact was a
part of growing up black; a part of the strange experience of being a
problem (DuBois, 1897); a part of learning "the weight of white people in the world" (James Baldwin, 1955); a response to being "lost in

one big white fog" and discovering the "adversary is next door to him, on the street, on the job, in the school" (Richard Wright, 1940, 1957).[21] Black Americans, in other words, became accomplished actors at an early age.[22] One contemporary white commentator, reminiscing of his discovery of the mask, wrote:

> These coons were—theatrical! They adopted, in their inter-course with me, with every white man, the voice and gesture familiar to all mimes. They were enacting, ineffably, very per-suasively, a self-imposed role. They were playing a part in a comedy! . . . That is to say, I saw the Africano, back of the smokescreen of his constitutional guarantees, all wispy and valueless, facing an elementary biological necessity—the nec-essity of adapting himself to a harsh and often lethal environment.[23]

Not only did the Afro-American learn to hide his true feelings about whites behind the mask; he also learned to shut the white out of his life as a way of protecting his self and defeating the white world. In Phillip Kay's *Taffy*, the father of the boy whose name gave the book its title passes along the advice that many parents in black America must have delivered to their children:

> "You can't beat white folks that way. You can't do it fight-ing . . . . You can't lose patience or spend yourself just like you want to. You got to learn not to feel, not to want, not to see what's outside. That beats the white man. You got to live in his world, but shut him out."[24]

Being black in a white society meant making an adjustment to that society—but not capitulating to it.[25] There were "Uncle Toms," in modern parlance, true enough, but as Thomas Pettigrew noted, "So effective is this impassive facade [this mask], many white Amer-icans have long interpreted it as proof that Negroes are happy and contented with their lot."[26] It is just this that makes the white claim of "knowing the Negro" so ironic.

The white, confident in his assumed superiority, never bothered to hide his feelings in the presence of Negroes. "The blacks haven't been working with and for the white folks all these decades and centuries for nothing . . . ," said critic and satirist George Schuyler. "Practically every member of the Negro aristocracy of physicians, dentists, lawyers, undertakers and insurance men has worked at one time or another for white folks as a domestic, and observed with cynical detachment their orgies, obsessions and imbecilities, while contact with the white proletariat has acquainted him thoroughly with their gross stupidity and often very evident inferiority.[27] "My God! the things I've seen!" cried one of Claude McKay's characters. "Working with white folks, so dickty and high-and-mighty, you think theyse nevah oncet naked and thim feets nevah touch ground."[28] William Faulker asserted: "No white man understood Negroes and never would so long as the white man compelled the black to be first a Negro and only then a man, since this, the impenetrable dividing wall, was the black man's only defense and protection for survival."[29]

Here, in the wearing of the mask, is some irrefutable evidence of the isolation of the Negro from the larger society. The ordinary Negro simply did not trust the white man; distrust, dislike, and contempt for whites characterize his view of the world outside. Part of the main axis of black life, these feelings cut across class lines as well as across regions. Suspicion of whites and white motives was endemic. Of his own early experiences, the highly articulate J. Saunders Redding of Hampton Institute (presently Professor Emeritus of American Studies at Cornell University), wrote, "My landlady, though she had been born and had lived all her life in New England and though she thought that this was in itself some sort of victory or credit for a Negro—my landlady was only less suspicious of white people than she was of Negroes who consorted with them."[30] Arnold Rose reported, "A leading Negro social scientist admitted in private conversation that he believed *all* Negroes hated whites. Of course, there is considerable variation in this hatred. . . . Most Negroes spend only a few minutes in each day hating whites, and they may not hate every day."[31] A character in Ann Petry's *The Street*, addressing a white, says, "I ain't prejudice. . . . I just ain't got no use for white folks. I don't want 'em any where near me. I don't even wants have to look at 'em. I put up with you because you don't ever stop to think whether folks are white or black and you don't really care. That sort of takes you out of the white folks class."[32]

Perhaps all Negroes did not hate, or at least hate all the time and with a blinding, crippling hatred.[33] But that whites were the object of a deep enmity that flowed widely through the black community cannot be doubted. "How many times have I heard Negroes mutter, when witness to some misfortune befallen a white person, 'What the hell! He's white, isn't he?'" noted Saunders Redding.[34] "So that's the way white people feel," Langston Hughes's Harriett explodes in his *Not Without Laughter.* "They wouldn't have a single one of us around if they could help it. . . . You can pray for 'em if you want to, mama, but I hate 'em! . . . I hate white folks! . . . I hate 'em all!"[35] One of Rudolph Fisher's characters avers, "I hate fays. Always have. Always will. Chief joy in life is making them uncomfortable."[36] Badly beaten during the Chicago riot of 1919, the protagonist of *Behold a Cry* was in bed.

> Son remembered how Ed opened one eye. It glittered with hate.
> "Look good!" he said.
> Son turned his head away.
> "Look good! he commanded. "Because I want you to remember what you see. Think about this when you hear all that fancy talk about white folks and how much a friend they is!"
>   . . .
> ". . . You too young to understand, I guess. But first and last, remember you a nigger. Look at me and see what it means. I'm your father, yes, but we tied together in another way. We all niggers together! That's something special because it only happens to us. Lots of times being niggers is most important of all!"[37]

This medley could be extended. The distrust of—and the contempt for—the white spread into almost every facet of black existence. Writing of his teaching experiences, W. E. B. DuBois made the point succinctly. When asked by his students if he trusted white people, he answered yes, but, he wrote, "All the while you are lying and every level, silent eye there knows you are lying, and you sit and lie on, to the greater glory of God."[38]

The black American's life experiences quite simply gave him few reasons to trust the white. Wherever he turned the correctness of this one simple guide to life was brought home to him: in matters of religion, in matters of simple justice, in matters of just living from one day to the next. For example, in the late nineteenth century Negro Catholics were to be barred from membership in Boston's cathedrals. Negroes were evidently to be excluded, remarked one Negro newspaper, "on the grounds that both races cannot get the Virgin Mary's attention at the same time, nor should both dip their hands into the holy water during the same service."[39] It might be noted that even though Catholicism was gaining ground among Negroes, there were still but five black priests in the country as late as 1911.[40]

After the turn of the century, the color line in Boston's churches rose ever higher as the Negro population of the city increased. So high was it by the end of the first decade that a large donation by a wealthy Negro was refused in one parish.[41] In New York City the white churches reacted similarly. St. Andrew's Episcopal church preferred that Negroes did not attend, perhaps, remarked the *Colored American Magazine*, because the pastor thought "Christ was running his missionary propaganda with a 'Jim Crow' attachment."[42]

When the population pressures created by the northward migration caused some churches to become white islands in residential areas turned black, the complaints of white congregations became almost frenzied.[43] These displays of color phobia by white churches served to heighten the Negro's sense of blackness. The migrant brought strong denominational feelings northward with him, but these fell to one side as he faced the northern variety of white racism.[44]

These everyday results of the white idea of brotherhood could be avoided, though. The black city dweller had his own religious institutions into which he could retreat. But such was not the case when it came to simple legal justice. The Negro press provided its readers with no end of comment in this area, comments often served up with sardonic exposition on white hypocrisy. Perhaps the judge believes in separate heavens, commented the *Broad Ax*, after a

Savannah member of the bench had freed the white woman involved in a miscegenation trial while sentencing the man to three years on the chain gang.[45] In New York in 1910, George W. Griffin, a porter, was awarded a $2,500 verdict by a jury after he had been falsely arrested for stealing some valuable papers from a passenger. The verdict was set aside, however, by a justice who ruled that a Negro could not "suffer the same amount of shame as a result of false arrest as a white man."[46] In 1911 it was charged that the Detroit police were trying to close Negro businesses that had white patronage. A few years later the Detroit police were said to be under orders to arrest any Negro man accompanied by a white woman.[47]

An especially bitter example of so-called equal justice was provided black America in the war years when "work or fight" edicts were issued in some places across the labor-short South. These edicts were interpreted as meaning that Negroes would work where, when, and for what wages whites decided.[48] Commenting on white law, Alva tells Emma Lou, protagonist of novelist Wallace Thurman's *The Blacker the Berry* . . . , "The only thing the law bothers niggers about is for stealing, murdering, or chasing white women, and as long as they don't steal from or murder ofays, the law ain't none too particular about bothering them."[49]

Charges of police brutality were common. Deaths resulting from police use of needless force in dealing with the Negro were frequently reported. These facts of black life continually reminded the Negro, as DuBois wrote at the turn of the century, that justice in both the North and the South was marked "For White People Only." "The Negro," he said, "is coming more and more to look upon law and justice, not as protecting safeguards, but as sources of humiliation and oppression."[50]

Perhaps nothing hammered blackness into the ordinary Negro's existence more than the day-to-day discriminations to which he was subjected and against which he had to be continually on guard. At the same time, of course, these discriminations further revealed the white man to the Negro.[51] In New York City at this time it was impossible for a Negro to eat in the downtown area. "Boots" Smith, a character in Ann Petry's novel, says to his white underworld boss,

" . . . you ain't never known what it's like to live somewhere where you ain't wanted and every white son-of-a-bitch that sees you goes out of his way to let you know you ain't wanted. Christ, there ain't even so much as a cheap stinking diner in this town that I don't think twice before I walk into it to buy a cup of lousy coffee, because any white bastard in there will let me know one way or another that niggers belong in Harlem."[52]

Refusals to serve Negroes in restaurants, to sell them theater tickets or anything but gallery tickets, overcharging Negroes to discourage patronage, and the continued introduction of discriminatory bills into state legislatures, were all designed to keep the Negro in his place.[53] It was just such public demonstrations of the Negro's inferior social position that made possible the larger wrongs against him. In his autobiography, Claude McKay asserted, "Right here in New York there are children of mixed parentage, who have actually hated their white mother after they had grown up to understanding. When they came up against the full force of the great white city on the outside and went home to face a helpless white mother (a symbol of that white prejudice) it was more than their Negroid souls could stand."[54]

The petty tokens of his assigned position thus came to be offered to the Negro in increasing proportions after the nation entered upon its search for a new social order in the last years of the nineteenth century. They increased further as the migration north altered the relationship between the old settlers and the white communities. They tore apart the old black-white equilibrium, such as it was, and forced new patterns of accommodation upon the Negro community.[55] But they also ensured the continued development of the sense of peoplehood that would pervade the black urban North.

The World War I era gave the Negro his most forceful lesson about the white world since the 1890s when Jim Crow began his more vociferous visits to northern cities. During the war the Negro responded to the government's needs in spite of the fact Mr. Crow was still an active old bird. There was dissent. "The Huns of Alsace have never threatened the Negro's life, liberty, and property like the Huns of Alabama," said the militant *Boston Guardian.*[56] The tired old joke about the Negro saying, "I hear you white folks is at war," may well have got its start here.

Noting that black opinion was set in New York and Chicago, Negro scholar Ira DeAugustine Reid later asserted that most Negro communities were not particularly enthusiastic about the war. "Not uncommon was the expression, 'The German ain't done nothin' to me, and if they have, I forgive 'em.'"[57] Jake, protagonist of Claude McKay's *Home to Harlem,* had enlisted, eager to fight, but he later deserted and was "on the white man books." He explains to his girl Felice:

> "I didn't run away because I was scared a them Germans. But I beat it away from Brest because they wouldn't give us a chance at them, but kept us in that rainy, sloppy, Gawd-forsaken burg working like wops. They didn't seem to want us niggers foh no soldiers . . . .
> ". . . You ain't telling me a thing, daddy [answers Felice] . . . What right have niggers got to shoot down a whole lot of a Germans for? Is they worse than any other nation a white people?"[58]

In his *Colored Soldiers,* a series of humorous vignettes in dialect that exploits stereotypes for the purpose of propaganda, one of author William MacIntyre's characters declares:

> I didn't perzactly know what de war wuz 'bout but be preacher say some white folks frum 'cross de ocean wuz tryin' ter take dis here country from our white folks. He say dese white folks us got gibes us trouble enough, Lord knows, but ef a bran' new crowd, what don't understand us at all, gits a hold ter us he jes' don't know what dey poor cullud folks gwine ter do . . . . So all us cullud boys, dat is, dem what wuz enybody, 'lowed dat dis is sho de time fer ter back up de white folks.[59]

There is a sentiment here that must be acknowledged. Many Afro-Americans of the lower strata looked at the white folks' war and rhetoric about democracy with a rather jaundiced eye born of past treatment. The sharp-tongued George Schuyler said as much a decade after the war:

> Is it generally known that large numbers of Negroes, though they openly whooped it up for Uncle Sam, would have shed no

tears in 1917-18 if the armies of the Kaiser had by some miracle suddenly swooped down upon such fair cities as Memphis, Tenn., Waycross, Ga., or Meridian, Miss.? The Negro upper class, in press and pulpit, roared and sweated to keep the dinges in line by telling them how much the white folks would do to improve their status after the war if they would only be loyal, but the more enlightened Ethiopes were frankly skeptical, a skepticism justified later on. On several occasions during that struggle for democracy I sounded out individual Sambos here and there, and was somewhat surprised to find many of them holding the view that it made no difference to them who won the war since the Germans could hardly treat them any worse than the Nordics of the U.S.A., and might treat them a lot better. Any number of intelligent Negroes expressed the opinion under their breath that a good beating would be an excellent thing for the soul of America.[60]

Yet even with such an underlying sentiment, the black community permitted its hopes to be swept upward. The future would hold better things for all after Germany had been vanquished; the Negro's burden of discrimination would be lightened by his contributions. In a conflict to make the world safe for democracy he could hardly fail to reap significant rewards. Moreover, the crisis would permit the black man an opportunity to prove his worth to white skeptics. "Let us, while this war lasts, forget our special grievances and close our ranks shoulder to shoulder with our white fellow citizens and the allied nations that are fighting for democracy," said W. E. B. DuBois in an often-quoted editorial in *The Crisis*. "We make no ordinary sacrifice, but we make it gladly and willingly with our eyes lifted to the hills."[61]

Nearly 400,000 Negroes saw military service, about half serving overseas. Mostly restricted to labor units by traditional prejudices, black Americans found that these prejudices endured even in the face of creditable service when assigned to combat units. Certainly discrimination did not abate.[62] During the peace-making period after the war some blacks agreed to be patient: "We know that public sentiment is not remolded overnight," allowed one influential Negro newspaper.[63] But if it was hard to be patient, it soon became impossible to be so: "The President is abroad . . . securing equality for all. Yet in the homeland he thinks it no shame to come into close affiliation with elements whose chief political prepossession is that democracy shall cease functioning when it approaches the cabin of the man of color."[64]

The nation's gratitude, like everything, was labeled "white," said the *New York Age* a few weeks later.[65] "One by one," wrote James Weldon Johnson in mid-1919, "the idealistic war dreams are vanishing; and as they vanish, the solid outlines of the old, prewar conditions loom up clearer and nearer."[66] New York's *Challenge Magazine* stated flatly:

> We are ignored by the President and law-makers. When we ask for a full man's share they cry "insolent." When we shoot down the mobist that would burn our properties and destroy our lives, they shout "Bolshevist." When a white man comes to our side armed with the sword of righteousness and square dealing, they howl "Nigger-lover and bastard." If we take our grievances to Congress they are pigeon-holed, turned over to moth. We are abandoned, cast off, maligned, shackled, shoved down the hills towards Golgotha in "The Land of the Free and the Home of the Brave."[67]

The extent of the disappointed hopes is a measure of the convergence of expectancies that had been tied to victory in the Great War. In spite of his suspicions of the white, the Negro had allowed himself to be swept along, perhaps because of the way wartime labor shortages had rapidly improved his relative economic position.[68] Yet his hopes vanished when racial violence swept across the country in the Red Summer of 1919.

The Negro's world was a dangerous place in the last decades of the nineteenth century and only marginally less so throughout the first three decades of the twentieth century. *Violent* can serve as a one-word description of interracial relations during the whole period. "What's goin' to happen to th' naygur?" Finley Peter Dunne's Mr. Hennessy asked of Mr. Dooley soon after the turn of the century:

"Well," said Mr. Dooley, "he'll ayther have to go to th' north an' be a subjict race, or stay in th' south an' be an objick lesson. 'Tis a har-rd time he'll have annyhow. I'm not sure that I'd not as lave be gently lynched in Mississippi as baten to death in New York . . . .

"I'm not so much throubled about th' naygur whin he lives among his oppressors as I am whin he falls into th' hands iv his liberators. Whin he's in th' south he can make up his mind to be lynched soon or late an' give his attintion to his other pleasures . . . , an' wurrukin' f'r th' man that used to own him an' now on'y owes him his wages. But 'tis th' divvle's own hardship f'ir a coon to step out iv th' rooms iv th' S'ciety f'r th' Brotherhood iv Ma-an . . . an' be pursooed by a mob iv aboli-tionists till he's dhriven to seek polis protection, which, Hinnissy, is th' polite name f'r fracture iv th' skull."[69]

Much of the responsibility for this state of affairs and the con-tinued hateful white racial attitudes lay with white newspapers, the Negro press frequently asserted. They engaged in the "manufacture of prejudice," *The Crisis* charged.[70] One black newspaper, the Chicago *Broad Ax,* said at the turn of the century that white news-papers handled news involving the Negro's shortcomings so badly that "to accuse a black man of any kind of crime now is to notify the undertaker for a coffin."[71] With the average number of lynchings per year during the 1890s approaching 200, the charge was well placed. Even in the 1920s, when the number of lynchings had fallen by half, the average was still one a week.[72]

The violence took all forms, to be sure, but worst of all was the savagery of lynching. "Savage" is actually too weak an adjective to describe many of the open acts of murder.

In the presence of nearly 2,000 people, who sent aloft yells of defiance and shouts of joy, Sam Hose (a Negro who committed two of the basest acts known to crime) was burned at the stake in a public road, one and a half miles from here. Before the torch was applied to the pyre, the Negro was deprived of his ears, fingers and other portions of his body with surprising fortitude. Before the body was cool, it was cut to pieces, the bones were crushed into small bits and even the tree upon which the wretch met his fate was torn up and disposed of as souvenirs.

"The Negro's heart was cut in several pieces, as was also his liver. Those unable to obtain the ghastly relics directly, paid more fortunate possessors extravagant sums for them. Small pieces of bone went for 25 cents and a bit of the liver, crisply cooked, for 10 cents."[73]

This particular incident took place in the South and was not unique. In the North, the supposed killing of a constable in Coatesville, Pennsylvania, led Zach Walker to be burned alive on his hospital bed. Pennsylvania's governor was only moved to remark that mistakes happen even in such orderly places as Coatesville. Such attitudes, the *New York Age* warned, meant that the white north was "Sowing the Wind." "Another lynching in Pennsylvania would wreck the State." Despite such protests no one was indicated for the crime.[74]

The Chicago *Broad Ax* wryly observed that "since the practice of lynching has found its way into many Northern states, the country seems to take it as an American institution to be cherished and defended like other institutions."[75] "Two Italians were lynched in Florida," noted the first issue of *The Crisis* in 1910. "The Italian Government protested, but it was found that they were naturalized Americans. The inalienable right of every free American citizen to be lynched without tiresome investigation and penalties is one which the families of the lately deceased doubtless deeply appreciate."[76] It was *The Crisis* that also noted that lynching had led to a new art form. Pictures of victims, often with the mob displaying the body as a trophy, were making their appearance on postcards.[77] Claude McKay's poem "The Lynching" caught the macabre horrors of the practice.

> *Day dawned, and soon the mixed crowds came to view*
> *The ghastly body swaying in the sun.*
> *The women thronged to look, but never a one*
> *Showed sorrow in her eyes of steely blue.*
> *And little lads, lynchers that were to be,*
> *Danced round the dreadful thing in fiendish glee.*[78]

The Negro press kept the existence of this universal threat to the black man continually before their readers, especially after the turn of the century and in the wake of the mob outbreaks that at this time seemed to rock northern cities periodically. New York City, 1900; Springfield, Ohio, 1904 and 1906; Springfield, Illinois, 1908: each was a personal lesson to the Negro, a reminder of his individual weakness, his position of inferiority, and his blackness. As reflected in the Negro press and periodicals the certainty that the "crime of color" was behind interracial violence was everywhere accepted. The unashamed attitudes of the white residents of Springfield, Illinois, plainly indicated as much. "'Why, the niggers came to think they were as good as we are!' was the final justification offered [for the riot], not once, but a dozen times," wrote William English Walling in an article credited with bringing the NAACP into existence. The North seemed to be moving toward open race warfare.[79]

Each act of violence by white against black seemed to threaten every black man everywhere. Sex, class, or economic success made no difference. It was self-deception to think that distinctions in individual industriousness and sobriety were of any consequence to a mob. Each attack was directed not at just John Brown, Negro American, central figure of white lawlessness at the moment, but at the "Negroness" of all John Browns. Says a character in Rudolph Fisher's *Walls of Jericho*, "Fays don' see no difference 'tween dicty shines [those blacks who measured their success by their ability to imitate white middle-class ways] and any other kind o' shines. One jig in danger is ev'y jig in danger. They'd lick *them* and come down on *us*."[80] What better lesson was there of the pervasive universal nature of the threat than the attack on the person of Booker T. Washington in New York City?[81]

In just two months, the *New York Age* noted in mid-1909, nearly every state had had lynchings for all manner of alleged offenses.[82] There followed, however, a relative respite from violence, although it did not last long. 1915 saw a surge of lynchings, and more than twice as many black Americans fell victim to mobs in 1919 as had in 1917.[83] And the temporary respite had not changed white attitudes toward racial violence. "The burning was under the supervision of the [Ellisville, Mississippi] city authorities, who characterized it as 'orderly,'" reported the *Chicago Defender* of a lynching in mid-1919.[84]

Increasing migration to labor-short industrial centers contributed to the again aroused racial tensions, especially when industrial managers sought to employ Negroes as strikebreakers. As an economic threat the Negro worker was suddenly no longer "invisible." Migration "has reached the point where drastic action must be taken . . . to get rid of a certain portion of those who are already here," said an East St. Louis white labor leader in early 1917.[85] Racial violence bathed the city in July of that year. A further example is found in the disorders that washed across the meatpacking industry as attempts were made to unionize it. The resulting turmoil provided a backdrop to the bloody Chicago riot of 1919.[86]

Eighteen major interracial conflicts occurred from 1915 to 1919, according to sociologist Allen Grimshaw's count, a fair portion of them in northern urban centers.[87] The San Juan Hill riot in May 1917 when New York police went on the rampage according to the *New York Age*, killing one and wounding two others, was just a preliminary to the 1917 wave of riots.[88] There were Chester and Philadelphia, Pennsylvania, and later, Houston, Texas, with its high death toll. Then in July 1917 came East St. Louis with at least forty-eight dead.

Each such instance demonstrated to the individual Negro the need to nurture the protective facade that isolated him from the white world. But now the collective facade that masked the community as a whole seemed to slip more often. The Chicago riot of July 1919 showed the measure of vehemence possible when both the white community's awareness of the Negro was awakened and black anger spilled over. At least thirty-eight persons died, twenty-three of them Negroes.[89] Claude McKay's often-quoted "If We Must Die" captured the now-common sentiment of the ordinary black in the cities.

> *If we must die, let it not be like hogs*
> *Hunted and penned in an inglorious spot,*
> *While round us bark the mad and hungry dogs,*
> *Making their mock of our accursed lot.*
> *If we must die, O let us nobly die,*
> *So that our precious blood may not be shed*

In vain; then even the monsters we defy
Shall be constrained to honor us though dead!
O kinsmen! we must meet the common foe!
Though far outnumbered let us show us brave,
And for their thousand blows deal one deathblow!
What though before us lies the open grave?
Like men we'll face the murderous, cowardly pack,
Pressed to the wall, dying, but fighting back![90]

Certainly the Chicago riot was not the first in which Negroes offered resistance to white mobs.[91] New York Negroes, it was found, had armed themselves quite precipitantly after the August riot of 1900.[92] The number of whites killed in Houston and East St. Louis in 1917 provides a stern measure of black resistance. But the Washington, D.C., riot of 1919, the press noted, was "the first time on any considerable scale, the negroes met 'mobs with mobs,' and inflicted at least as many casualties as were inflicted on them."[93] The old-style Negro was gone, asserted the *Chicago Defender*. "The younger generation of black men are not content to move along the line of least resistance as did their sires."

On all sides we have been made to feel the humiliating pressure of the white man's prejudice. In Washington it was a case of "teaching us our place." In Chicago it was a case of limiting our sphere of metes and bounds that had neither the sanction of law or sound common sense. In both cases we resent the assumption. Hence the race riots.[94]

In sum, the war had completed the destruction of the old status quo. The Negro had worked in the factory and ridden in the front of the streetcar; had received good wages, made inroads into formerly closed occupations and skills, and spent his pay on "white-style" entertainments; had been drafted and had seen Paris. That the war had produced a "new Negro" seems to have been the general consensus of the times, even in the case of the racists who screamed that it was bound to happen with so many "French-women-ruined niggers" around.[95] Certainly the individual Afro-American continued to use his defensive mask in personal interracial relations, but the community as a whole emerged from behind its protective cloak of passiveness.

In overview, the violence concentrated in this short span of years might best be seen as a period of social turbulence growing out of the need for accommodative adjustment. The search for order in the white community and the resolution of the black community, especially in the northern cities, into a viable if distorted image of white society made it imperative that a new balance be struck. But white society was not willing to acknowledge the need and it reacted accordingly. As Allen Grimshaw has suggested, the violence was "determined more by the reaction of the dominant white community to attacks on the accommodative patterns by Negroes than by any conscious determination of policy by the white group."[96] There were, obviously, numerous areas in which adjustments had to be made: housing, employment, public recreation and transportation, political power and authority, education—literally all areas where inequality was the Negro's lot.

Most of the adjustments that did come about between the black and white communities were made through sullen give and take. Garveyism, the continued resolution of the new black social structure, the burgeoning growth of black enclaves within the larger communities all worked to relieve some of the tensions within the black community. But there was, certainly, no concerted effort on the part of white America to relieve the strained conditions. Even in Chicago there was no dearth of events that could have triggered another conflict.[97] The remainder of 1919 and 1920 provided ample provocation for the *Chicago Defender's* assertion that

> so common has become lynching of a black man or woman, the fiends, for diversion, occasionally inflict the same torture on one of their own. But when a white man is the victim the whole world is shocked and from the pulpit, press, and platform, condemnations are heaped upon the savages . . . . The life of a black man has been held so cheap it has brought the price of a white man's life far below par, and still dropping.[98]

Still, the marked decrease in the number of racial conflicts in the cities and the decreasing number of lynchings over the next decade can be taken as indications that some manner of accommodation did follow these violent years.[99]

As America entered the 1920s, racial violence remained the black American's most vivid reminder of his blackness. A hysterical white woman could still place a black man's life in jeopardy, James Weldon Johnson protested in 1921.[100] The resurrection of the Klan contributed to the continuing violence as well. "Hooded Band Attacks Man's Home," read the headlines. "Farmer Forced to Hide in Woods as Terrorists Rule."[101] The scene was western Pennsylvania, not Mississippi. In short, white America was at least as preoccupied with race in the 1920s as it had been before the Great War, or so it seemed to many from its public responses to the need for accommodation of the "Problem of Problems." Bolshevism, even the Kaiser's Germany, was not much of a threat when compared to that of the dark-skinned races, proclaimed America's most formidable racist of the period, Lathrop Stoddard.[102] Langston Hughes's Mr. Simple seems almost to be speaking to the Stoddard's of the 1920s and later when he remarks, "I love Harlem."

"What is it you love about Harlem?"
"It's so full of Negroes," said Simple. "I feel like I got protection."
"From what?"
"From white folks," said Simple.[103]

Had white America been listening over these decades, it would have heard the voices of innumerable Mr. Simples expressing their opinions of white America—expressing their opinions and laughing. But white America was not really listening. It chose to interpret the generous measure of humor in black life as a racial trait. As W. E. B. DuBois put it, "That we do submit to life as it is and yet laugh and dance and dream is but another proof that we are idiots."[104]

Humor provided ordinary black Americans with a means to soften the hurt involved in their everyday dealings with the white world as well as providing a means of openly criticizing and attacking it. Many of the items cited above, especially the newspaper items, emphasize this most prominent mode of response when dealing with the white world. There is a thread of a sardonic humor to be

found weaving through editorials on black-white relations, James
Weldon Johnson noted around the turn of the century.[105] Humor
kept things in perspective; as an old Negro observation had it,
"When your head is in the lion's mouth you have to pat it a little."[106]

There exists a scholarly and popular consensus that humor was
adopted early by the Negro in America as an outlet to drain off some
of the frustration stemming from his assigned role. Without the outlet the frustrations could have otherwise boiled over and jeopardized
the individual and the group. "Putting it on" for the white man,
skillful deceptions that provided a measure of self-protection for the
individual, was born of slavery. For the group, the resulting humor
provided a means of openly criticizing black-white relations.[107]
"That's how Negro America lived for three hundred years," anthologist Philip Sterling maintains, "and that's what a good deal of its
humor has been about."[108]

Many of the most perceptive comments on the white are the
product of the period of slavery that maintained their applicability.
"God made de world and de white folks made work," is one of the
folk expressions that retained its cutting edge. Another, concerning
the origins of the races, ended with the observation, "And de white
man been sittin' up figgerin', ought's a ought, figger's a figger; all
for de white man, none for de nigger."[109] The same kind of observations are found in "secular" spirituals.

> *Our Father, who are in heaven,*
> *White man owe me 'leven, and pay me seven,*
> *Thy kingdom come, thy will be done,*
> *And if I hadn't tuck that, I wouldn't a got none.*[110]

It has been noted of minority groups in general that "sarcasm,
humor or parody of a prejudice's absurdity, primarily function to
preserve the ego identity of minority group members." As a matter
of mental health, humor serves "through sublimating the anger,
anxiety, shock and emotional disgust" to permit the expression of
protest against the dominant group.[111] "In part," DuBois held, the
Negro's humor "is a defense mechanism; reaction from tragedy; op-
positions set out in the face of the hurt and insult. In part it supplies
those inner pleasures and gratifications which are denied in broad

outline to a caste-ridden and restricted people."[112] As an example: "It says in the white folks' newspaper that our women are trying to ruin the white folks' homes—by quitting their jobs as maids."[113] The accommodative and conflict functions of humor have, in short, served the Afro-American well throughout the years.[114] "You've got to kid white folks along," says a Langston Hughes character. "When you're depending on 'em for a living, make 'em *think* you like it."[115]

Certainly the use of sardonic humor in newspaper items noted above scarcely hid the fact that distrust of the white was common and hardly at all masked the Negro's contempt for the white and hatred for his prejudices. In fact many of the expressions of this contempt used white stereotypes and turned them back upon the white. A rather recent, though applicable, story may serve as an example.

> In an Eastern college city a torrid romance between a light-skinned colored boy and white girl was interrupted by the draft. A year later he was back on furlough; to his surprise she had become a mother.
>
> "Why didn't you write me you were married?"
>
> "I'm not, and this is your child."
>
> "Why didn't you tell me. I would have come home and married you."
>
> "I know, but I talked it over with my family and they decided they'd rather have an illegitimate child in the family than a nigger."[116]

Utter hatred was not unusual in Negro humor relating to whites, however, nor was it necessarily camouflaged. Other jokes reflected the separation between the black and white worlds and the impact of the white world upon the black. The white was often hard pressed to understand such humor because the situations were unfamiliar, although this kind of humor also depended heavily upon stereotypes, and the comments on white prejudice actually contain a minimum of exaggeration of the truth.[117] A story of "equal justice" summarized by Sterling Brown illustrates this: "A Negro gets off free in traffic court by telling the judge that he saw whites drive on the green light so he knew the red light was for him."[118] It is thus rather ironic that the white who "knew" the Negro so well took white jokes in blackface as being representative of Negro humor. The humor that came out of World War I provides an excellent example here.[119]

Black laughter thus reveals much in the way of the Negro's attitudes toward the white world. "We of the vanguard often looked with despair at these very characteristics of the masses," James Weldon Johnson admitted. But, he noted, the vanguard was prone to underestimate them, for "no account [was taken] of the techniques for survival that the masses have evolved through the experience of generations."[120]

It made little difference which way the ordinary Negro turned, for he ran into the effects of white racism in every direction. Black Americans were being shortchanged, they knew it, and the knowledge is visible in the manner in which they viewed the white world. They knew, as the *New York Age* observed in 1919, that "the difference between white and black in this country is that the white man is compelled to struggle only against conditions that are within his possibility to change, while the black man . . . is confronted by conditions that are not within his possibility to change[.] [H]e cannot change his race and color."[121]

The axis of Negro-white relations impinged upon black experience in almost its every facet. Black Americans were victims of "Ezekielism," a delightfully simple and cogent revelation of white America's racist mannerisms presented by reformer Mary Ovington in her *Half a Man.* Ezekiel Jordan, a little black boy, is made the representative of the entire race.

> Ezekiel was too young to understand his position, but the white world about him never forgot it. When he arrived late to school, he was a dilatory representative; when, obliging little soul, he promised three people to weed their gardens all the same afternoon, he was a prevaricating representative. He never happened to steal ice-cream from the hoky-poky man or to play hookey, but if he had, he would have been a thieving and lazy representative. . . . Ezekiel's position is that of each Negro child and man and woman in the United States today.[122]

The burden of caste was especially heavy for the woman: not only was she not secure from any unwanted advances by the white man, she was scorned by her white sister. "I cannot conceive of such a creation as a virtuous black woman," an article in a national periodical asserted early in the century.[123] Their social position, like the man's, was such that they were continually reminded of their assigned role and could find escape only within the black community. But even there the force of the white world was felt, and behind the mask that all offered to the white world, distrust and contempt for whiteness was a common binding adhesive. "The attitude of the Northern white folks," said George Schuyler in the late 1920s, ". . . puzzles and incenses him. Very often he feels that they are more dangerous to him than the Southerners. Here are folks who yawp continuously about liberty, justice, equality and democracy, . . . but toward the Negro in their midst they are quite as cruel as the Southern crackers."[124]

From the 1890s, these attitudes continued to force the Negro toward higher and higher levels of racial consciousness. The disappointment of the World War I expectations completed the process, and ordinary black America entered the 1920s with a sense of peoplehood that matched its distrust of white society. By the time the depression burst upon the nation, modern black America had come into being.

That there were exceptions to the views of the white world presented here is obvious. There were, to be sure, many instances of affection, of trust, of mutual respect. Many of the mainstream cultural values were also those of the black subculture. But in the makeup of the characteristic spirit of the black community, the variations on the theme counted for little.

146   BLACK ON WHITE

NOTES

[1]From "Tiger," by Claude McKay in *The Selected Poems of Claude McKay* (Bookman Associates, 1953), 47.

[2]There are decisive groups of primary interests in the ethos of any group, sociologist Samuel Strong noted a generation ago in mapping out a method of analysis that is both productive and descriptive. See Samuel M. Strong, "Social Types in a Minority Group; Formulation of a Method for Studying a Minority: The Negro Community in Chicago," *AJS* 48 (March 1943): 565. See also Charles S. Johnson, *Growing Up in the Black Belt: Negro Youth in the Rural South* (Washington, D.C.: Prepared for the American Council on Education, 1941), 305-325. Johnson points to the white-black population ratio as being an important factor (how "visible" the Negro was in the larger community) and sees a direct correlation between class and racial consciousness. If it can be assumed that Negro youth mirror their parents' opinions in any way, Johnson's evidence here may be given added weight. For example, investigation in the 1930s showed northern urban Negro youth demonstrated less prejudice toward the white and held the Negro in higher regard than did southern Negro youth. Ibid., 250-255.

It also might be noted here that the relationship of visibility and prejudice has been questioned. Several recent studies find no significant correlation between the number of Negroes in a community and the amount of discrimination. See Hubert M. Blalock, Jr., "Per Cent Non-White and Discrimination," *ASR* 22 (December 1957): 677-682.

[3]*Crisis* 10 (July 1915): 114.

[4]Nick Aaron Ford, *The Contemporary Negro Novel* (Boston: Meador Publishing Co., 1936), 96-97.

[5]Thomas F. Pettigrew, *A Profile of the Negro American* (Princeton: D. Van Nostrand Co., 1964), 25. It is just this reality of black life that prompts social scientists such as Gordon Allport to state, "The Negro in America is socially a better example of caste than he is of race." Gordon Allport, *Nature of Prejudice*, abridged ed. (Doubleday, Anchor Books, 1958), 304. Myrdal noted, "The definition of the 'Negro race' is thus a social and conventional, not a biological concept. The social definition and not the biological facts [with some placing the number of American Negroes with some white ancestry as high as 70 percent of the black population] actually determines the status of an individual and his place in interracial relations." Gunnar Myrdal, *An American Dilemma,* 20th anniversary ed. (Harper & Row, 1962), 115, 133.

[6]James Weldon Johnson, *The Autobiography of an Ex-Coloured Man* (1912; reprint ed., Hill & Wang, 1960), 21.

[7]Ralph Ellison, *Shadow and Act* (Signet Books, 1966), 167.

[8]Ann Petry, *The Street* (Boston: Houghton Mifflin Co., 1946), 57.

[9]W. E. B. DuBois, *Dusk of Dawn* (1940; reprint ed., Schocken Books, 1968) 135.

[10]Rudolph Fisher, *The Walls of Jericho* (1928; reprint ed., by Arno Press, Inc., 1969), 61, 62.

[11]"For a Lady I Know," in Countee Cullen, *On These I Stand: An Anthology of the Best Poems of Countee Cullen* (Harper and Brothers, 1927), 33.

[12]See also Claude McKay, *A Long Way from Home* (1937; reprint ed., Harcourt, Brace and World, 1970), 345.

[13]Ralph Ellison, *Invisible Man* (Modern Library, 1952), 3.

[14]Richard Wright, *Native Son* (1940; reprint ed., Signet Books, 1964), 109.

[15]W. E. B. DuBois, *Darkwater* (1920; reprint ed., Schocken Books, 1969), 223. See also Walter White, "The Paradox of Color," in Alain Locke, ed., *The New Negro* (1925; reprint ed. by Arno Press, 1968), 362.

[16]W. E. B. DuBois, "The Black North," *New York Times*, November 24, 1901; Richard Wright, "The Man Who Went to Chicago," in *Eight Men* (1961; reprint ed., Pyramid Books, 1961), 180, 192; Johnson, *Growing Up in the Black Belt,* 294-296.

[17]C. S. Johnson, *Growing Up in the Black Belt*, 297; Pettigrew, *Profile of the Negro American*, 51.

[18]James Baldwin, "A Talk to Teachers," *Saturday Review* 46 (December 21, 1963): 43.

[19]Verses 1 and 4 of "Me And My Captain," in *"Me And My Captain," Chain Gang Negro Songs of Protest,* from the collection of Laurence Gellert (Hours Press, c. 1939), 5.

[20]"We Wear the Mask," in *The Complete Poems of Paul Laurence Dunbar* (1921; reprint ed., Dodd, Mead and Co., 1962) 71.

[21]W. E. B. DuBois, "Strivings of the Negro People," *Atlantic Monthly* 80 (August 1897): 194; James Baldwin, *Notes of a Native Son* (Boston: Beacon Press, 1955), 88; Richard Wright, *Uncle Tom's Children* (Harper & Row, 1940), 130, and *White Man, Listen!* (Doubleday and Co., 1957), 43.

[22]Allport, *Nature of Prejudice*, 287-288; Thomas F. Pettigrew, "Negro American Personality: Why Isn't More Known," *Journal of Social Issues* 20 (April 1964): 7.

[23]L. M. Hussey, "Homo Africanus," *American Mercury* 4 (January 1925): 84-85. The term *coon* was not used derogatorily but rather in the theatrical sense of the 1920s. *Crisis* 29 (February 1925): 181, it might be noted, commented at some length upon the accuracy of Mr. Hussey's observations.

[24]Phillip B. Kay, *Taffy*, quoted in James W. Byrd, "The Portrayal of White Characters by Negro Novelists, 1900-1950" (Ph.D. diss., George Peabody College for Teachers, 1955), 264. See also Pettigrew, "Negro American Personality," 7.

[25]In a paper presented to the National Medical Association meeting in San Francisco in August 1969, Carl S. Jenkins prefaced his remarks with the assertion, "I feel that every black person . . . in the United States today, has to make some sort of adjustment to the white community. This adjustment must be made at a very early age if he is to be able to function in society. From the time he first starts playing in the neighborhood, he is aware that he is black, he is different, and he must make some changes in his interpersonal relations." "HAT," *Journal of Human Relations* 17 (Summer 1969): 162.

[26]Pettigrew, *Profile of the Negro American*, 50. See also William M. Tuttle, Jr., "Views of a Negro During the 'Red Summer' of 1919: A Document" [Letter, Stanley B. Norvell, Chicago, to Victor F. Lawson, Chicago, August 22, 1919], *JNH* 51 (July 1966): 213.

[27]George S. Schuyler, "Our White Folks," *American Mercury* 12 (December 1927): 387.

[28]Claude McKay, *Home to Harlem* (Harper and Brothers, 1928), 86.

[29]Quoted in Pettigrew, *Profile of the Negro American*, 51.

[30]J. Saunders Redding, *On Being Negro in America* (1951; reprint ed., Indianapolis: Bobbs-Merrill Co., 1962), 63. See also Donald L. Noel, "Correlates of Anti-White Prejudice" (Ph.D. diss., Cornell University, 1961), 136.

[31]Arnold Rose, *The Negro's Morale* (University of Minnesota Press, 1949), 113. See also Baldwin, *Notes of a Native Son*, 38; Bone, *Negro Novel in America*, 6.

[32]Petry, *The Street*, 251.

[33]See, for example, Baldwin, *Notes of a Native Son,* 112; Langston Hughes, *The Big Sea* (1940; reprint ed., Hill & Wang, 1963), 14; Noel, "Correlates of Anti-White Prejudice," 161. Ralph Ellison regards the assertion of universal hatred of whites as a most "questionable proposition." *Harper's Magazine* 235 (July 1967): 4.

[34]Redding, *On Being Negro in America*, 15.

[35]Langston Hughes, *Not Without Laughter* (1930; reprint ed., Alfred A. Knopf, 1963) 85.

[36]Fisher, *Walls of Jericho*, 37. The origin of the term "fay" or "ofay," meaning a white, is obscure. Michael Harrington, *The Other America* (Penguin Books, 1963), 65, using a double-f spelling, asserts that it is pig Latin for foe.

McKay, through his character Ray in *Banjo*, observes: "We Negroes have humorous little words of our own with which we replace unpleasant stock

words. And we often use them when we are among white people and don't
want them to know just what we are referring to, especially when it is anything delicate or taboo between the races. For example, we have words like
ofay, pink, fade, spade, Mr. Charlie, cracker, peckawood, hoojah, and so
on—nice words and bitter. The stock is always increasing because as the
whites get on to the old words we invent new ones." Claude McKay, *Banjo,
A Story Without a Plot* (1929; reprint ed., Harcourt Brace Jovanovich,
1970), 217.

[37]Alden Bland, *Behold a Cry* (Charles Scribner's Sons, 1947), 163-164.

[38]DuBois, *Darkwater*, 82.

[39]Salt Lake City *Broad Ax,* February 25, 1899.

[40]*New York Age,* August 24, 1911; *Crisis* 1 (January 1911): 8.

[41]*New York Age,* April 1, 1909.

[42]"Negroes in White Churches," *Colored American Magazine* 12 (April
1907): 247.

[43]"The White Church," *Crisis* 14 (May 1917): 10.

[44]*The Negro in Detroit* (Detroit Bureau of Governmental Research,
1926), sec. X, 20-21. The Negro church in the urban north is discussed in
some detail in chap. 7. For a summary of the "compartmentalization" of
black-white religious life, as it has been termed, see Joseph R. Washington,
Jr., *Black Religion: The Negro and Christianity in the United States*
(Boston: Beacon Press, 1964), chap. 4, and Liston Pope, "The Negro and
Religion in America," *Review of Religious Research* 5 (Spring 1964):
142-152.

[45]Salt Lake City *Broad Ax*, February 11, 1899. Although of a generation
later, Arthur Raper's "A Day at Police Court," *Phylon* 5 (Third Quarter
1944): 225-232, conveys the maddening frustration that the poor—especially the poor black—met everyday in the courts.

[46]The case was later retired and an award of $1,000 made. *New York Age*,
April 7, 1910; *Crisis* 1 (February 1911): 20.

[47]*Crisis* 2 (May 1911): 6-7; ibid. 6 (August 1913): 189.

[48]Ibid. 18 (June 1919): 97; see also letter, "Somewhere in South Georgia,"
November 5, 1918, sender unknown, to John R. Shillady, New York,
NAACP MSS, File Box C-226, Library of Congress.

[49]Wallace Thurman, *The Blacker the Berry . . . , A Novel of Negro Life*
(1929; reprint ed., Collier Books, 1970) 162.

[50]W. E. B. DuBois, *The Souls of Black Folk* (1903; reprint ed., Fawcett
Publications, 1965), 151, 176.

[51]The white as revealed to black eyes shows up starkly in Eric D.
Walrond, "On Being a Domestic," *Opportunity* 1 (August 1923): 234.
George S. Schuyler in "Blessed Are the Sons of Ham," *Nation* 124 (March
23, 1927): 313-315, uses satire to the same end.

[52]Petry, *The Street*, 260.

[53]Some of the legislation introduced was patently ridiculous, as for example, when Indianapolis sought to separate Negro and white divorce cases. *Crisis* 2 (May 1911): 7. As a further example, see the medley of such Jim Crow legislation compiled for the first months of 1913 in ibid. 6 (May 1913): 15.

[54]McKay, *A Long Way from Home*, 347.

[55]*Crisis* 2 (October 1911): 242; E. Franklin Frazier, "The Negro Community: A Cultural Phenomenon," *Social Forces* 7 (March 1929): 416.

[56]Quoted in Robert T. Kerlin, *Voice of the Negro: 1919* (1920; reprint ed., Arno Press, Inc., 1968), 12.

[57]Ira DeA. Reid, "A Critical Summary: The Negro on the Home Front in World Wars I and II,"*JNE* 12 (Summer 1943):514.

[58]McKay, *Home to Harlem*, 331-332.

[59]William Irwin MacIntyre, *Colored Soldiers* (Macon, Ga.: The J.W. Burke Co., 1923), 54.

[60]Schuyler, "Our White Folks," 386.

[61]"Close Ranks," *Crisis* 16 (July 1918): 388. See also Robert Russa Moton, "The American Negro and the World War," *World's Work* 36 (May 1918): 74-77, and "The Patriotism of the Negro Citizen," *Outlook* 120 (November 20, 1918): 451-452; "What the Negro Is Doing to Help Win the War," *Literary Digest*, 58 (July 27, 1918): 39-40; Kerlin, *Voice of the Negro*, 39.

[62]John Hope Franklin, *From Slavery to Freedom,* 3rd ed., (1966; Vintage Books, 1969), 455-470; Emmett J. Scott, *The American Negro in the World War* (Chicago: Homewood Press, 1919), chaps. 11-19. The appendixes of U.S. Army War College, *The Colored Soldier in the U.S. Army* (Washington, D.C.: Historical Section, Army War College, May 1942), are awash with all of the prejudices of this time. They present solid "evidence" of the Negro's unfitness for combat services, cowardliness, and so forth.

[63]*New York Age*, January 11, 1919.

[64]Ibid., January 4, 1919. This pickup item from the *New York Globe* was captioned "High Professions a Sham."

[65]*New York Age*, February 15, 1919.

[66]Ibid., June 7, 1919.

[67]*Challenge Magazine* (October 1919), quoted in Kerlin, *Voice of the Negro*, 19.

[68]Kenneth B. Clark, "Morale of the Negro on the Home Front: World Wars I and II," *JNE* 12 (Summer 1943): 423-424; E. Franklin Frazier, "Ethnic and Minority Groups in Wartime, with Special Reference to the Negro," *AJS* 48 (November 1942): 369-377. See also Richard M. Dalfiume,

Desegregation of the U.S. Armed Forces: Fighting on Two Fronts, 1939-1953 (University of Missouri Press, 1969), 7-22; C. Vann Woodward, *The Strange Career of Jim Crow* (Oxford University Press, 1966), 114-115; Constance McLaughlin Green, *The Secret City: A History of Race Relations in the Nation's Capital* (University of Princeton Press, 1967), 187-190; Hughes, *The Big Sea*, 51; W. E. B. DuBois, "The Negro Soldier in Service Abroad During the First World War," *JNE* 12 (Summer 1943): 324-334; Franklin, *From Slavery to Freedom*, 478ff; "Returning Soldiers," *Crisis* 18 (May 1919): 13-14; Ford, *Contemporary Negro Novel*, 89-90.

[69]Finley Peter Dunne, *Mr. Dooley's Philosophy* (R. H. Russell, Publishers, 1902), 217-218.

[70]See, for example, *Crisis* 5 (February 1913): 195-196. Such items became familiar to *Crisis* readers.

[71]Chicago *Broad Ax*, February 2, 1901.

[72]Myrdal, *American Dilemma*, 561; U.S., Bureau of the Census, *Historical Statistics of the United States, Colonial Times to 1957* (Washington: GPO, 1960), 218 (Table, series H 452-454). There was not, evidently, any set criteria for counting victims of Judge Lynch before 1940. See *Historical Statistics of the United States,* 216. For a description of the parade of violence see Ida Wells-Barnett, *On Lynchings* (reprint ed., Arno Press, 1969), a series of three pamphlets originally published in 1892, 1895, and 1900; and Walter White, *Rope and Faggot: A Biography of Judge Lynch* (1929; reprint ed., Arno Press, 1969).

[73]*New York Tribune*, April 24, 1899, quoted in NAACP, *Thirty Years of Lynching in the United States, 1899-1918* (NAACP, April 1919) 13.

[74]*New York Age*, August 17, 1911, 4; *Crisis* 2 (September, 1911), 185; NAACP, *Thirty Years of Lynching*, 19.

[75]Chicago *Broad Ax*, December 30, 1911.

[76]*Crisis* 1 (November 1910): 11.

[77]Ibid. 3 (January 1912): 110. A series of these grisly pictures is found in Scott Nearing, *Black America* (1929; reprint ed., Schocken Books, 1969) 189-195.

[78]From "The Lynching," in *Selected Poems of Claude McKay*, 37.

[79]William E. Walling, "The Race War in the North," *Independent* 65 (September 3, 1908): 530; James L. Croutthamel, "The Springfield Race Riot of 1908,"*JNH* 45 (July 1960): 164-181; Kelly Miller, "The Attitude of the Intelligent Negro Toward Lynchings," *Voice of the Negro* 2 (May 1905): 307-312. See also Charles Crowe, "Racial Violence and Social Reform—Origins of the Atlanta Riot of 1906," *JNH* 53 (July 1968): 234-356, and "Racial Massacre in Atlanta, September 22, 1906," *JNH* (April 1969): 150-173.

For a first-hand account of the Atlanta riot and being guilty of blackness, see Walter White's autobiography, *A Man Called White* (1948; reprint ed., Indiana University Press, 1970) 4-12.

The Brownsville, Texas, affair of 1906 was a cause célèbre in the black world because of President Theodore Roosevelt's ordered discharge of Negro troops without regard to guilt. See Joseph Smith, "The True Story of the Brownsville Affair," *Alexander's Magazine* 3 (January 15, 1907): 158-162; Emma Lou Thornbrough, "The Brownsville Episode and the Negro Vote," *JNH* 44 (December 1957): 459-493; Archibald Grimké, "Hon. Joseph Benson Foraker, or, the Man and the Hour," *Alexander's Magazine* 4 (May 15, 1907): 31-42, and "The Black Battalion," *Alexander's Magazine* 5 (April 1908): 189-224.

[80]Fisher, *Walls of Jericho*, 8.

[81]*Crisis* 2 (May 1911): 13, presents a medley of press comment expressing just this theme.

[82]*New York Age*, June 3, 1909.

[83]*Historical Statistics of the United States*, 218. Seventy-six Negroes were killed by mobs in 1919 versus thirty-six in 1917. The number of white victims also increased. See Myrdal, *American Dilemma*, 563. White, *Rope and Faggot*, 213 (table 1), gives strikingly different figures for the war years, especially for 1915.

[84]*Chicago Defender*, July 5, 1919.

[85]Quoted in August Meier and Elliott Rudwick, "Attitudes of Negro Leaders Toward the American Labor Movement from the Civil War to World War I," in Julius Jacobson, ed., *The Negro and the American Labor Movement* (Anchor Books, 1968), 46. See also Elliott M. Rudwick, *Race Riot at East St. Louis, July 2, 1917* (Southern Illinois University Press, 1964), 16-26; NAACP, "The Massacre of East St. Louis," *Crisis* 14 (September 1917): 219-238.

[86]Sterling Spero and Abram L. Harris, *The Black Worker: The Negro and the Labor Movement,* (1931; reprint ed., Atheneum, 1968), 128-131; William M. Tuttle, Jr., *Race Riot: Chicago in the Red Summer of 1919* (Atheneum, 1970), 108-123.

The relationship of labor and the ordinary black American needs to be more closely examined. At this point it seems certain that the ordinary Negro wanted little to do with white labor organizations; he distrusted their motives and had many a lump on his head to remind him of their attitudes toward black workers. There is, moreover, little that would indicate that ordinary black Americans were listening very closely to Negro leaders who were calling for solidarity with white labor. The comments found on this subject in the imaginative literature were almost invariably negative.

[87]Allen D. Grimshaw, "A Study in Social Violence: Urban Race Riots in the United States" (Ph.D. diss., University of Pennsylvania, 1959), 179.

[88]*New York Age*, May 31, 1917.

[89]St. Clair Drake and Horace R. Cayton, *Black Metropolis* (1945; revised ed., Harper Torchbooks, 1962), 65-69; Myrdal, *American Dilemma*, 563, 567; Tuttle, *Race Riot*, 32-66.

[90]*Selected Poems of Claude McKay*, 36.

[91]A reporter for the *Chicago Tribune* characterized the Chicago riot scene as a war battle zone. "On the Firing-Line during the Chicago Race-Riots," *Literary Digest* 62 (August 23, 1919): 44-46.

[92]Gilbert Osofsky, "Race Riot, 1900: A Study of Ethnic Violence," *JNE* 32 (Winter 1963):22

[93]"Our Own Subject Race Rebels," *Literary Digest* 62 (August 2, 1919): 25.

[94]*Chicago Defender*, August 2, 1919. See also Kerlin *Voice of the Negro*, 24-25.

[95]"Our Own Subject Race Rebels," 25; Myrdal, *American Dilemma*, 193, 563, 745; Grimshaw, "Study in Social Violence," 48, 50-51. In a survey of opinion as to the cause of the riot, *Literary Digest* gave prominent place to the Illinois state attorney, Maclay Hoyne, who saw the riot as the product of a conspiracy, a planned uprising by Negroes. He recommended segregation after the Black Belt had been disarmed. "Why the Negro Appeals to Violence," *Literary Digest* 62 (August 9, 1919): 11. Hoyne, it might be added, had political axes to grind at the time, and the Negro was a handy stone. See Tuttle, *Race Riot*, 252-253, 254.

The southern press, of course, had a holiday with the outbreaks of these racial disturbances in the North. "What the South Thinks of Northern Race-Riots," *Literary Digest* 62 (August 16, 1919): 17-18.

[96]Grimshaw, "Study in Social Violence," 21.

[97]Tuttle, *Race Riot*, 248-258.

[98]*Chicago Defender*, September 4, 1920.

[99]Grimshaw, "Study in Social Violence," 179; White *Rope and Faggot*, 131-132.

[100]*New York Age*, June 18, 1921.

[101]*Pittsburgh Courier*, August 11, 1923.

[102]Frederick Lewis Allen, *Only Yesterday: An Informal History of the 1920's* (1931; Harper & Row, Perennial Library ed., 1964), 53.

[103]Langston Hughes, *The Best of Simple* (Hill & Wang, 1961), 20. Clements Wood's grisly short story "The Mother," *Opportunity* 3 (July 1925): 214-216, illustrates the force of this continual personal threat. See also McKay, *Home to Harlem*, 265-266.

[104]Quoted in Green, *The Secret City*, 148. Humor, it has been pointed out, depends upon a thorough knowledge of its object to be effective. Here again is good evidence of the Negro's knowledge of white America—and of the hidden irony in white claims of "knowing the Negro." See James Weldon Johnson, *Along This Way: The Autobiography of James Weldon Johnson* (Viking Press, 1933), 120-121; Ellison, *Shadow and Act*, 153.

[105]Johnson, *Autobiography of an Ex-Coloured Man*, 183.

[106]Philip Sterling, ed., *Laughing on the Outside* (Grosset and Dunlap, 1965), 168.

[107]Myrdal, *American Dilemma*, 960-961.

[108]Sterling, ed., *Laughing on the Outside*, 168 (emphasis removed). See also Nancy Levi Arnez and Clara B. Anthony, "Contemporary Negro Humor as Social Satire," *Phylon* 29 (Winter 1968): 339-346; A. Russell Brooks, "The Comic Spirit and the Negro's New Look," *CLA Journal* 6 (September 1962): 35-43; John H. Burma, "Humor as a Technique in Race Conflict," *ASR* 11 (December 1946): 710-715.

[109]Both quoted in Sterling Brown, "Negro Folk Expression," *Phylon* 11 (October 1953): 325, 326.

[110]Sterling Brown, in introduction to folk literature section, *The Negro Caravan: Writings by American Negroes,* ed. by Sterling Brown, Arthur P. Davis, and Ulysses Lee (Dryden Press, 1941), 422.

[111]Donald C. Simmons, "Protest Humor: Folkloristic Reaction to Prejudice," *American Journal of Psychiatry* 120 (December 1963): 567.

[112]Quoted in Sterling, ed., *Laughing on the Outside*, 24.

[113]Cited by Myrdal, *American Dilemma*, 961.

[114]S. P. Fullwinder, *The Mind and Mood of Black America* (Homewood, Illinois: Dorsey Press, 1969), 216, observes: "Rural folk-humor ran on the fine line of tragedy. City humor, on the other hand, always threatened to explode into violence. Here again, humor was a type of aggression. It grew directly out of the disorganization of family and community life in the ghetto." More emphasis should be afforded to humor as an alternative to overt aggression, however. See, for example, Ulf Hannerz, *Soulside: Inquiries into Ghetto Culture and Community* (Columbia University Press, 1969), 66-67.

The function of intragroup criticism evidently did not develop in the Negro community until quite recently, although the Negro certainly always has been able to laugh at himself. See Irwin Rinder, "A Note on Humor as an Index of Minority Group Morale," *Phylon* 26 (Spring 1965): 117-121.

[115]Langston Hughes, "A Good Job Gone," in *Something in Common and Other Stories* (Hill & Wang, 1963), 36.

[116]Burma, "Humor as a Technique," 713.

[117]Rose, *The Negro's Morale*, 118.

[118]Brown, "Negro Folk Expression," 327.

[119]See, for example, "Some War-Time Humor of the Negro Soldier," *Literary Digest* 61 (April 12, 1919): 88, and "The Colored Fighters Never Lose Their Sense of Humor," *Literary Digest* 61 (May 10, 1919): 63-64; Charles E. Mack, *Two Black Crows in the A.E.F.* (Indianapolis: The Bobbs-Merrill Company, 1928). See also Edgar A. Toppin, *"The New York Times'* Idea of Humor about the Negro in the Early Part of the Twentieth Century," *Negro History Bulletin* 14 (June 1951): 205-206; David L. Cohen, "White Folks Are Easy to Please," *Saturday Review of Literature* 27 (November 25, 1944): 12.

[120]Johnson, *Along This Way*, 120.

[121]*New York Age*, February 1, 1919.

[122]Mary White Ovington, *Half a Man* (1911; reprint ed., Schocken Books, 1969), 219. See also the comments on "Ezekielism" in *Crisis* 3 (November 1911): 26.

[123]Quoted in Sylvanie Francaz Williams, "The Social Status of the Negro Woman," *Voice of the Negro* 1 (July 1904): 298. See also Elise Johnson McDougald, "The Task of Negro Womanhood," in Locke, ed., *The New Negro*, 369-370; Petry, *The Street*, 45-46. Ovington, in *Half a Man*, 162-168, presents a "Half a Woman" theme.

[124]Schuyler, "Our White Folks," 388.

6

BLACK ON BLACK I

Hello, Central, What's the matter with this line?
I want to talk to that high Brown of mine. . . .[1]

AS THE nation neared the turn of the century, ambiguity and inconsistency were found everywhere in the Negro's everyday life. On the one hand he had come to be judged from without by the standards of the white community—or rather, by standards that reflected what the white community thought itself to be. On the other hand he was set apart from that society as an inferior being and deemed by the majority incapable of ever measuring up to white standards.[2] Though many of the mainstream cultural values were those of the black subculture, many—perhaps even most of those that were involved in everyday life—were also the offspring of white racism and the color line. Limited job opportunities, restricted educational opportunities, poor and crowded housing, and all other manner of discriminations worked to shape the black world and its attitudes about itself. Even as late as the 1950s and 1960s Saunders Redding found that the force with which whiteness operates upon blackness could only be described as "daeomonic." He refuses to believe that any black can escape the force even now. "One's heart is sickened at the realization," he asserts, "of the primal energy that goes undeflected and unrefined into the sheer business of living as a Negro in the United States—in any one of the United States. Negroness is a kind of superconsciousness that directs thinking, that dictates action, that perverts the expression of instinctual drives which are salutary and humanitarian."[3]

In a very measurable way a sense of frustration, of futility, was built into black American existence by the impact of whiteness on blackness. It was part of being black—and the reality of being black is a force that must be recognized to appreciate the meaning of being a "special kind of American." Of it, DuBois wrote:

> It is a peculiar sensation, . . . the sense of looking at one's self through the eyes of others, of measuring one's soul by the tape of a world that looks on in amused contempt and pity. One ever feels his two-ness,—an American, a Negro; two souls, two thoughts, two unreconciled strivings; two warring ideals in one dark body, whose dogged strength alone keeps it from being torn assunder. [4]

"From adolescence to death there is something very personal about being a Negro in America," Saunders Redding writes in the same vein. "It is like having a second ego which is as much the conscious subject of all experience as the natural self." [5] In an autobiographical sketch, Richard Wright wrote: "While working as a porter in Memphis I had often stood aghast as a friend of mine offered himself to be kicked by the white men; but now, while working in Chicago, I was learning that perhaps even a kick was better than uncertainty . . . . I could now sympathize with—though I could never bring myself to approve—those tortured blacks who had given up and had gone to their white tormentors and had said: 'Kick me, if that's all there is for me; kick me and let me feel at home, let me have peace!'" [6] "I am telling you," says Hughes's Mr. Simple, "we has so many problems, life is liable to kill us before death does." [7]

Yet for all of the shaping force the white community exerted on the black and for all of the frustrations it introduced from day to day, day in, day out, the ordinary Negro's life in the northern cities was not itself something grotesque. Within his community, limited though it was, he functioned quite freely. Some adjusted so well to the manifestations of white racism that the white world itself was an existence to be ignored when possible. And when the white world could not be disregarded, it became a fact of life to be suffered, not necessarily in silence. "Identified as a Negro," journalist and historian Lerone Bennett, Jr., maintains, "treated as Negro, provided with Negro interests, forced whether he wills or not, to live in Negro communities, to think, love, buy and breathe as a Negro, the Negro comes in time to see himself as a Negro, . . . he comes, in time, to invent himself."[8]

Black Americans built their communities, as Charles S. Johnson noted, "around the idea of adjustment to being a Negro," an idea that rejected "escape into the white world."[9] That is to say, race consciousness was nurtured by white racism, and it in turn ensured that the Negro community would evolve an ethos well able to protect its ordinary resident.

"Adjustment to being a Negro," as C. S. Johnson put it, involved more than assuming a role dictated by the dominant white society. The Negro could, Johnson said, criticize the race and could even dislike Negroes—as long as he remembered that he was himself a Negro.[10] On the surface, this rule of "adjustment to being a Negro" seems rather paradoxical, but it is indicative of two primary and interrelated facets of Negro life: the force with which the values of the white society shaped those of the black and the force with which racial self-hatred could impinge on and hammer at everyday life. Both of these facets were especially manifest in the existence of a rather ubiquitous concern with color within the Negro community. In all of its various aspects this concern with color amounted to a "color complex" that tore at intraracial harmony and served more to disrupt than to foster the development of institutions within the growing black urban communities. It even maintained a good deal of its force in the face of the ever-increasing sense of peoplehood during the period.

One of the most striking facets of the color complex was the color caste that forever got in the way of racial solidarity. This color caste demonstrates most forcefully that "the only factor common to *all* Negroes is color," as one student of the phenomenon expressed it.[11] It was inevitable, of course, that color would enter the black ethos when it had so prominent a place in the larger society. For example, the "tragic mulatto" had become a common character in white American fiction, as had other stock characterizations that perpetuated old stereotypes.[12] He had also found his way into Negro literature. While giving a lecture, a minister in Pauline Hopkins's *Contending Forces* abruptly "touched upon the Negro, and with impressive gesture and lowered voice thanked God that the mulatto

race was dying out, because it was a mongrel mixture which combined the worst elements of two races."[13]

But the mulatto and color were every day afforded more continuous and special attention than this. The mulatto was at the root of
America's race problem. He, in the eyes of whites, caused the tract-
able black to be discontented. Control this product of miscegenation
and the race problem would be easily solved.[14] Some blacks agreed,
for the color mania led many in the community to place a high value
on lightness of skin color. "The pride of the Negro is in the color of
the white, and is a confession of inferiority as to himself and of superiority as to the white man," said one Negro critic.[15] "It is well
known," the vitriolic William Hannibal Thomas wrote in 1901,
"that the black man is morbidly sensitive regarding his color."

> That negroes have a conscious sense of degradation which they
> falsely attribute to their color, is shown by their eagerness to
> get as far as possible away from black shades. It is this craving
> for a light color and better hair for their offspring, which is re-
> sponsible for many of the illegitimate children of negro
> motherhood.[16]

Thomas was given to overstatement, but here at least he well
caught what lightness of skin color meant to many Negroes. The Negro's "looking-glass self," in other words, was being shaped by what
others said he was. "Thus, the Negro's ego structure is [still] largely
a reflection of the actual and legal status he enjoys," a close commentator recently observed.[17] A character in Wallace Thurman's
color-critical novel, *The Blacker the Berry . . . ,* says: "We are all
living in a totally white world, where all standards are the
standards of the white man, and where almost invariably what the
white man does is right, and what the black man does is wrong, unless it is precedented by something a white man has done."[18]

As in other aspects of black life, South and North, rural and
urban attitudes were different. Sociologist Charles S. Johnson, for
instance, in an early study of rural Black Belt life in Alabama, found
that "black" was equated with good, solid respectability.[19] In the
urban setting, however, light skin color was of singular social value
at the end of the nineteenth century and was closely related to social
class and position.[20] In a *Harper's* story, Carter was seven-eighths

white and longed to be "white," but he knew he was a Negro. He confessed his tainted blood to a white girl, and when she was un- impressed, declared, "I can't have anything to do with a woman who'd marry a nigger."[21]

The existence of self-hatred stemming from the tendency of a dispossessed group to assimilate the values of the dominant group was first introduced into the social science field by the noted social psychologist Kurt Lewin, according to one authority.[22] But Negro America knew it for what it was all along. It was the other side of the we-group, the racial pride, coin.[23] "For now nearly twenty years," W. E. B. DuBois wrote in 1914, "we have made ourselves mudsills for the feet of this Western world.

We have echoed and applauded every shameful accusation made against 10,000,000 victims of slavery. Did they call us inferior half-beasts? We nodded our simple heads and whis- pered: "We is." Did they call our women prostitutes and our children bastards? We smiled and cast a stone at the bruised breasts of our wives and daughters. Did they accuse of laziness 4,000,000 sweating, struggling laborers, half paid and cheated out of much of that? We shrieked: "Ain't it so?" We laughed with them at our color, we joked at our sad past, and we told chicken stories to get alms.

And what was the result? We got "friends." I do not believe any people ever had so many "friends" as the American Negro today! He had nothing but "friends" and may the good God deliver him from most of them, for they are like to lynch his soul.[24]

Black self-hatred clearly resulted from the humiliation heaped upon all blacks by whites. "My father hated Negroes," Langston Hughes said. "I think he hated himself, too, for being a Negro. He disliked all of his family because they were Negroes and remained in the United States, where none of them had a chance to be much of anything but servants—like my mother, who started out with a good education at the University of Kansas, he said, but had sunk to working in a restaurant, waiting on niggers, when she wasn't in some white woman's kitchen."[25] "Oh, it's no curse to be a Negro," read the anonymous diary entry of a short story, "if you are content to live a black existence. But I am not. I can't. My inside is different from my outside. For as far back as I can remember, I have realized that I was different from my Negro people."[26]

It is pretty well accepted that skin color and class associations in the United States date back to the period of slavery "when white masters gave positions as house servants to 'nice-looking' Negroes or granted special privileges to their own mulatto children."[27] Noting that after the Civil War "a free and mulatto ancestry became the basis of important social distinctions," sociologist E. Franklin Frazier went on to remark that "even in the Methodist and Baptist denominations there were separate church organizations based upon distinctions of colour and what were considered standards of civilized behavior."[28] Yet this facet of color consciousness seems to have been largely a northern and urban phenomenon.[29] Certainly there existed all through the 1890-1930 period a correlation between class and color.[30] The old "blue veins" were losing out, but light skin color was to remain almost a prerequisite for entry into the upper strata of Negro society. In the form of a dialogue between two female gossips of the "best" people portion of black society, satirist George Schuyler brings up the subject of the color mania and the "voluntary Negro." One gossip says:

> "Those two gentlemen have admitted they are Negroes, and have been accepted as such by Negro society. Of course, they *are* white men, but what are we to do? When they cannot make a living in white society and the future looks rather doubtful, they just come over to us, claiming that they possess the necessary drop of Negro blood. Who can deny it? And, since the American Negro psychology is such that a man or woman rises higher and higher in our esteem, the whiter they are, it is only natural that these people immediately jump to a prominent position in Negro society. And no one will deny that a high position and usually a fat job in Negro society, is better than being a nonentity and possessing a low job or no job in white society."[31]

Color, in a very real sense, came to describe the layers of black society. In picturing a "race" affair to which all in the black commu-

nity were welcome, Rudolph Fisher related the following in one of
his best stories:

> Those who between dances repaired only as far as the ter-
> races and sat at the round-top tables and drank Whistle, per-
> haps tinctured with corn, were either just ordinary respectable
> people or rats [the lowest of the lowly]. But those who mounted
> the stairs and crowded into or about the boxes, who kept wait-
> ers busy bringing ginger ale, which they flavored from silver
> hip flasks—those were dicties and fays.
>
>   . . .
>
> Ordinary Negroes and rats below, dicties and fays above, the
> floor beneath the feet of the one constituting the roof over the
> heads of the others. Somehow, undeniably, a predominance of
> darker skins below, and, just as undeniably, of fairer skins
> above. . . . One might have read in that distribution a com-
> plex philosophy of skin-color, and from it deduced the past,
> present, and future of this people.[32]

Black Washington, D.C., is the most often cited example of
this class-color phenomenon—and also the most ridiculed. At the
turn of the century and up into the 1930s, it had the most thoroughly
exclusive black elite in the nation, backed as its members were by a
long history of visible relationship to the very center of white authority. Washington was the social capital of Negro America, and as one
observer noted of its elite, "A majority of the women too possess
Caucasian exteriors. To be able to 'pass' [for white] is almost a req-
uisite."[33] Langston Hughes observed it first hand. "As long as I have
been colored I have heard of Washington society," he wrote in 1927.
"Yet I found that their ideals seemed most Nordic and un-
Negro . . . . Speaking of a fraternity dance, one in a group of five
college men said proudly, 'There was nothing but pinks there,—
looked just like' fay women. Boy you'd have thought it was an o'fay
dance!'"[34]

Closely akin to skin color in the color complex is the factor of
"good" hair, as illustrated by the poem, "Baby Hair," by Constance
Nichols.

> *I took a peek for the very first time*
> *At the tiny brown mite on the bed.*
> *He blinked his eyes and doubled plump fists,*
> *and I ran to his mother and said,*
> *"The most cunning baby I ever did see."*
> *But she, patiently lying there,*
> *Touched my arm and with anxious voice*
> *Whispered, "Does he have good hair?"*[35]

"It's just by luck that you even got good hair," asserts the mother of the protagonist in a Langston Hughes short story.

"What's that got to do with being an American?"
"A mighty lot," said his mama, "in America."[36]

"Always the same tune," Pauli Murray wrote in her *Proud Shoes.* "Good hair! Bad hair! Stringy hair! Nappy hair! Thin lips! Thick lips! Red lips! Liver lips! Blue veined! Blue gummed!

> Brush your hair, child, don't let it get kinky! Cold-cream your face, child, don't let it get sunburned! Don't suck your lips, child, you'll make them too niggerish! Black is evil, don't mix with mean niggers! Black is honest, you half-white bastard. I always said a little black and a little white sure do make a pretty sight! . . .
> To hear people talk, color, features and hair were the most important things to know about a person, a yardstick by which everyone measured everybody else.[37]

There is some rather striking evidence of the importance of "good" physical features in the advertisements that urged the use of cosmetics to assist the darker brother and sister in reaching the ideal. Negro publications were replete with advertisements that commanded: "Lighten Your Dark Skin." One such proclamation, which featured a picture of an attractive "light" Negro girl, read: "Race Men and Women Protect Your Future by Using Black and White Ointment. By Mail 25c. See What it did for Viola Steele."[38] Yet the use of cosmetics was quite widespread in America by this time, regardless of race, and too much can be made of the use of hair straighteners, skin bleaches, and other such aids. Their use did not in all cases mean racial self-hatred, only the pervasive force of whiteness on blackness.[39]

Socially, black life was dominated by the color complex. This even included the term *black*. That sharp observer, Claude McKay, noted in one short story:

> There is no greater insult among Aframericans than calling a black person black. That is never done. In Aframerican literature, perhaps, but never in social life. A black person may be called "nigger" as a joke in Aframerica, but never "black," which is considered a term of reproach in the mouths of colored people quite as contemptuous as "nigger" in the mouths of whites.[40]

A Rudolph Fisher short story catches the point well. The scene is an employment office. The agency clerk asks an applicant:

> "What makes you think you can cook?"
> "Why, brother, I been in the neighborhood o' grub all my life!"
> "Humph! Fly bird, you are."
> "Pretty near all birds fly, friend."
> "Yes—even black birds."
> The applicant for the cook's job lost his joviality. "All right. I'm a black bird. You're a half-yaller hound. Step out in the air an' I'll fly down your dam' throat, so I can see if your insides is yaller, too!"[41]

The felt need to differentiate skin color led to the invention of quite an extensive list of euphemisms. One listing of the mid-1920s read: "black, brown, high-brown, yellow, red-brown, high yellow, dark-brown, chocolate-brown, ginger-brown, fair, fair-brown, red, pink, tan, olive, copper-colored, blue (an extremely dark complexion), cream-colored, smooth black, rough black, bronze and banana-colored, . . . [and] such slang terms as stove-pipe blonde or tantalizing brown."[42]

One finds insightful examples of these affectations everywhere. Take, for instance, the great W. C. Handy's "Hesitating Blues" (1915):

> *Hello, Central, what's the matter with this line?*
> *I want to talk to that high Brown of mine.* . . . [43]

Or take the Langston Hughes commentary on black life in which Mr. Simple is going to have his picture taken to please his girl Joyce:

"I asked, 'Joyce, what color do you want me to be?' "Joyce said, 'A little lighter than natural. I will request the man how much he charges to make you chocolate.' "[44]

Then there is the old Negro folk song that is especially revealing:

> *I wouldn't marry a black gal, tell you de reason*
> *   why,*
> *Her hair so short and kinky, break eve-y comb*
> *   I buy.*
> *I wouldn't marry a black gal, she so black, you*
> *   know,*
> *When I see her comin' she look like a crow.*
> *I wouldn't marry a black gal, tell you de reason*
> *   why,*
> *She got so many kin-folks dey make yo' biscuits*
> *   fly.*
> *I don' like a nigger nohow,*
> *Nigger an' a mule is a mighty big fool,*
> *I don' like a nigger nohow.*
> *Nigger be a nigger, whatever you do,*
> *Tie a red rag roun' de toe of his shoe,*
> *Jerk his vest on over his coat,*
> *Snatch his britches up roun' his throat.*
> *God make a nigger, make him in de night,*
> *Make him in a hurry an' forgit to paint him*
> *   white.* [45]

Even Negro humor contributes its insights:

> "You're so black till lightin' bugs follow you at twelve o'clock
> in the day thinkin' it's midnight." "You're so black till they
> have to throw a sheet over your head so the sun c'n rise every
> morning."[46]

The color mania, in short, reached out to touch the individual
in almost all aspects of his existence. In the selection of a mate, Melville Herskovits noted that "the dark man with a wife of lighter color
finds many social and economic doors open which would otherwise
be closed to him; his lighter wife brings him the prestige he desires."[47] A respondent told him in an interview: "Of course a man
wants to marry a lighter woman. . . . Doesn't he want his children
to be lighter than he is, and doesn't he want to lift up the race?"[48]

"Of course they think I'm white," says Joanna in Jessie
Fauset's, *There Is Confusion*. "There are a lot of young men in the
office and I flirt with them outrageously. At first I did it only to an-
noy mother, she hated it so. You know, the funny thing is she
doesn't like white people any better than I do—she just didn't want
me to marry a dark man because, she says, in this country a white
skin is such an asset."[49] In Fauset's novel *Plum Bun*, the dark-
skinned man was astonished at the light-skinned Mattie's attitude:
"You don't mind my being so black then? Lots of colored girls I
know wouldn't look at a black man."[50] Wallace Thurman wrote in
his sharply critical *The Blacker the Berry* . . . that

> the people who . . . really mattered, the business men, the
> doctors, and lawyers, the dentists, the more moneyed pullman
> porters, hotel waiters, bank janitors, and major-domos, in fact
> all of the Negro leaders and members of the Negro upper class,
> were either light skinned themselves or else had light skinned
> wives. A wife of dark complexion was considered a handicap
> unless she was particularly charming, wealthy, or beautiful.
> An ordinary looking dark woman was no suitable mate for a
> Negro man of prominence.[51]

The color mania reached even to the grave. The undertaker in
Rudolph Fisher's black detective novel, *The Conjure Man Dies,*

allows that many of his "customers" want to go out looking lighter and brighter.[52]

It was the economics of the color complex that gave it much of its force, of course. The help-wanted advertisement usually read "light coloured man wanted," James Weldon Johnson noted, around the turn of the century.[53] And that not much had changed by the 1920s is obvious from such assertions as this from *The Messenger:*

A business man advertises for a stenographer. Two or three girls apply. Assuming that all three are equally competent, the best looking one (meaning the one with the lightest complexion and the straightest hair) will most likely get the job—even in the office of Marcus Garvey.[54]

Nor was it just the higher ranking occupations that were "color coordinated." Wallace Thurman's protagonist, Emma Lou, thinks introspectively:

She was black, too black, there was no getting around it. Her mother thought so, and had often wished that she had been a boy. Black boys can make a go of it, but black girls. . . .

No one liked black anyway. . . .

Wanted: light colored girl to work as waitress in tea-room. . . .

Wanted: Nurse girl, light colored preferred (children are afraid of black folks). . . .

"I don' haul no coal [meaning men do not go out with dark girls] . . . ."[55]

Employment agencies were told: " 'Send me a maid of Spanish type.' 'I want a cook, but please don't send me a black one.' 'Mother's helper wanted . . . light colored girl preferred.' "[56]

The logical extreme of the color mania in black America was "passing" for white. And though passing meant denying the race, something universally condemned in the black community, the act was accepted and even admired. "It's funny about 'passing,' " says Nella Larsen's character, Irene. "We disapprove of it and at the

same time condone it. It excites our contempt and yet we rather ad-
mire it. We shy away from it with an odd kind of revulsion, but we
protect it."[57]

The assessment seems strikingly accurate. "1,000 Passing in
Washington," read the caption to an article in a New York newspaper. The article condemned those who so turned their backs on
the race, but went on to allow that those who passed only occa-
sionally should not be judged too harshly.[58] Of course the white
man, secure in his self-declared superiority, ignored or denigrated
the idea that a "nigger" could really pass for white. Blood would tell
in every case, and there were all manner of readily detectable manifestations of the telltale taint. Speaking of Walter White, the
"Nordic"-looking secretary of the NAACP in the 1930s, Calude
McKay mused in his autobiography:

> The White stories of passing white among the crackers were
> delightful. To me the most delectable was one illustrating the
> finger-nail theory of telling near-white from a pure-white.
> White was traveling on a train [in a "white" coach as he often
> did] on his way to investigate a lynching in the South. The
> cracker said, "There are many yaller niggers who look white,
> but I can tell them every time."
> "Can you really?" Walter White asked.
> "Oh sure, just by looking at their finger nails." And taking
> White's hand, he said, "Now if you had nigger blood, it would
> show here in your half-moons."[59]

Passing could obviously be enjoyed as a joke on white society.
But neither the joys of deception nor some manner of revenge seem
to have been the main impulse. Very real advantages accrued.
Passing represented, according to at least one psychological study,
"an opportunity for the light-skinned Negro to avoid prejudice,
escape restriction, and perhaps to ally the anxiety implicit in being a
Negro."[60]

Passing was also sometimes a form of revolt. Nick Aaron Ford
argues that the Negro who passes is in a sense taking by subterfuge
that which the white world would otherwise deny to him.[61] At other

times the black who could pass felt he had no choice, as suggested in Rudolph Fisher's short story, "High Yaller." Rejected by the white world when he acknowledged the race and repudiated by many in the black world as the product of black and white mixing, he escaped an intolerable situation by passing. "Cain' none of us go but so fur back in our fam'ry hist'ry, 'fore we stops," a character notes in this short story by Fisher. "An' doan nobody hav' t' ask why we stops. We jes' stops . . .—dey's a white man in de woodpile somewha'."[62]

Of great significance were those who could pass but did not. These "optional" Negroes, as George Schuyler termed them, found it to their advantage, at least most of the time, to stay in the black world.[63] The social value assigned to light skin color enhanced their position there, whereas in the white world they would fall in relative status. And, of course, if they were among the business or professional elite, they had the advantage of an ever-increasing marketplace as the black urban communities expanded. This small group could also more easily avoid painful contact with the white world because of their better economic position. Light-skinned Negro women provide the best example of this social paradox.[64]

Casual or temporary passing was indulged in by all who could manage it, though, including the "optional" Negro. This was readily accomplished in the northern cities, even by those of a marked swarthiness. Few would be suspected—or at any rate challenged—in a theater or restaurant where dark-skinned migrants from southern Europe were a common sight. Some also passed daily in their occupations but otherwise remained in the Negro community.[65]

There were those—how many will never be known—who left the black world for good. They crossed over the color line so completely that they were totally accepted, and many subsequently rose to significant heights in the white world.[66] For some in this group a total rejection of the race was involved. So it was with the protagonist of *The Autobiography of An Ex-Coloured Man*: "I know that it was shame, unbearable shame. Shame at being identified with a people that could with impunity be treated worse than animals."[67]

Others, rationalizing their defection, perhaps saw their passing as a way of gaining a position from which they could ameliorate American racism. In all events, to most who completely abandoned the race, passing was simply the means to gain all that whites would deny them.[68]

Black literary artists made passing a subject for some telling social satire. "My sociology teacher," wrote George Schuyler in his satirical novel *Black No More*, ". . . once said that there were but three ways for the Negro to solve his problem in America. . . . 'To either get out, get white, or get along.'"[69] But black artists also came close to accepting the white "tragic mulatto" stereotype by appealing to an unbreakable racial bond that drew the passer back to the Negro world, often tragically.[70] The mysticism of this bond was not as infallible as some would have had it, though, considering the many who permanently disappeared across the color line with no backward glances. A sophisticate in Wallace Thurman's *Infants of the Spring* reassures a potential passer:

My dear, you've been reading novels. Thousands of Negroes in real life cross the line every year and I assure you that, few, if any, ever feel that fictional urge to rejoin their own kind. That sort of nostalgia is confined to novels. Negroes who can and do pass are so glad to get away they probably join the K.K.K. to uphold white supremacy.[71]

How many Negroes crossed the color line to stay between 1890 and 1930? No one really knows. One estimate puts the figure for the first four decades of the twentieth century at 25,000 a year, but this figure has been largely discredited.[72] Statistical manipulations of population data indicate about one-tenth this number would be more nearly correct.[73] There are also indications that the number permanently forsaking the race decreased as the century wore on. If true, this fact would be consistent with the argument here that racial consciousness increased and there was a growing sense of peoplehood during the period. But the estimates still ran large.[74] Novelist Jessie Fauset, who often dealt with the question of passing and color consciousness in her works, said that in 1929, 20,000 were passing in New York City alone.[75] That same year the NAACP guessed that 5,000 crossed the line to stay every year, impressive evidence of the meaning of being black in white America.[76]

The intraracial tensions caused by the color complex in black America are obvious in the above citations. If passing actually declined after 1900, the causes of the decline did not affect the importance of "good" physical attributes very much. Not even the immense force of Garveyism made a lasting impression on it. In an anecdotal sketch of Harlem in 1924, a colorful (and stereotype-ridden) black charlatan is found fleecing Negro women by touting a diet of fish. This "sci'ntist and di'tishion and chemist" saw the black man's color as coming from the inside. If he ate "cold" foods as the white did—fish, for instance—he would become whiter each passing generation.[77] "More and more dusky damsels are getting their epidermics calcimined," said the sharp-tongued George Schuyler in commenting on the continued widespread striving for the "right" shade.[78] "There aren't any more dark girls," Rudolph fisher declared in his short story "High Yaller." "Skin bleach and rouge have wiped out the strain."[79] The desire for "good" physical traits was so strong, in fact, that one observer feared for the continued existence of "black" America. The advantages, he said, were all the more in favor of the girl with "good skin" and "good hair" in 1927 than they had been at the turn of the century. "The black girl's case is tragedy, hopeless," he continued. "Relegated to the rear economically, shunned socially, barred from propagating her kind, she passes."[80] A more cogent comment on the color complex is difficult to imagine.

NOTES

[1]From W. C. Handy, "The Hesitating Blues," in Arna Bontemps, ed., *Golden Slippers* (Harper and Brothers, 1941), 87.

[2]Thus, Gunnar Myrdal would observe, "In practically all of its divergences, American Negro culture is not something independent of general American culture. It is a distorted development, or a pathological condition, of the general American culture." Gunnar Myrdal, *An American Dilemma*, 20th anniversary ed., (Harper & Row, 1962), 928 (emphasis removed). The observation, quite in keeping with Myrdal's theme that a real dilemma was embodied in white American racial thought, registers nicely the peculiar relationship that exists between the black and white worlds, one visible even from an "integrationist" viewpoint.

[3]J. Saunders Redding, *On Being Negro in America* (1951; reprint ed., Indianapolis: Bobbs-Merrill Co., 1962), 25-26, 122. See also Nick Aaron Ford, *The Contemporary Negro Novel* (Boston: Meader Publishing Co., 1936), 83; Andrew Billingsley, *Black Families in White America* (Englewood Cliffs, N.J.: Prentice-Hall, 1968), 4. Sociologist Wilson Record in "Sociological Theory, Intra-Racial Color Differentiation and the Garvey Movement," *JNE* 25 (Fall 1956): 394-395, lays out a series of seven points that summarized the complexity of the shaping force of the white society on the black.

[4]W.E. Burghardt DuBois, *The Souls of Black Folks* (1903; reprint ed., Fawcett Publications, 1965), 16-17.

[5]Redding, *On Being Negro in America*, 12. Such expressions as these are common. See, for example, Richard Wright, *White Man, Listen!* (Doubleday and Co., 1957), 40; Albon L. Holsey, "Learning How to Be Black," *American Mercury* 16 (April 1929): 421-425.

[6]Richard Wright, "The Man Who Went to Chicago," in *Eight Men* (1961; reprint ed., Pyramid Books, 1969), 173.

[7]Langston Hughes, *Simple's Uncle Sam* (Hill & Wang, 1965), 148.

[8]Lerone Bennett, Jr., *The Negro Mood* (Chicago: Johnson Publishing Co., 1964), 49.

[9]Charles S. Johnson, *Growing Up in the Black Belt* (Washington D.C.: Prepared for the American Youth Commission, American Council on Education, 1941), 301. Elsewhere Johnson noted that Negroes "may never escape the insistent implication of their status and race. Attention and interest are centered on themselves. They become race concious. Opinion and feelings on general questions must always be filtered through this narrow screen that separates them from their neighbors. Their opinions are therefore, largely negative products, either disparagement of difficulties or

protest." Charles S. Johnson, "Public Opinion and the Negro," from *Proceedings of the National Conference in Social Work, 1923*, quoted in Bernard Magubane, "The American Negro's Conception of Africa: A Study in the Ideology of Pride and Prejudice" (Ph.D. diss., University of California, Los Angeles, 1967), 19.

In her novels, Jessie Fauset addresses the problem of the personal confusion that results from being black but at the middle-class level. See her *There Is Confusion* (Boni and Liveright, 1924), 179, by way of example.

[10]Johnson, *Growing Up in the Black Belt*, 301.

[11]Elizabeth A. Ferguson, "Race Consciousness Among American Negroes," *JNE* 7 (January 1938): 33.

[12]Sterling Brown, *The Negro in American Fiction* (1937; reprint ed., Atheneum, 1969), 145-146.

[13]Pauline E. Hopkins, *Contending Forces: A Romance Illustrative of Negro Life North and South* (Boston: The Colored Co-operative Publishing Co., 1900), 150.

[14]See, for example, Alfred Holt Stone, "The Mulatto Factor in the Race Problem," *Atlantic Monthly* 91 (May 1903): 658-662; "Old Ben Tillman and the Negro," *Chicago Broad Ax*, May 29, 1909; Albert Ernest Jenks, "The Mulatto—Crux of the Negro Problem," *Current History and Forum* 19 (March 1924): 1065-1070.

[15]Quoted in Bertram Wilbur Doyle, "Racial Traits of the Negro as Negroes Assign Them to Themselves" (Master's thesis, University of Chicago, 1924), 114. Nannie H. Burroughs, "Not Color But Character," *Voice of the Negro* 1 (July 1904): 277, is typical of these attacks on the color-phobia within the race.

[16]William Hannibal Thomas, *The American Negro* (Macmillan Co., 1901), 407, 408. DuBois reviewed this volume in *Dial*; he saw the book as "a sinister sympton—a growth and development under American conditions of life which illustrates peculiarly the anomalous position of black men and the terrific stress under which they struggle." He then goes on to present, side by side, Thomas's writings in 1890 and those of 1901, showing a complete reversal of his opinion concerning just such aspects of black life as reflected here. W. E. B. DuBois, "The Storm and Stress in the Black World," *Dial* 30 (April 16, 1901): 262. See also Charles W. Chesnutt, "A Defamer of His Race," *Critic* 38 (April 1901): 350-351.

[17]Clemmont E. Vontress, "The Negro Personality Reconsidered," *JNE* 35 (Summer 1966): 211. See also Royal D. Colle, "The Negro Image and the Mass Media" (Ph.D. diss., Cornell University, 1967), 6; Henry J. Myers and Leon Yockelson, "Color Denial in the Negro," *Psychiatry* 11 (February 1948): 41.

[18]Wallace Thurman, *The Blacker the Berry* . . . (1929; reprint ed., Collier Books, 1970), 145. See also Melville J. Herskovits, *The American Negro* (1928; reprint ed., Indiana University Press, 1964), 60-62.

[19]Charles S. Johnson, *Shadow of the Plantation* (1934; reprint ed., University of Chicago Press, 1966) and his *Growing Up in the Black Belt*, 266-267.

[20]Color consciousness in the black community today is something quite different from that of the period of this discussion, although the rhetoric of Garveyism harked forward to the current theme of blackness. See, William C. Kvaraceus et al, *Negro Self Concept: Implications for School and Citizenship* (McGraw-Hill Book Co., 1965), 43.

[21]Don Marquis, "The Mulatto," *Harper's Magazine* 132 (April 1916): 728. The setting of the story was the urban North, of course; in a southern setting Carter would have been recognized immediately by some telltale trait as a "yaller nigger."

[22]Donald L. Noel, "Correlates of Anti-White Prejudice" (Ph.D. diss., Cornell University, 1961), 189, 190.

[23]Ibid., 229.

[24]W. E. B. DuBois, *An ABC of Color* (International Publishers, 1969), 66. This is a selection DuBois made of his own writings in 1963, just prior to his death.

[25]Langston Hughes, *The Big Sea* (1940; reprint ed., Hill & Wang, 1963), 40.

[26]Rose Dorothy Lewin, "A Fragment," *Crisis* 12 (September 1916): 223. See also Wright, "The Man Who Went to Chicago," in *Eight Men*, 173-174; Vontress, "The Negro Personality Reconsidered," 211-212; Langston Hughes, "The Negro Artist and the Racial Mountain," *Nation* 132 (June 23, 1926): 692-693; Thomas F. Pettigrew, *A Profile of the Negro American* (Princeton: D. Van Nostrand Co., 1964), 8-11, 36. Noel, in "Correlates of Anti-White Prejudice," 193-236, provides a review and discussion of the literature on this topic.

[27]Arnold Rose, *The Negro's Morale* (University of Minnesota Press, 1949), 59.

[28]E. Franklin Frazier, *The Negro Church in America* (Schocken Books, 1963), 30, 31. The reference to "civilized behavior," to respectability as a measure, should be again noted.

[29]See Johnson, *Shadow of the Plantation* and *Growing Up in the Black Belt*. "Our results indicate that there is little correlation between class and color in the Southern rural area. Differences in complexion and hair create problems of adjustment, but do not mark class lines within rural Negro groups." Johnson, *Growing Up in the Black Belt*, 272.

³⁰This continued to persist. E. Franklin Frazier, in commenting upon the storm his *Black Bourgeoisie* kicked up when first published, said, "some working class Negroes got the impression I had written a book attacking 'upper-class, light-skinned' Negroes. As a consequence I was even stopped on the street by working-class Negroes who shook my hand for having performed this long overdue service." *Black Bourgeoisie* (Free Press, 1957), 8. LeRoi Jones reiterates the theme in his poem of the same title:

> has a gold tooth, sits long hours
> on a stool, thinking about money.
> sees white skin in a secret room
> rummages his sense for sense
> dreams about Lincoln(s)
> conks his daughter's hair
> sends his coon to school
> works very hard
> grins politely in restaurants
> has a good word to say
> never says it
> does not hate ofays
> hates, instead, himself
> him black self.

LeRoi Jones, "Black Bourgeoisie," *Rights & Reviews* (December 1964).

³¹George S. Schuyler, "At the Darktown Charity Ball," *Messenger* 6 (December 1924): 377. See also Eugene Gordon, "The Negro's Inhibitions," *American Mercury* 13 (February 1928): 159-165, a firsthand account of Boston's black "400." He also notes the importance of a "good" skin color in ascribed status and the class tension between the "dicty" and those below them.

³²Rudolph Fisher, *The Walls of Jericho* (1928; reprint ed., Arno Press, 1969), 72, 74.

³³Eugene Gordon, "Negro Society," *Scribner's Magazine* 88 (August 1930): 141.

³⁴Langston Hughes, "Our Wonderful Society: Washington," *Opportunity* 5 (August 1927): 226. For earlier parallel comment, see "The Negroes and the Near-Negroes," *Colored American Magazine* 13 (July 1907): 9-10.

³⁵"Baby Hair," by Constance Nichols, in Beatrice M. Murphy, ed., *Ebony Rhythm: An Anthology of Contemporary Negro Verse* (1948; reprint ed., Freeport, New York: Books for Libraries Press, 1968) 110.

[36]From Langston Hughes, "Spanish Blood," in *Laughing to Keep from Crying* (Henry Holt and Co., 1952), 37. See also Lewin, "A Fragment," 222.

[37]Pauli Murray, *Proud Shoes* (Harper & Row, 1956), 270.

[38]*New York Age*, February 15, 1919.

[39]James Weldon Johnson, "A Negro Looks at Race Prejudice," *American Mercury* 14 (May 1928): 52. These advertisements were often the target of criticism and ridicule in Negro publications. It was a facet of the "Afro-American Boobocracy," said George Schuyler, without even a nod toward H. L. Mencken. "Shafts and Darts," *Messenger* 6 (August 1924): 238. See also Frederick G. Detweiler, *The Negro Press in the United States* (1922; reprint ed., College Park, Maryland: McGrath Publishing Co., 1968), 115.

[40]Claude McKay, "Mattie and Her Sweetman," in *Gingertown* (Harper and Brothers, 1932), 63-64. The same observation was recorded by Langston Hughes in his autobiography, *The Big Sea*, 103-104.

[41]Rudolph Fisher, "The South Lingers On," *Survey Graphic* 53 (March 1, 1925): 645.

[42]Melville J. Herskovits, "The Color Line," *American Mercury* 6 (October 1925): 206.

[43]From Handy, "The Hesitating Blues," in Bontemps, ed., *Golden Slippers*, 87.

[44]Langston Hughes, *The Best of Simple* (Hill & Wang, 1961), 107.

[45]Quoted in John A. Lomax, "Self-Pity in Negro Folk Songs," *Nation* 105 (August 9, 1917): 143-144. The author badly misinterpreted these songs; protest and an awareness of his social position are actually more evident than any measurable self-pity.

[46]Philip Sterling, ed., *Laughing on the Outside* (Grosset and Dunlap, 1968), 166.

[47]Herskovits, *The American Negro*, 64.

[48]Ibid. See also Ulysses S. Poston, "The Negro Awakening," *Current History and Forum* 19 (December 1923): 474.

[49]Fauset, *There Is Confusion*, 199-200.

[50]Jessie Fauset, *Plum Bun* (Frederick A. Stokes Co., 1929), 31. See also Claude McKay's short story "Brownskin Blues" in *Gingertown*, 8-13.

[51]Thurman, *The Blacker the Berry*, 47. Note again the description of those belonging to the "upper" class.

[52]Rudolph Fisher, *The Conjure Man Dies: A Mystery Tale of Dark Harlem* (Covice-Friede, 1932), 91.

[53]James W. Johnson, *The Autobiography of an Ex-Coloured Man* (1912; reprint ed., Hill & Wang, 1960), 155.

[54]*Messenger*, November 1923, quoted in Doyle, "Racial Traits of the Negro," 126.

[55]Thurman, *The Blacker the Berry*, 118-119.

[56]Floyd C. Covington, "Color: A Factor in Social Mobility," *Sociology and Social Research* 15 (November-December 1930): 145-152.

[57]From Nella Larsen, *Passing*, quoted in Hugh Morris Gloster, *Negro Voices in American Fiction* (University of North Carolina Press, 1948), 146.

[58]*New York Age*, September 16, 1909.

[59]Claude McKay, *A Long Way from Home* (1937; reprint ed., Harcourt, Brace and World, 1970), 110-111. A brief rundown on the various telltale traits is found in Redding, *On Being Negro in America*, 116-117.

[60]Myers and Yockelson, "Color Denial in the Negro," 41.

[61]Nick Aaron Ford, "The Negro Author's Use of Propaganda in Imaginative Literature" (Ph.D. diss., University of Iowa, 1946), 73-74.

[62]Rudolph Fisher, "High Yaller," *Crisis* 30 (October 1925): 281-286 (quote from p. 284), and 31 (November 1925): 33-38. One can find the vocabulary of "whiteness" and passing here, as well as excellent comment on blackness in a white world.

[63]*Black and Conservative: The Autobiography of George S. Schuyler* (New Rochelle, New York: Arlington House, 1966), 89.

[64]Myrdal, *American Dilemma*, 686; Ferguson, "Race Consciousness Among American Negroes," 34; E. B. Reuter, "Sex Distribution in the Negro and Mulatto Population of the United States," *Sociology and Social Research* 7 (January-February 1923): 130-138.

[65]Walter White, "The Paradox of Color," in Alain Locke, ed., *The New Negro* (1925; reprint ed., by Arno Press, Inc., 1968), 364-365; Rollin Lynde Hartt, "When the Negro Comes North," *World's Work* 48 (June 1924): 188-189; Myrdal, *American Dilemma*, 686. See also Walter White, *Flight* (Alfred A. Knopf, 1926), 199-200.

[66]Redding, *On Being Negro in America*, 116.

[67]Johnson, *Autobiography of an Ex-Coloured Man*, 191. See also Rose, *The Negro's Morale*, 5; Myers and Yockelson, "Color Denial in the Negro," 40.
    Total rejection was naturally not restricted to those with a light skin color, as highlighted by this news item captioned, "Lives Entirely Too Long": "Dempsey Hare, the richest Negro in Eastern Virginia, and owner of 2,000 acres of farm land, died January 30. . . . Hare, who would not associate with Negroes . . . once applied to a surgeon to remove the Negro blood from his veins." Chicago *Broad Ax*, March 2, 1901.

[68]Ford, *Contemporary Negro Novel*, 48; Gloster, *Negro Voices in American Fiction*, 39. For a brief review of the motives involved, based on literature and questionnaire data, see James E. Conyers and T.H. Kennedy, "Negro Passing: To Pass or Not to Pass," *Phylon* 24 (Fall 1963): 215-223.

[69]George S. Schuyler, *Black No More: Being an Account of the Strange and Wonderful Workings of Science in the Land of the Free, A.D. 1933-1940* (1931; reprint ed., Negro Universities Press, 1969), 13.

[70]Ford, *Contemporary Negro Novel*, 51, 52, 81-82; Brown, *The Negro in American Fiction*, 144-145. Brown adds that the novel makes passing "a much more acute and frequent problem than it is in ordinary Negro middle class experience."

[71]Wallace Thurman, *Infants of the Spring* (Macauley Co., 1932), 262. An editorial in *Opportunity* 7 (July 1929): 206, concurred wholeheartedly with this view.

[72]John H. Burma, "The Measurement of Negro 'Passing,' " *AJS* 52 (July 1946): 21.

[73]Ibid.; E.W. Eckhard, "How Many Negroes 'Pass'?" *AJS* 52 (May 1947): 498-500.

[74]Rose, *The Negro's Morale*, 60, 114; *Pittsburgh Courier*, October 15, 1927, February 23, 1929.

[75]*Pittsburgh Courier*, May 11, 1929.

[76]Ibid., August 10, 1929. Estimates continued to run high; Walter White in the late 1940s said 12,000 Negroes "disappeared" every year. Roi Ottley estimated 40,000 to 50,000. Figures cited in Wm. M. Kephart, "The 'Passing' Question," *Phylon* 9 (4th Quarter, 1948): 336.

[77]Konrad Bercovici, "The Black Blocks of Manhattan," *Harper's Magazine* 149 (October 1924): 615.

[78]George S. Schuyler, "Shafts and Darts," *Messenger* 5 (November 1923): 862.

[79]Fisher, "High Yaller," 282.

[80]G.A. Steward, "The Black Girl Passes," *Social Forces* 6 (September 1927): 103.

7

BLACK ON BLACK II

I am the darker brother.
They send me to eat in the kitchen
When company comes.
But I laugh,
And eat well,
And grow strong.[1]

MANY OF the intraracial tensions that continually surfaced to plague the ordinary Afro-American's everyday life were by-products of the white color mania. The magnitude of these tensions at any given time might be regarded as a function of white racism; they might even be regarded as barometers of race relations. The level of the intraracial tension in the black community between the old settlers in the northern urban centers and the southern migrants, for instance, responded to changes in the white color mania. The black color complex was obviously fed by the white color mania. So were such other marked intraracial tensions in the black community as those between the upper and lower social strata and between the Afro-American and the West Indian immigrant.

Almost as marked as the color tension was the class tension that helped to keep the black community and its developing institutions off balance. The ordinary black did not trust the higher-status (and so often lighter-colored) Negro, while those of the upper reaches looked down upon those below them, often with despair. Examples of this particular intraracial tension are plentiful. A Langston Hughes character in an engaging short story observed of a pretty girl: "She wasn't a bit hinkty like so many folks when they're light-complexioned and up in the money."[2]

Much of the antagonism in this area stemmed from the nebulous nature of the class divisions—from the weakness of the distinction between the various social levels. The female passenger held herself aloof from the protagonist of DuBois's 1928 novel, *Dark Princess:*

> She was afraid to be familiar with a porter. He might presume. . . . She was dressed with taste, and Matthew [the protagonist] judged that she was probably a teacher or a clerk. She had a cold half-defiant air which Matthew understood. This class of his people were being bred that way by eternal conflict.[3]

Will Thomas writes that being city bred in a racially mixed area he had thought "nigger" was just another epithet to be fought over, like "Hunkie." Such does not appear to be in keeping with the usual black experience, but later, in Kansas City, he found differently. "So you think you ain't no nigger just 'cause you're lighter than somebody," an antagonist challenges. "Li'l yella nigger, you think you're cute just 'cause you're father is a doctor. Just 'cause you come from Shee-cau-go."[4]

The coming of an actual middle class in the black community did little or nothing to bridge the great gulf between the top and the bottom. And this new middle class, although basically serving the black community, had its values determined by whiteness, as did all groups up and down the social ladder.[5] The noted entertainer Ethel Waters writes thus of her childhood in Pennsylvania in the early years of the twentieth century:

> In her whole life Mom [her grandmother] never earned more than five or six dollars a week. Being without a husband, it was hard for her to find any place at all for us to live, a place she could afford. And even then she never got a chance to live with my aunts and me, could only visit us on her day off. Being with white people so much, she stopped living colored, thinking colored.
>
> What broke Mom's heart was realizing that her children knew nothing and cared nothing about the better side of life.

From the white people she worked for she had learned there could be a nice side. But Vi and Ching and Charles took no interest in that. Mom might as well have tried to read poetry to cows.[6]

Joyce, the girl friend of Langston Hughes's Mr. Simple, might typify those at the middle of the social ladder. Jesse Semple says to her:

"One thing, Joyce, for which I admires you is your culture. Was your old man cultured? I mean, your *father*?"

"He is a bricklayer," said Joyce, "but my mother was a Daughter of the Eastern Star, also a graduate of Fessenden Academy. She always worked around fine white folks. She never did work for no poor white trash. In fact, she wouldn't. Poor folks have nothing to give nobody—least of all culture. I come by mine honestly."[7]

At the upper end of the ladder rested the "better class." They tended to make much of their professional status, their own culture, and their connections with white authority. For some here the competition for social distinction remained as fierce as it had been in the old blue vein circles.[8] "Tempy?" scoffs Langston Hughes's Harriett in *Not Without Laughter*:

"So respectable you can't touch her with a ten-foot pole, that's Tempy! . . . Annjee's all right, working herself to death at Mrs. Rice's, but don't tell me about Tempy. Just because she's married a mail-clerk with a little property, she won't even see her own family any more. When niggers get up in the world, they act just like white folks—don't pay you no mind. And Tempy's that kind of a nigger—she's up in the world now!"[9]

As indicated by Harriett's derision, the most marked class antagonism in the black community was reserved for that between the better class and those at the bottom of the ladder. "Aw, man, whut you talkin' 'bout?" asked a Rudolph Fisher character. "Hyeh's a dicky trying' his damnedest to be a fay—like all d' other dickties.

When they get in hot water they all come cryin' to you and me fo' help."[10] Or later, "If this bird wasn't a dickty he'd be o.k. But there never was a dickty worth a damn."[11] This was a widespread and open antagonism. By the 1920s, for instance, Ethel Waters had risen up through the ranks of the entertainment world and knew such white intellectuals as Carl Van Vechten, author of the celebrated novel *Nigger Heaven* (1927). He told her, she writes, "that other colored people were never quite themselves when he was around them and that I was the only Negro he'd ever met who was completely natural with him. I told Carl that was because he'd been hanging around mostly with dictys who tried to be as much like white people as possible."[12]

There was, quite simply, a line segregating the ordinary black American from his more sophisticated brother. But the lowly were ever tripping on the line. Unable to escape as their betters often could the manifestations of the color line that separated *all* blacks from the white world, they had a hard time discerning this intra-racial line. This is nowhere better illustrated than in the often-noted refusal of a Negro domestic to work for a Negro family. The upper class at best took such refusals as being indicative of a misconception of individual independence and at worst as indicating that some white stereotypes were correct after all. One prominent black, Justice Terrell of Washington, D.C., reportedly said on one public occasion, "I am sorry to be compelled to say [anything like] this in the presence of white men because it is the deepest indication of a lack of self-respect." He then went on to relate a story about a prominent Negro family that had advertised for domestic help. When one Negro applicant found her prospective employer to be Negro, she said, "Lady, I can't wash for you because I am in society myself."[13]

The color complex quite clearly led to much of the confusion about status within the black community, a point that is explicit in the above citations. The white man drew only one color line, a black critic said, but "when the negro takes his brush in hand he draws a hundred."[14]

At the same time, class differentiation came more and more to be based upon occupation and life-style, as the evolving social structure came to resemble that of the larger society.[15] But the lines of economic and occupational differentiation within the black community were further complicated by the community's relationship to the dominant white society; it diluted the new middle-class member's ability to demonstrate his right to deference. Forced into close quarters with all others of his race by white discriminations, he found it difficult to discriminate himself, W. E. B. DuBois noted. "He recoils from appeal to the white city even for physical protection against his anti-social elements, for this, he feels, is a form of self-accusation, of attack on the Negro race. It invites the smug rejoinder: 'Well, if you can't live with niggers, how do you expect us to?'"[16] As a result, conspicuous consumption came to provide a ready means of distinction, as strikingly demonstrated by E. Franklin Frazier in his controversial *Black Bourgeoisie.* It is "in the absence of a true upper class based upon old family ties and wealth," G. Franklin Edwards says of Frazier's theme, that "the Negro middle class simulates the behavior of the white upper class without possessing the fundamental bases upon which such behavior rests."[17]

Regardless of the form it took, this need to demonstrate social distance placed the Negro middle class in a peculiar position. Those at the very edge of the white-designated social mudsill looked at them and ruled—"dickty." "Trying to be something you ain't." They stood, paradoxically, between the black and the white, and were tempted to maintain their position by discriminating against the lowly and by minimizing and ignoring as much as possible the white discriminations directed against themselves.[18] Langston Hughes captured such attitudes in his poem "High to Low."

> *God knows*
> *We have our troubles too—*
> *One trouble is you:*
> *you talk too loud,*
> *cuss too loud,*
> *look too black,*
> *don't get anywhere,*
> *and sometimes it seems*
> *you don't even care.*
> *The way you send your kids to*
>   *school*
> *stockings down,*

(not Ethical Culture)
the way you shout out loud
  in church
(not St. Phillips)
and the way you lounge on
  doorsteps
just as if you were down South
  (not at 409)
the way you clown—
the way, in other words,
you let me down—
me, trying to uphold the race
and you—
well, you can see,
we have our problems,
too, with you. [19]

Little of such critical comments on intraracial affairs spread outside the black community prior to the first decade of the twentieth century. Perhaps this fact reflects the sway of the accommodationist philosophy at the time. Much of the comment up to this time was confined to observations on racial traits and public conduct and toward the need for racial solidarity, a need demonstrated by the lack of support for Negro businesses. Typical of these comments is the observation in the first volume of the *Voice of the Negro* that "our race habit of looking up to somebody as superior to ourselves, of asking for everything and creating but little, . . . is a great handicap to the cultivation of manhood, courage and pride of race."[20] One observer digested the outlook when he remarked, "A Negro editor would be mobbed if he told the truth about Negroes; they say let the white people do it."[21]

But as the first decade of the twentieth century wore on, more and more intraracial criticism leaked out into the open. The previous kinds of comments continued to be issued, but the impression gathered from the periodical literature is that the castigations became sharper, so much so that one editor in 1907 charged: "This constant washing of dirty linen in the limelight is hurtful of race progress, and exhibits an inherent weakness that militates powerfully against the boasted capability of the race for self-government."[22] "The besetting sin of the race is idle gossip and the dissemination of evil report," the *Broad Ax* asserted in labeling the Negro himself the greatest enemy of the Negro race.[23] "The Gentlemen of Leisure," read the cartoon caption in a New York paper. It showed a well-dressed black leaning against a lamp post, a black workingman rebuking him with the charge, "You mean you live on servant girls!"[24]

Certainly as northward migration continued to swell the Negro districts of the urban industrial centers, censure of public conduct became more frequent and immediate. Black men and women on the streets, "uncouth in appearance, rude in deportment, and boisterous of utterance," wounded the desired Negro image, one paper charged.[25] Negro organizations issued broadsides on public manners as the Great Migration came into full flood during World War I. One, directed toward the female migrant, was worded in the form of a pledge:

"I desire to help bring about a new order of living in this community. I will attend to the neatness of my personal appearance on the street or when sitting in the doorway. I will refrain from wearing dust-caps, bungalow aprons, house clothing and bedroom shoes when out of doors. I will arrange my toilet within doors and not on the front porch."[26]

The Detroit branch of the NAACP, in a 1920 throwaway, charged parents to attend to their children's appearance in the new school year, for "everything in our power must be done to prevent the increase of prejudice and to secure justice for our people."[27] Another broadside early in 1921 continued the attack, adding such cautions as, "If you have a place of business do not permit the grounds outside your door and in front of your show windows to be used as a Rest Room."[28]

Most migrants were obviously not trained in the ways of the city when they first arrived. Thus the continuous streams that moved north repeatedly elicited public rebukes. "Heads stuck *out* and rags stuck *in* windows should not be tolerated," said one.[29] There were as well rejoinders to the effect that "we have little reason to point to their faults, their awkwardness, their crude customs, their revolvers and their lack of decorum, until we are sure they have been taught by us all the nicer things known to our community life."[30]

To the old settlers especially, these new arrivals seemed to epitomize all that was the worst in the race. The tension produced within the community was striking and evidently consistent across the North. The two gossips of the George Schuyler satire already mentioned, "At the Darktown Charity Ball," discuss this topic:

> "Do you see that group over in the corner by themselves?"
> "Yes."
> "Well, they are the super-snobs—the sacred cows of every Negro community."
> "Who are they? What is their claim to distinction?"
> "Well, they are the *old residents*. You meet them in every town. In New York, they are 'Old New Yorkers'; in Philadelphia, 'Old Philadelphians'; in Boston, 'Old Bostonians'; . . . and so on in every city and town. Their conversation usually consists of 'viewing with alarm' the younger generation; the 'influx of those Southerners,' and . . . deploring the passing of the alleged social equality they enjoyed in 'the old days before the migration,' when they could 'go anywhere,' and so on *ad nauseam*."[31]

Schuyler, of course, correctly labeled the "social equality" being lamented as "alleged," yet there was that coincidence with the northward migration. The older resident's proclivity to blame the heightening of white prejudice upon the influx of southern migrants was not entirely unfounded.[32] The situation in fact provided some of the rationale for appeals to race consciousness and solidarity. A speaker told the Brooklyn branch of the Urban League in 1920:

> "These migrants are going to destroy your status. If you think you don't want an Urban League; if you think you are alright without welfare organizations, let something happen like it did in Chicago [the 1919 riot], and they [whites] will not ask whether you are the old settlers or the new settlers but will settle you. The thing to do is to keep things like that from hap-

pening by keeping these people [the migrants] up to the standards of the community where they live."[33]

Some of the newcomers soon picked up many of the old settlers'
attitudes. But most of the new arrivals ended up merging with the
largely undifferentiated mass at the bottom of the black social heap.
Since many of the migrants had seen the northern city as a kind of
Canaan, this reality was difficult to cope with.[34] John A. Williams,
in his recent novel *Sissie*, puts it bluntly. Emma, long disillusioned,
shrills at Sissie (who is still clutching to her dreams):

> "It's hopeless. All you niggers from down South comin' up
> here lookin' for streets made outa gold bricks, but they ain't
> none. Not one goddamn gold brick, unless you-all gonna shit
> it. We niggers just like you-all. Only trouble is, we livin' the
> life you folks was dreamin' about. This is the way it is. Oh'
> don't be thinkin' about them niggers livin' on the side of the
> hill; they's damned few of them; it's us that counts, 'cause we
> ain't suckin' nobody's ass to live."[35]

The migrant reciprocated the northerner's animosity, of course.
And in spite of continued cityward movement, this enmity displayed
a rather remarkable durability. The root of some of this antagonism
is to be found in the suspicions the northern Negro aroused in the
minds of southern whites, which in turn tended to nurture the per-
petual threat of violence to all blacks in a southern community.
When they moved North they brought this feeling with them. Also,
those Negroes who visited the South were often the economically
better off and seemed to flaunt or lord it over the poorer southern
Negro.[36] Then too there was the remarkable persistence of the idea
that long residence in the North somehow conveyed credit and
stature in the community. For quite a number this often remained,
as Arnold Rose observed, "as important as the number of generations a white man's forebearers have been in the United States."[37]
But the antagonism between the old settler and the southern
migrant had yet another peculiarity. Even though the migrants belonged to the same religious denominations as the old established
residents, for the most part they found the big established Baptist

and Methodist churches cold and forbidding.[38] The migrant desired something more familiar; the old settler desired that the old ways be left behind and more decorous conduct be followed in worshipping God. Two migrants in Rudolph Fisher's "The South Lingers On" were attending Ebeneezer Church, "but dey doan like it 'tall. Says hit's too hifalutin for 'em de way dese Harlem cullud folks wushup; Ain' got no Holy Ghos' in 'em, dass what. Jes' come in an' set down an' git up an' go out. Never moans, never shouts, never even says 'amen.'"[39]

"Emphasis upon 'preaching the Word,' salvation by faith, worship as fellowship, and vernacular singing," identified by Raymond Jones as characteristic of many Negro denominations, were not unknown in northern Negro churches.[40] But these churches could not satisfy the religious needs of many migrants. In their study of the Negro church, Benjamin Mays and Joseph Nicholson report that more than one pastor was moved to start a new church because of this dissatisfaction. One pastor told them that "he talked with a large number of southern people who desired a church similar in worship to the churches in the rural South. As a minister, this man felt obliged to start a church for these people."[41] Another pastor, the minister of a Detroit storefront church, told Mays and Nicholson:

> He could not pray in the big Detroit church as he was accustomed to praying in the rural church of the South. His long loud prayer would not be in place in the semi-sophisticated Detroit church. He therefore organized a church of his own.[42]

Until the era of the Great Migration, the development of the Negro's church was continuous and predictable (in retrospect), given the social structure in which it was forced to evolve. For the greater part of the nineteenth century, Liston Pope of the Yale Divinity School notes, the Negro church was "a defensive and accommodating institution, but it often modified the harshness of caste and was the birthplace of schools, social organizations, and other facilities that have improved the conditions of the Negro community as a whole."[43] The associational functions of the church gave the Negro an arena in which he could perform without caste restrictions and in which he could gain status, an arena in which the white man

did not intrude.[44] The northward and cityward movement of the
southern Negro, however, disrupted the pattern. It was "the inade-
quacy, from a religious standpoint, of the institutional denominations," E. Franklin Frazier asserts, that "accounts for the 'storefront' churches which one finds in Negro communities in American
cities."[45]

The institutional denominations grew as a result of northward
migration, certainly, and some storefront churches came into being
to handle the overflow.[46] But it was because they were unable to deal
with the needs of all blacks regardless of class and economic background that the storefronts proliferated. There were 140 churches in
150 blocks in New York's Harlem in 1926, one study noted, 126 of
them having come into existence after 1911. Only a little over one-
third of these churches were housed in "regular church edifices";
the remainder were storefront churches.[47] Narrowly speaking, the
storefront churches, the sects, and the cults grew because they satisfied the emotional needs of those at the bottom of the social ladder
(although some cults attracted blacks—and whites—of higher social
status, as for instance, Father Divine's Peace Mission Movement).
Most of the storefronts were more revivalistic or evangelistic in
nature than the established urban churches. More to the liking of
the migrant, the services leaned toward long sermons suitably punc-
tuated at just the right time by shouts of "Hallelujah" from the con-
gregation; sermons, says Raymond Jones, "featuring polemics
against the so-called 'sins of the flesh,' . . . and the dogmatic assertion by each [church] of its monopoly on the 'only true gospel' of
Jesus."[48]

Worship and the fulfillment of ritualistic demands ranked high
in the hierarchy of values of those wanting this manner of service.
The pull of the supernatural was especially strong. Ease of access
and the level of individual emotional involvement provided relief
from the routine of life at the bottom of the heap. In short, the storefront church or cult was a vehicle of adjustment. This was especially
the case for the southern Negro, thrown as he was into the fluid social structure of the northern urban centers in the teens and twenties
of this century.[49]

Also contributing to the growth of storefront churches and to
the various cults and sects that sprang up in the first decades of the

twentieth century was the rising sense of racial consciousness in the black community. The awareness of being a black man in a white society, of not being able to be an American, a Christian, and a Negro all at the same time, brought to many an urgent sense of racial solidarity. The mushrooming of religious sects and cults can best be seen, as one student of them has noted, as part of "a chain of movements [that arose] out of the disillusionment and race consciousness of recent Negro migrants to northern industrial cities."[50] Marcus Garvey's African Orthodox church, with its appeal to racial consciousness and its lively spirit of blackness, is only one example.[51]

But the growth of storefronts stemmed from intraracial tensions as well. Aspects of class tension and the color complex contributed to their proliferation. A person's social class could almost be determined by knowing the denomination of the church he attended, and his skin color would all but confirm it. Gwendolyn of Wallace Thurman's *The Blacker the Berry* . . . had rejected the idea of trying to join the Episcopal church, "for she knew that most of its members were 'pinks' and despite the fact that a number of dark-skinned West Indians. former members of the Church of England, had forced their way in, . . . the Episcopal Church in Harlem, as in most Negro communities, was dedicated primarily to the salvation of light-skinned Negroes."[52]

The ordinary black urban dweller could in some manner understand his betters' attitudes, but he could not accept them. The white man's color line was burden enough for him. This explains (in part at least) the endurance, even thoughout these years of rising racial consciousness, of the intraracial tensions that continued to plague the black community. It helps explain, for instance, the reaction of the ordinary Negro to the continual admonishments to support black businesses.

Many of the old elite and rising middle class enjoyed at least partial monopolies: the teacher, barber, beautician, minister, and undertaker, for example. Others, such as insurance agents, gained a monopoly as a result of white refusals to deal with blacks. But the small merchant, and such professionals as the doctor and the lawyer, while restricted from competing for white business, were hard pressed to gain a real share of the black market. Calls to racial solidarity thus served to advance the personal position of these "disadvantaged."

Negro periodicals are replete with editorials decrying the fact that blacks did not recognize their responsibilities and failed to support Negro enterprises. At the same time there was no dearth of comment on the failure of Negro enterprise to measure up. The shortcomings ranged wide: incompetence, overcharging, social pretensions, even the charge that Negro proprietors continually displayed unwarranted familiarity toward their black patrons. None seemed to hesitate to ask all manner of personal questions even of a total stranger, an editorial charged in 1909, as long as that stranger had a black skin.[53]

For all of the rising racial consciousness and growth of the black business sphere by 1930, these rebukes continued. "An energetic young Negro in the mercantile business," wrote George Schuyler in the radical journal *Messenger* in 1924, "bombarded sable Harlem with tracts and handbills for two or more years, tearfully urging Negroes to trade with their own race:"

> His arguments were masterpieces; his logic was excellent. Most of his merchandise was only about 20 percent higher than the same goods in ofay stores, and the quality was nearly the same. He urged Harlem blacks to stretch out the hand of racial cooperation, but he went into the hands of the receiver.[54]

"Deep down in its heart, I fear," lamented the secretary of the National Negro Business League in 1928, "the Negro mass prefers to trade at white grocery and dry-goods stores. How else could we account for such familiar expressions as:

> "I gets my money from white folks and I'se gwine give it back to 'em."
> "What do niggers know about runnin' a store?"
> "I ain't gwine spend my money wid dem niggers. First thing I know dey'll be thinkin' dey's rich and tryin' look down on me."
> "Nigger stores don' carry nothin' but cheap stuff."[55]

The Negro professional pleaded for support from the race as well. He complained not infrequently that even other professionals carried their needs to whites rather than to their own people: the Negro doctor went to the white lawyer, the Negro lawyer to the white doctor.[56] Such admonishments continued for many years—as did the ordinary Negro's suspicion of the competence of the Negro professional. The Chicago *Broad Ax* related the following story in commenting in late 1899 on the Negro's inability to earn equal recognition for equal accomplishment—not from the white but from the black portion of the community.

> While conversing with one of the leading white professors of one of our medical colleges, recently, he informed us that many colored people came to the college for examination, but as soon as they entered the door, they blubbered out in a loud voice that they did not want "no Niggah doctor to examine them," and the professor said that "many colored women would permit young white students who had just come from the farm and who knew nothing about anatomy to examine them, in preference to a first class Negro doctor."[57]

The ordinary Negro's lack of confidence in the abilities of his professionals may be traced to white opinions concerning their competency. (G. Franklin Edwards's observation that "the attitudes of the Negro toward himself are merely reciprocals of the attitudes of other groups toward him" finds applicability here.[58]) Still, the attitude revealed by this and like intraracial critiques points to the fact that the Negro had reason to lack confidence in the professional class. Prone though he was to exaggeration, Negro critic William Hannibal Thomas's assertion that the Negro community at large was "overrun with incompetent teachers, incapable lawyers, illiterate doctors, and immoral preachers" was not groundless.[59] Furthermore, the assertions in large measure were equally applicable to white America at the time. Historian Robert Wiebe noted of the late nineteenth century that "the so-called professions meant little as long as anyone with a bag of pills and a bottle of syrup could pass for a doctor, a few books and a corrupt judge made a man a lawyer, and an unemployed literate qualified as a teacher."[60]

Those intraracial tensions—light against dark, migrant versus old settler, ordinary, lower-class black in opposition to the upper class, often light-colored "dickty"—were commonplace in the northern urban communities. So too was yet another intraracial ten-

sion, the enmity toward the foreign-born black, although comparatively few of these black immigrants from the West Indies and Central and South America settled outside the East Coast urban centers.
Most were drawn to New York, Massachusetts, and Florida.[61]

There were few foreign-born Negroes in the country prior to
1880. Between 1900 and 1930, however, there was a 232 percent increase, although this increase still only brought their numbers to
181,981. Sixty-five percent resided in New York City, thereby creating quite a significant minority within a minority.[62]

The immigrant from the West Indies and South America found
himself in a rather odd position. To them, the word *Negro* referred
to only full-blooded blacks. A person of mixed racial heritage was a
"person of color" and, as such, enjoyed a different status back
home. But the color line in America made no such distinctions—and
neither did the ordinary Afro-American.[63] All were forced to adopt
to the role of being Negro in white America—a rather different position from that of being Negro or a "person of color" in, say,
Jamaica. More than this, these "foreigners" became subject to all
manner of black American prejudice.[64]

The Afro-American constructed stereotypes in this case that
mirrored those of the larger society almost exactly. Eight-Ball, in
Rudolph Fisher's biting short story "Ringtail," is talking:

"You jigs are worse 'n ofays," he accused. "You raise hell
about prejudice and look at you—doin' just what you're raisin'
hell over yourselves."

"Maybeso," Red rejoined, "but that don't make me like
monks ["monkey-chasers"] any better."

"What don't you like about 'em?"

"There ain't nothin' I do like about 'em. They're too damn
conceited. They're too aggressive. They talk funny. They look
funny—I can tell one the minute I see him. They're always
startin' an argument an' they always want the last word. An'
there's too many of 'em here."

"Yeah," Eight-Ball dryly rejoinded. "An' they stick too
close together an' get ahead too fast. They put it all over us in
too many ways. We could stand 'em pretty well if it wasn't for
that. Same as ofays an' Jews."[65]

Migration from the Caribbean area peaked in the early 1920s, keeping this particular intraracial tension running high throughout the decade. The conflict at the lower social levels was a function of American Negro nativism as well as status and economic competition. At the higher social levels, though the hostilities were publicly decried, the animosities also existed. This, it is generally agreed, stemmed from the fact the West Indian was more community and politically oriented than his Afro-American brother, and he came into community leadership competition with the native aspirant.[66] The prejudice against the "monkey-chaser" seems, thus, to have been the product of the nonconformity of the foreign-born black to the norms of the black community. In the 1930s, however, this migration all but ceased (actually, greater numbers left than came in), and this aspect of intraracial enmity slowly faded, at least temporarily.[67]

Leadership in the black community, the last black-on-black commentary to be discussed, has never been clearly defined. That delightful character Mr. Simple, for example, once got to thinking about Negro leaders and

> how there is so many leaders I don't know that white folks know about, because they are always in the white papers. Yet *I'm* the one they are supposed to be leading. Now, you take that little short leader Dr. Butts. . . . If he ever made a speech in Harlem it were not well advertised. From what I reads, he teaches at a white college in Massachusetts, stays at the Commodore when he's in New York, and ain't lived in Harlem for ten years. Yet he's leading me.[68]

Except for Marcus Garvey, the national Negro leadership of the period simply failed to reach the black masses. "One thing is certain," sociologist Bertram Doyle noted in 1924, "the Negro is not satisfied with his leaders, of the past or the present."[69] A persistent gulf existed between the ordinary Negro and those who claimed leadership. The central character in John Arthur's *Dark Metropolis* was going to name his Harlem hotel after Booker Washington but "found that the good old doctor's name [was] held in reverence only by whites and a few very old-fashioned colored folks."[70]

Only the Negro church managed to span the leadership gulf to any significant degree. Even in slavery the church exerted a measure of influence and was to become "the chief means by which a structured or organized social life came into existence among the Negro masses," E. Franklin Frazier maintained.[71] But this does not alter the fact that the ordinary Negro was suspicious of his leadership, that he did not really trust its motives. As a result, the goals and possibilities that he could express through his leadership have never been very clear. Many of the above quotations hint at this state of affairs. Even in recent years the average Negro has said that his leaders are ashamed of him. How, he is likely to ask, can they lead anyone in such a case.[72] Three quarters of a century ago he was asking the same question. The worst enemy of the race, a New York paper observed in 1909, was the leader who had "no faith in the capacity of the race to perform any laudable enterprise."[73]

There were, for all practical purposes, only two national leaders throughout the whole period considered here, Booker T. Washington and W. E. B. DuBois. Booker Washington and his "Tuskegee Machine" were viewed by his critics as the epitome of the accommodationist school of race relations. His philosophy of race relations may even be seen as being addressed to white America rather than to black America. Certainly it offered no open challenge to white America.[74] As far as white America was concerned, Arnold Rose observed, Washington was "already marked as a 'good nigger,'" even before "he clinched his position by his famous Atlanta speech in 1895, in which he gave up the Negro demand for social and political equality."[75]

Yet it is possible to see a different Booker Washington from different vantage points. The white world saw only his conciliatory attitude and was given no reason to doubt it. All of his public expressions seemed reasoned calls for interracial cooperation that would not assail the social-political barriers of the color line. In his methods, historian C. Vann Woodward writes, the Tuskegeean "sought out the very type of men whom Southern whites were trying to interest in the development of Southern industry. He thus identified himself with the Eastern affiliations of the conservative South."[76] "His was a practical, canny mind," Eric Goldman says, "operating in a situation that suggested bargaining Negro equality for some Negro advances."[77]

But Booker Washington wore the mask—or rather, a mask for each of the many roles he played. In what is perhaps the best sketch of the enigmatic Washington, Louis Harlan writes:

> Washington's life and thought were layered into public, private, and secret and also segmented according to which subgroup of black or white he confronted. For each group he played a different role, wore a different mask. . . . Yet there were so few slips of the mask that it is no wonder his intimates called him "the wizard."

> In each of these compartmentalized worlds Washington displayed a different personality, . . . played a different role. At Tuskegee he was a benevolent despot. To Northern whites he appeared a racial statesman; to Southern whites he was a safe, sane Negro who advised blacks to "stay in their place." To Southern Negroes he was a father, to Northern blacks a stepfather; to politicians he was another political boss. In his paradoxical secret life he attacked the racial settlement that he publicly accepted, and he used ruthless methods of espionage and sabotage that contrasted sharply with his public Sunday-school morality.[78]

It seems likely that Washington could not have responded otherwise considering the times and his life experiences.[79] The "secret" side of Washington's life does not modify this assessment. That he worked clandestinely against the policy he publicly espoused cannot be doubted, but just how effective this militancy may have been—other than to enhance his own political strength—is open to question. It certainly does not seem that the ordinary Negro could have been influenced by Washington's secret political activities.[80]

In retrospect Washington's errors in formulating the economic basis of his program are apparent.[81] At the very time white America was pursuing a new social order congruent with its evolving urban-industrial institutions, Washington was calling for economic self-sufficiency on the basis of small agricultural and business pursuits.[82] Yet he succeeded in building a following unrivaled until his death in 1915, even though his power had waned considerably by that time. It was true, as journalist Joel Rogers said bluntly, that "Washington got along well in the South because he knew just how to tickle the color-vanity of the white."[83] But the timing and tone of his appeal were obviously critical.

Of equal significance is the fact that Washington came to control black communications in the South.[84] Black Belt communications were on a personal basis at this time, and they were delivered into Washington's hands through the black ministry, a group that saw him as giving voice to their own thoughts. Moreover, his agreeable message was freely carried in the white Southern press. "Washington never could have monopolized so effectively Negro leadership" in these years, one observer assessed in the mid-1920s, "had not the masses of Negroes been confined to the South." The end result was that "a veritable 'legend' sprang up embodying in the mind of the [southern] Negro masses their concept of the man."[85]

Politically, Washington was all powerful until the time of the Taft administration, and although his power ebbed significantly by the time of the Wilson administration, it lasted Washington's lifetime. At its peak few were in a position to challenge him, for he controlled patronage through his so-called black cabinet and was in a position to dictate the distribution of the funds white philanthropic foundations provided for Negro education. Through a combination of methods he also was able in varying degree to counter and even control the expression of criticism against him in the northern Negro press.[86]

Washington's policies and power did draw fire, however. Dissent was evident although not very effective throughout the early years of his career. But as northward migration progressed, as experience demonstrated again and again that the accommodationist approach produced no individual security or benefits for the ordinary Negro, as racial tension prodded racial consciousness to higher levels, as dissenters gained public voice with the proliferation of race newspapers, Washington was faced with challenges from quarter after quarter.[87] The black urban community was walled in by white racism, but there growing black peoplehood was already contesting the idea that everything must be measured by whiteness. "The time is not far distant," said the *Broad Ax* in 1899, "when Booker T. Washington will be repudiated as the leader of our race, for he believes that only the mealy-mouthed negroes like himself should be permitted to participate in politics." Washington alone, the article said, would be responsible for the disfranchisement of the Negro in Alabama.[88]

The preliminaries of what is usually cast as the Washington-DuBois controversy certainly registered the dissatisfaction that was growing by the turn of the century. Then in 1905 DuBois openly challenged Washington's leadership with the so-called Niagara Movement. According to the Tuskegeean's supporters, the Movement had only one aim: the destruction of Washington's programs and influence.[89] Washington did not sit idly by and allow the challenge to go unanswered. His counterattacks are among the best examples of the "secret" Booker Washington and his use of undercover methods: paid and unpaid spies to infiltrate organizations, attempts to squelch publicity for the Movement, bribes for favorable editorial comment concerning his views, paid propaganda agents.[90] That DuBois later admitted that the Tuskegeean's activities had in fact kept the Niagara Movement from achieving its objectives is acknowledgment of their effectiveness.[91]

The Niagara Movement had no broad popular base, however, and lacked strong white support. One black editor said the Movement was all noise and no action and only gave support to the "bourbon South."[92] Nor were the participants "interested in building Negro race pride," Arnold Rose writes; "in fact, some of them personally tended to look down upon the Negro masses themselves. They were the talented tenth."[93] Still, though it failed, the Niagara Movement prepared the ground for what would become the first effective national Negro protest and defense organization, the NAACP.[94]

The attacks on Washington's leadership were highly critical by the time the NAACP was officially launched in 1910. Said one newspaper, "The False Leader of Tuskegee . . . is proving himself to be the greatest arch enemy and traitor of the Negro race."[95] The NAACP did not, however, attack Washington, and the founders tried to keep a rein on the polemical W. E. B. DuBois in the hopes of reaching a rapprochement with the governor of the "Tuskegee machine."[96] This was not to be realized, though. By 1912, criticism of Washington was being broadcast by *The Crisis*—much of it shotgun fashion by reprinting critical reports from widespread sources.[97]

Washington, for his part, continued his attempts to undermine the new organization and stifle its national voice, *The Crisis*, in one instance, according to Louis Harlan, through "a devastating secret attack on the white liberals who were working with his black enemies.[98]

The way the Washington-DuBois controversy is often related, the central issue was segregation versus integration, accommodation versus confrontation.[99] Presented in this manner, however, the story leaves out much. The policies of the two men may have differed but their basic philosophies did not. "'Actually,' W. E. B. DuBois once remarked," historian Eric Goldman reports, "'Washington had no more faith in the white man that I do,' which was saying that he had little faith indeed."[100] Both Washington and DuBois, Ralph Bunche observed a generation ago, "confined their thinking within the periphery of race."

> Both . . . strove for: (1) improved living conditions for Negro city-dweller; (2) greatly increased educational facilities; (3) equality of economic opportunity; (4) equal justice in the courts; (5) emphasis on racial consciousness and dignity.[101]

Furthermore, the usual manner of presenting the Washington-DuBois dispute tends to camouflage the fact that a power shift from South to North was underway even as Washington reached the peak of his power. Without the northward migration and the rising sense of peoplehood, DuBois would have been without an audience.[102] But more importantly, the simplified story of the controversy tends to conceal the wide gulf that existed between the ordinary Negro and race leadership on all levels. All of the Mr. Simples in the urban centers saw that their leaders' reputations were based upon white approbation, not his own approval. This was especially applicable to national leadership—including Booker Washington.[103] At a meeting of the top black leadership in George Schuyler's satirical *Black No More*, "They all listened with respect to Dr. Gronne. He had been in turn a college professor, a social worker and minister, had received the approval of the white folks and was thus doubly acceptable to the Negroes. Much of his popularity was due to the fact that he very cleverly knew how to make statements that sounded radical to Negroes but [were] sufficiently conservative to satisfy the white trustees of his school."[104]

It would be difficult to depict national Negro organizations as resting upon any broad popular base at any time before the 1940s or 1950s. Even at the local branch level, the national organization—be it the NAACP or Washington's Negro Business League—fostered middle-class, color-conscious values. They performed invaluable services to the black community, but this does not mean that a sense of identification was thereby fostered throughout the community. There was, for one thing, no real economic tie to bind the organization to the community.[105] And little has really changed. Nathan Hare recently wrote:

> Consider this: the total membership of the NAACP, CORE, Southern Christian Leadership Conference, and the Urban League (even throwing in the Black Muslims and the "marches on Washington" for good measure) totals only about one-eighteenth of the Negro population. And this after years and, in some cases, decades of "membership drives." It is readily apparent that none of today's leaders is accepted by Negroes as a group.[106]

White racism dictated that race leadership come from within the race. At the same time all of the intraracial tensions made it impossible for the black community to function in a really cohesive manner. Class tension, the color mania, the very instability of the white man's color line in the urban North, all worked against full unity even as a sense of racial peoplehood spread widely among the masses. Nowhere is this better demonstrated than in the color antagonism that existed between the NAACP and Garvey's UNIA as both of these organizations matured rapidly at the end of World War I. The importance of this in the dramatic success of Garveyism can hardly be overemphasized.[107] "Being black," wrote Garvey, "I have committed an unpardonable offence against the very light colored negroes in America and the West Indies by making myself famous as a negro leader of millions. In their view, no black man must rise above them."[108]

Much of Garvey's plebeian appeal rested upon just this facet: he not only spoke to those most harried by the discriminations of the white color line but for those most tried by all of the intraracial tensions. Looking from the top down, all was still chaos in the black community. Looking from the bottom up there was a sentiment, a sense of peoplehood, an ethos, that made the "beaten and baffled, but determined not to be wholly beaten" mass, as Langston Hughes lovingly called these people he knew so well, into the progenitors of modern black America.[109]

NOTES

[1]"I, Too," by Langston Hughes, in Alain Locke, ed., *The New Negro* (1925; reprint ed., Arno Press, Inc., 1968), 145.

[2]Langston Hughes, "A Good Job Gone," in *Something in Common and Other Stories* (Hill & Wang, 1963), 36.

[3]W.E.B. DuBois, *Dark Princess* (Harcourt, Brace and Co., 1928), 50.

[4]From *The Seeking*, by Will Thomas, in Jay David, ed., *Growing Up Black* (William Morrow & Co., 1968), 42. See also Willard Motley, "The Almost White Boy," in Herbert Hill, ed., *Soon, One Morning: New Writings by American Negroes, 1940-1962* (Alfred A. Knopf, 1963), 391.

[5]Edward A. Shils, "The Bases of Social Stratification in Negro Society" 18-19, memorandum, Carnegie-Myrdal Study, Schomburg Collection, New York Public Library; Gunnar Myrdal, *An American Dilemma*, 20th anniversary ed. (Harper & Row, 1962), 1389n.2; Donald L. Noel, "Correlates of Anti-White Prejudice" (Ph.D. diss., Cornell University, 1961), 222-223. See also E. Franklin Frazier, *Black Bourgeoisie* (Free Press, 1957), passim, in which this is a central theme.

[6]Ethel Waters, with Charles Samuels, *His Eye Is on the Sparrow* (Doubleday and Co., 1951), 8-9.

[7]Langston Hughes, *The Best of Simple* (Hill & Wang, 1961), 100. See also Wallace Thurman, *The Blacker the Berry* . . . (1929; reprint ed., Collier Books, 1970), 162; Walter White, *Flight* (Alfred A. Knopf, 1926), 13. Eugene Henry Huffman, *"Now I Am Civilized"* (Los Angeles: Wetzel Publishing Co., 1930), devotes his satirical and stereotype-ridden novel to this topic. The protagonist is a Negro cook who gains his culture parrotlike and on the job.

[8]See chap. 6 regarding the relationship between "color" and class. See also Eugene Gordon, "The Negro's Inhibitions," *American Mercury* 13 (February 1928): 163-164; Langston Hughes, *The Big Sea* (1940; reprint ed., Hill & Wang, 1963), 206-208; Langston Hughes, "Our Wonderful Society: Washington," *Opportunity* 5 (August 1927): 225-226; White, *Flight,* 210-212; George Schuyler, *Black and Conservative* (New Rochelle, New York: Arlington House, 1966), 29.

[9]Langston Hughes, *Not Without Laughter* (1930; reprint ed., Alfred A. Knopf, 1963), 44-45.

[10]Rudolph Fisher, *The Walls of Jericho* (1928; reprint ed., Arno Press, Inc., 1969), 8.

[11]Ibid., 51.

[12]Waters, *His Eye Is on the Sparrow*, 196.

[13]*Colored American Magazine* 9 (November 1905): 632-633. See also Myrdal, *American Dilemma*, 1389n.2; Fenton Johnson, "The Servant," in *Crisis* 4 (August 1912): 189; Elise Johnson McDougald, "The Task of Negro Womanhood," in Locke, ed., *The New Negro*, 371.

[14]" 'Color Lines' Among the Colored People," *Literary Digest* 72 (March 18, 1922): 42.

[15]Howard E. Freeman, J. Michael Ross, David Armor, and Thomas Pettigrew, "Color Gradation and Attitudes Among Middle-Income Negroes," *ASR* 31 (June 1966): 365-374. "Color among American Negroes," say the authors, is still a factor to be considered but one that "can best be viewed, like occupation, as a contemporary status symbol shaping the individual's personal world, rather than as a status ascribed at birth and related to the total life experience of the individual."

[16]W.E.B. DuBois, *Dusk of Dawn* (1940; reprint ed., Schocken Books, 1968), 185.

[17]G. Franklin Edwards, "Community and Class Realities: The Ordeal of Change," *Daedalus* 95 (Winter 1966): 16. Thomas F. Pettigrew in his *A Profile of the Negro American* (Princeton: D. Van Nostrand Co., 1964), 34, allows that "though he clearly overgeneralized his description, Frazier saw this behavior as a desperate attempt to gain within the ghetto the recognition long denied in the larger society."

[18]Robert Bone, *The Negro Novel in America*, rev. ed. (New Haven: Yale University Press, 1965), 4-5; W.E.B. DuBois, "Black North," *New York Times*, December 1, 1901; Robert H. Brisbane, Jr., "The Rise of Protest Movements Among Negroes Since 1900" (Ph.D. diss., Harvard University, 1949), 2.

[19]Langston Hughes, "High to Low," in *Montage of a Dream Deferred* (Henry Holt, 1951), 43-44. The number "409" refers to a prestigious address in Harlem.

[20]Fannie Williams, "The Negro and Public Opinion," *Voice of the Negro* 1 (January 1904): 32.

[21]George L. Knox, in D.W. Culp, ed., *Twentieth Century Negro Literature* (1902), quoted in Bertram Wilbur Doyle, "Racial Traits of the Negro as Negroes Assign Them to Themselves" (Master's thesis, University of Chicago, 1924), 150.

[22]*Colored American Magazine* 12 (April 1907): 249.

[23]Chicago *Broad Ax*, April 10, 1909.

[24]*New York Age*, March 21, 1907.

[25]Ibid., April 14, 1910.

[26]Chicago Urban League, quoted in Carl Sandburg, *The Chicago Race Riots, July, 1919* (1919; reprint ed., Harcourt, Brace and World, 1969), 42.

[27]Bulletin No. One, Detroit Branch, NAACP, September 13, 1920. NAACP MSS, File Box G-95, Library of Congress.

[28]Bulletin No. Two, Detroit Branch, NAACP, April 22, 1921. NAACP MSS, File Box G-95, Library of Congress.

[29]*Chicago Defender*, February 17, 1923, quoted in Doyle, "Racial Traits of the Negro," 75. Doyle devoted a section to "Public Manners" (pp. 168-174) that provides a good sampling of such critiques.

[30]*Pittsburgh Courier*, June 16, 1923. For similar such comment see *Opportunity* 1 (November 1923): 346-347; Thurman, *The Blacker the Berry . . . , 36*.

[31]George Schuyler, "At the Darktown Charity Ball," *Messenger* 6 (December 1924): 378. See also Rollin Lynde Hartt, "When the Negro Comes North," *World's Work* 48 (May 1924): 86-87.

[32]This charge is a frequent one in the literature of the period. See, for instance, Otis M. Shackelford, *Lillian Simmons, or The Conflict of Section* (1915), quoted in Hugh M. Gloster, *Negro Voices in American Fiction* (University of North Carolina Press, 1948), 92; Waters Edward Turpin, *O Canaan* (Doubleday, Doran and Co., 1939), 23-24.

[33]*New York Age*, January 31, 1920.

[34]Turpin, *O Canaan*, 46-50 and passim.

[35]John A. Williams, *Sissie* (Doubleday Anchor Books, 1969), 155.

[36]See, by way of example, Waters, *His Eye Is on the Sparrow,* passim. Waters returns often to these points in her autobiography. See also Pauline E. Hopkins, *Contending Forces: A Romance Illustrative of Negro Life North and South* (Boston: The Colored Co-operative Publishing Co., 1900), 181.

[37]Arnold Rose, *The Negro's Morale* (University of Minnesota Press, 1949), 58. See also J. Saunders Redding, *On Being Negro in America* (1951; reprint ed., Indianapolis: Bobbs-Merrill Co., 1962), 63; *Opportunity* 7 (August 1929): 243; Schuyler, *Black and Conservative,* 3-4.

[38]Liston Pope a few years ago quoted Booker Washington as once remarking: "If you find a Negro who is not a Methodist or Baptist, it is a sure sign that some white man has been tampering with his religion." Liston Pope, "The Negro and Religion in America," *Review of Religious Research* 5 (Spring 1964): 144. See also E. Franklin Frazier, *The Negro Church in America* (Schocken Books, 1963), 8; White, *Flight*, 13.

[39]Rudolph Fisher, "The South Lingers On," *Survey Graphic* 53 (March 1, 1925): 645.

[40]Raymond Julius Jones, *A Comparative Study of Religious Cult Behavior Among Negroes with Special Reference to Emotional Conditioning Factors* (Washington, D.C.: Howard University Studies in the Social Sciences, 1939), 2.

[41]Benjamin E. Mays and Joseph W. Nicholson, *The Negro's Church* (1933; reprint ed., Russell and Russell, 1969), 98. See also St. Clair Drake, "Churches and Voluntary Associations in the Chicago Negro Community" (Official Report, W.P.A. Project, Chicago District, December 1940), 149; Carter G. Woodson, *The History of the Negro Church* (Washington, D.C.: The Associated Publishers, Inc., 1921), 301; Joseph R. Washington, Jr., *Black Religion: The Negro and Christianity in the United States* (Boston: Beacon Press, 1964), 113; Elmer T. Clark, *The Small Sects in America*, rev. ed. (Nashville, Tennessee: Abingdon, 1949), 117.

[42]Mays and Nicholson, *The Negro's Church*, 98. As used here, the term *storefront* includes houses or residences, halls, theaters, and the like that are used for religious services.

[43]Pope, "The Negro and Religion in America," 146.

[44]Frazier, *Negro Church in America*, 44-45; Drake, "Churches and Voluntary Associations," 10.

[45]Frazier, *Negro Church in America*, 53.

[46]By way of an extreme example, membership in one established Chicago church increased almost 2,000 percent during the period of the migration. Drake, "Churches and Voluntary Associations," 147. See also Mays and Nicholson, *The Negro's Church*, 115.

[47]Ira DeAugustine Reid, "Let Us Prey!" *Opportunity* 4 (September 1926): 274-275. The title of the article indicates its tenor. See also Mays and Nicholson, *The Negro's Church*, 219, 223; Drake, "Churches and Voluntary Associations," 183; Woodson, *History of the Negro Church*, 290, 303; Clark, *Small Sects in America,* 117.

[48]Jones, *Religious Cult Behavior,* 2-3. The language dates the study but not the conduct it describes as characteristic. See also Arthur Huff Fauser, *Black Gods of the Metropolis* (University of Pennsylvania Press, 1944), 76; Clark, *Small Sects in America*, 116. Descriptions of services can be found in Redding, *On Being Negro in America*, 140, Turpin, *O Canaan*, 258-261; Richard C. Minor, "The Negro in Columbus Ohio" (Ph.D. diss., Ohio State University, 1937), 104-115; Waters, *His Eye Is on the Sparrow*, 110; Langston Hughes, "Rock Church," in Hill, ed., *Soon, One Morning*; George W. Crawford, " 'Jazzin' God,' " *Crisis* 36 (February 1929): 45.

[49]Frazier, *Negro Church in America,* vii; Woodson, *History of the Negro Church*, 280; Washington, *Black Religion*, 113, 116, 121; Drake, "Churches and Voluntary Associations," 187, 194, 195; Hadley Cantrill, *The Psychology of Social Movements* (Wiley and Sons, 1941), 130, 141; Fauset, *Black Gods of the Metropolis*, 76-86; Benton Johnson, "Do Holiness Sects Socialize in Dominant Values?" *Social Forces* 39 (May 1961): 309; William A. Clark, "Sanctification in Negro Religion," *Social Forces* 15 (May 1937): 544-551.

[50]Erdmann Doane Beynon, "The Voodoo Cult Among Negro Migrants in Detroit," *AJS* 43 (May 1938): 894; Frazier, *Negro Church in America*, 67.

[51]E. David Cronon, *Black Moses: The Story of Marcus Garvey and the Universal Negro Improvement Association* (University of Wisconsin Press, 1955), 177-183.

[52]Thurman, *Blacker the Berry . . . ,* 206.

[53]Chicago *Broad Ax*, October 9, 1909.

[54]George S. Schuyler, "Shafts and Darts," *Messenger* 6 (March 1924): 73. See also Myrdal, *American Dilemma*, 803.

[55]Albon L. Holsey, "White Folks First, Please," *Messenger* 10 (February 1928): 46.

[56]See, for instance, *Colored American Magazine* 13 (November 1907): 328. Charges that professionals actually pushed for segregation in order to gain a monopoly were not infrequent. See *Pittsburgh Courier*, July 18, 1925.

[57]Chicago *Broad Ax*, November 11, 1899. See also Myrdal, *American Dilemma,* 802.

[58]Edwards, "Community and Class Realities," 3.

[59]William H. Thomas, *The American Negro* (Macmillan Co., 1901), 13-14.

[60]Robert Wiebe, *The Search for Order* (Hill & Wang, 1967), 13-14.

[61]Ira DeAugustine Reid, *The Negro Immigrant: His Background, Characteristics and Social Adjustment, 1899-1937* (Columbia University Press, 1939), 43-44, 85, 89.

[62]Ibid., 42, 85; W.A. Domingo, "Gift of the Black Tropics," in Locke, ed., *The New Negro,* 342.

[63]In *The Negro Immigrant*, 54-60, Reid outlines Caribbean color prejudice and sketches the backgrounds of the migrants from the various islands and countries. In a "collective autobiography" and through excerpts from personal narratives (pp. 171-213), the author provides insights into the lives of these migrants who were excluded from the "melting pot."

[64]Ibid., 215; Domingo, "Gift of the Black Tropics," in Locke, ed., *The New Negro*, 374; Rollin Lynde Hartt, " 'I'd Like to Show you Harlem!' " *Independent* 105 (April 21, 1921): 335.

[65]Rudolph Fisher, "Ringtail," *Atlantic Monthly* 135 (May 1925): 656-657. "Ringtail" equals "monkey-chaser." See also Langston Hughes, "Little Ham," in *Five Plays*, ed. Webster Smalley (Indiana University Press, 1963), 64-67; Gilbert Osofsky, *Harlem: The Making of a Ghetto* (Harper & Row, 1963) 134-135. Reid, in *The Negro Immigrant*, 107-108, provides a listing of the most prominent stereotypes.

[66]Domingo, "Gift of the Black Tropics," in Locke, ed., *The New Negro*, 346; Reid, *The Negro Immigrant*, 167-169; Roi Ottley, *New World A'Coming: Inside Black America* (Boston: Houghton Mifflin, 1943), 46.

[67]Osofsky, *Harlem*, 135.

[68]Langston Hughes, "Dear Dr. Butts," from *Simple Takes a Wife*, in James A. Emanuel and Theodore L. Gross, eds., *Dark Symphony: Negro Literature in America* (Free Press, 1968), 215. See also Hughes, *Simple's Uncle Sam* (Hill & Wang, 1965), 80-81.

[69]Doyle, "Racial Traits of the Negro," 139.

[70]John Arthur (Arthur Joseph) *Dark Metropolis* (Boston: Meador Publishing Co., 1936), 17.

[71]Frazier, *Negro Church in America*, 30. See also Ralph J. Bunche, "The Programs of Organizations Devoted to the Improvement of the Status of the American Negro," *JNE* 8 (July 1939): 547.

[72]Hughes, *Simple's Uncle Sam*, 145; Nathan Hare, *The Black Anglo-Saxons* (Marzani and Munsell, 1965), 121-122.

[73]*New York Age*, April 29, 1909.

[74]Roi Ottley and William J. Weatherby, eds., *The Negro in New York* (Praeger Publishers, 1969), 139; Louis R. Harlan, "Booker T. Washington in Biographical Perspective," *American Historical Review* 75 (October 1970): 1586; Bunche, "Programs of Organizations Devoted to the Improvement of the Status of the American Negro," 540.

[75]Rose, *The Negro's Morale*, 28.

[76]C. Vann Woodward, *Origins of the New South* (Louisiana State University Press, 1951), 358.

[77]Eric F. Goldman, *Rendezvous with Destiny: A History of Modern American Reforms*, rev. ed. abridged (Vintage Press, 1956), 63. See also Guy B. Johnson, "Negro Racial Movements and Leadership in the United States," *AJS* 43 (July 1937): 63.

[78]Harlan, "Booker T. Washington in Biographical Perspective," 1582, 1586. See also Donald J. Calista, "Booker T. Washington: Another Look," *JNH* 49 (October 1964): 250-251.

[79]Harlan, "Booker T. Washington in Biographical Perspectives," 1598-1599. See also Louis Harlan, "Booker T. Washington and the White Man's Burden," *American Historical Review* 71 (January 1966): 442; Woodward, *Origins of the New South*, 367; Myrdal, *American Dilemma*, 739-742; Rose, *The Negro's Morale*, 28; W.L. Brown, "Booker T. Washington as a Philosopher," *Negro History Bulletin* 20 (November 1956): 35.

[80]August Meier, "Toward a Reinterpretation of Booker T. Washington," *Journal of Southern History* 23 (May 1957): 227; Harlan, "Booker T. Washington in Biographical Perspective," 1586. It is in keeping with Washington's life experiences to see him as deliberately setting up a facade, with which the white would conveniently deceive himself, allowing him to pursue his real goals. See, for example, Jacqueline James, "Uncle Tom? Not Booker T.," *American Heritage* 19 (August 1968): 51-54, 95-100.

[81]For an early statement of Washington's philosophy of industrial training and economic advancement versus the pretensions of a liberal education, see Booker T. Washington, "The Awakening of the Negro," *Atlantic Monthly* 78 (September 1896): 322-328.

[82]Harlan, "Booker T. Washington in Biographical Perspective," 1584; Woodward, *Origins of the New South,* 366-367; John Hope Franklin, *From Slavery to Freedom* (Vintage Books, 1969), 395-396.

[83]J.A. Rogers, *From "Superman" to Man* (privately printed, 1965), 29.

[84]Calista, "Booker T. Washington," 248; Horace M. Bond, "Negro Leadership Since Washington," *South Atlantic Quarterly* 24 (April 1925): 116.

[85]Bond, "Negro Leadership Since Washington," 116-117; Charles S. Johnson, "The Rise of the Negro Magazine," *JNH* 13 (January 1928), 21; Brisband, "The Rise of Protest Movements Among Negroes," 32; Johnson, "Negro Racial Movements and Leadership," 63. Guy Johnson notes that Washington qualified as a hero in the typical sense and much of his strength is to be found in this fact. He fitted the Horatio Alger image almost exactly. This point is underscored by David Reisman in his noted analysis of the American character, *The Lonely Crowd.* "What the story of George Washington could be for a white child the story of Booker T. Washington could be for a black one." David Riesman, with Nathan Glazer, and Reuel Denny, *The Lonely Crowd: A Study of the Changing American Character,* abridged ed. (Garden City: Doubleday Anchor Books, 1950), 117.

[86]Harlan, "Booker T. Washington in Biographical Perspective," 1584-1585; Ottley and Weatherby, eds., *The Negro in New York,* 170; Mary L. Chaffee, "William E.B. DuBois Concept of the Racial Problem in the United States," *JNH* 41 (July 1956): 244-245; August Meier, "Booker T. Washington and the Negro Press," *JNH* 38 (January 1953): 67-90; Woodward, *Origins of the New South,* 365; Frazier, *Black Bourgeoisie,* 64.

[87]Daniel Walden, "The Contemporary Opposition to the Political and Educational Ideas of Booker T. Washington," *JNH* 45 (April 1960): 103-115; August Meier, *Negro Thought in America* (University of Michigan Press, 1966), 171ff; Elliot M. Rudwick, *W.E.B. DuBois: Propagandist of the Negro Protest* (Atheneum, 1969), 54ff.

[88]Salt Lake City *Broad Ax*, April 8, 1899.

[89]See, for example, "The Niagara Movement," *Alexander's Magazine* 2 (September 1906): 18-19. See also Rudwick, *W.E.B. DuBois,* 94-95. Saunders Redding, in the introduction to DuBois's *Souls of Black Folk* (Fawcett Edition, 1965), asserts that the changing black attitude is well marked by the publication of this work, although its publication did not

mean DuBois felt called to lead. See also Myrdal, *American Dilemma,* 742; Rudwick, *W.E.B. DuBois*, 68-69; J. Saunders Redding, "American Negro Literature," *American Scholar* 18 (Spring 1949): 142. An earlier statement of the "talented tenth" philosophy is found in, W.E.B. DuBois, "Of the Training of Black Men," *Atlantic Monthly* 90 (September 1902): 289-297.

[90]Louis R. Harlan, "The Secret Life of Booker T. Washington," *Journal of Southern History* 37 (August 1971): 392-416.

[91]Rudwick, *W.E.B. DuBois*, 118.

[92]*Colored American Magazine* 13 (October 1907): 247-248.

[93]Rose, *The Negro's Morale*, 32. A polemical but straightforward statement of the need for, and the objectives of, the movement is W.E.B. DuBois, "The Niagara Movement," *Voice of the Negro* 2 (September 1905): 619-622.

[94]Rudwick, *W.E.B. DuBois,* 98ff.

[95]Chicago *Broad Ax*, July 17, 1909.

[96]Rudwick, *W.E.B. DuBois,* 131, 137-139.

[97]Ibid., 178-179. See, for instance, the medley of press opinion repeated in *Crisis* 9 (November 1914): 17-18.

[98]Harlan, "Secret Life of Booker T. Washington,"413. See also Redding, "American Negro Literature," 144.

[99]S.P. Fullinwider, *The Mind and Mood of Black America* (Homewood, Illinois: Dorsey Press, 1969), 68.

[100]Goldman, *Rendezvous with Destiny*, 63.

[101]Bunche, "The Programs of Organizations Devoted to Improvement of the Status of the American Negro," 541.

[102]Bond, "Negro Leadership Since Washington," 118, 122.

[103]See, for example, *Colored American Magazine* 14 (June 1908): 328.

[104]George Schuyler, *Black No More* (1931; reprint ed., Negro Universities Press, 1969), 94-95.

[105]Brisbane, "The Rise of Protest Movements Among Negroes," 7-8, 76, 163; Bernard Magubane, "The American Negro's Conceptions of Africa: A Study in the Ideology of Pride and Prejudice" (Ph.D. diss., University of California, Los Angeles, 1967), 197-198, 215; Harold W. Cruse, "Revolutionary Nationalism and the Afro-American," *Studies on the Left* 2 (November 3, 1962): 21-22; T.G. Standing, "Nationalism in Negro Leadership," *AJS* 40 (September 1934): 187-192; Oliver C. Cox, "The New Crisis in Leadership Among Negroes," *JNE* 19 (Fall 1950): 459; Claude McKay, *A Long Way from Home* (1937; reprint ed., Harcourt, Brace and World, 1970), 113-114; Bunche, "The Programs of Organizations," 544, 546; E. Franklin Frazier, "Garvey: A Mass Leader," *Nation* 123 (August 18, 1926): 147.

[106]Hare, *Black Anglo-Saxons*, 42.

[107]Walter White, "The Paradox of Color," in Locke, ed., *The New Negro*, 366-367; Brisbane, "The Rise of Protest Movements Among Negroes," 90; Cruse, "Revolutionary Nationalism and the Afro-American," 20.

[108]Marcus Garvey, "The Negro's Greatest Enemy," *Current History and Forum* 18 (September 1923): 956. See also Harold R. Isaacs, "Blackness and Whiteness," *Encounter* 21 (August 1963): 18; Magubane, "The American Negro's Conceptions of Africa," 127, 214, 215; Redding, *On Being Negro in America*, 38-39. While Garvey was organizing the mass of ordinary Negroes, Kelly Miller called a "Sanhedrin" to bring together black intellectuals and the national Negro organizations. Both, paradoxically, were appealing to racial consciousness. Bernard Eisenberg, "Kelly Miller: The Negro Leader as a Marginal Man," *JNH* 45 (July 1960): 186-187.

[109]Hughes, *The Big Sea*, 264.

8

SUMMARY

What happens to a dream deferred?
Does it dry up
like a raisin in the sun?
Or fester like a sore—
And then run?
Does it stink like rotten meat?
Or crust and sugar over—
like a syrupy sweet?
Maybe it just sags
like a heavy load
Or does it explode?[1]

WHEN THE ordinary Negro in the northern urban centers of the 1890-1930 period looked about him, he found his vistas limited by his blackness. There was no change over these years in this aspect of black American life; there was, rather, a deadly sameness to the tenor of race relations during the whole first half of this century, as J. Saunders Redding has noted.[2]

Racial attitudes were not all that remained constant during these years. Even though the period encompasses the "search for order," as it has been termed, and the highly publicized Progressive reform era, all of the changes that came about, in the words of social-intellectual historian Charles Forcey, wrought only "inconsequential consequences":

The changes since (1900), while great, have been more those of degree than of kind . . . . This is no more than another way of stating the obvious fact that American social institutions have remained remarkably stable during tremendous economic, technological, military and diplomatic changes.[3]

Examine the "inconsequential consequences" in the black community. Did much in the economic, social, or political lot of the ordinary black American actually change? Not really. He was economically better off, quite substantially so in many instances, but he was still being exploited by whites (and other blacks). His occupation was largely determined by the wishes and whims of the white world—and his social position primarily by his occupation—even as a black economy developed in the burgeoning black urban centers of the North. A small but growing middle class altered the social structure of black America into a distorted replica of the dominant white society and continued to evolve in that direction, but the ordinary black was still at the mudsill.

Was the ordinary Negro's policital position any the less precarious or more potent? Instances can be pointed to that say it was both—the failure of Judge John J. Parker to be confirmed to the Supreme Court in 1930 because of his stand on Negro political participation, for example.[4] A good case can also be made that the black migrants who swelled the northern Meccas were not politically apathetic. Rather, they tended—in Chicago at least—to see the ballot as a measure of their changed status.[5] But as long as the black man remained, to use an appropriate phrase, the bete noire of both major political parties, politics remained something to be tolerated rather than participated in as far as the ordinary Negro was concerned.[6]

It would be erroneous, therefore, in the light of all of the inconsequential consequences, to look back on this period and regard Booker T. Washington and W. E. B. DuBois as symbols of the dilemma black America faced—as representing a dilemma of accommodation or confrontation, segregation or integration. The latter was an impossible option in the black South, but both were unacceptable choices to the growing black urban North. The ordinary Negro still found his everyday life molded by the white world in 1930, just as it had been in 1890. In his relationships with the dominant society he was still forced to function first as a Negro and only second as a man. He regarded the white world with dislike and distrust, and with disparaging contempt for the hypocrisies it so prominently displayed. Being Negro at this time was not just a biological fact; it was, as John Burma has noted, "a legal and social matter as well."[7] When Langston Hughes is critical of his Mr. Simple for forever bringing up race, Mr. Simple tells him:

> "I do . . . because that is what I am always coming face to face with—race. I look in the mirror in the morning to shave—and what do I see? *Me.* From birth to death my face—which is my race—stares me in the face."[8]

Yet this period saw the culmination of what historian C. Vann Woodward has termed "one of the most important developments in Negro history, . . . [the] rise of a whole separate system of society and economy on the other side of the color line."[9] In short, it is the "inconsequential consequences" of the changes in white America that made the changes in black America so significant.

By 1930, the ordinary black American thought almost exclusively in terms of blackness. The role the white world forced him to play launched him into one of his own, and he regarded all of his relationships with the dominant society in terms of blackness. Blackness was ubiquitous.

> *Once riding in old Baltimore,*
> *Heart-filled, head-filled with glee,*
> *I saw a Baltimorean*
> *Keep looking straight at me.*
> *Now I was eight and very small,*
> *And he was no whit bigger,*
> *And so I smiled, but he poked out*
> *His tongue, and called me, "Nigger."*
> *I saw the whole of Baltimore*
> *From May until December;*
> *Of all the things that happened there*
> *That's all that I remember.*[10]

The acceptance of blackness was actually the only choice open to the Negro. The changes that took place in white America, though they wrought inconsequential consequences there, in short made blackness *the* difference in black America. "Negro-ness" entered everywhere. Both the black and the white communities drilled the ordinary Negro with it. Garvey appealed to him with blackness. So did the Negro Business League. So did his church, his job, his streets in Harlem or Bronzeville, his newspapers, his manner of entertainment, his whole life-style. Blackness walled him in.

The black urban North did not announce a choice of blackness and embark on a reasoned drive toward a cultural nationalism, of course. But the tone of sentiment that grew up—the ethos of the community—reflected a heightened racial awareness, a press to think in terms of blackness first and foremost. It started at the bottom but all in the community, from the "rat" to the "respectable," to the "dickty," to the "talented tenth," were forced by the role assigned to the Negro in America to bring a "racial" interpretation to everyday matters, to just living from one day to the next.[11] The ordinary Negro became inherently nationalistic while at the same time he retained his American identity. He was not trying to preserve a cultural heritage in his nationalism; he was building one. A "state of mind," not a political state was involved.[12] The ordinary black American was thus building an ethos capable of supporting him in his new urban environment, a plan for living that described the social reality of his world. Only at the start of the Great Depression would the choice that he had for the most part unconsciously elected become even partially apparent, however.

When the Great Depression rocked all America, the Negro in his new urban setting was yet unsettled. The depression was disastrous economically for him because of his "first fired" position in the larger society. Many, as historian S. P. Fullinwider argues, sought escape, or rather security, in the preachings of such cult leaders as "Daddy" Grace and Father Divine and in the strident black nationalism of the newly founded Nation of Islam—the Black Muslims.[13] Those who had risen a peg and been rudely shoved back to the mudsill by the economic disaster now began to more clearly understand the ordinary Negro's lack of enthusiasm for the programs of the respectable protest organizations. They recognized now that his previous lack of support was grounded in the dictum, "We are all niggers together to the white man." The recognition of this fact by those who had long been the major source of support for the NAACP, for instance—the recognition of the essential weakness of the ordinary Negro's position—brought a reordering of the objectives of that organization.[14]

Something of the viewpoint from the bottom of the heap and the sense of peoplehood that had grown up in ordinary black America percolated upward. The flow was sufficient to sustain the whole of the black community in spite of the toll extracted by the depression. When the nation entered World War II, the Negro's morale was not very high, but it was grounded upon blackness.[15] Upon this, *the ethos of ordinary black America*, the opening battles of the modern civil rights revolution, rested securely.

NOTES

[1]"Lenox Avenue Mural" by Langston Hughes, *The Panther and the Lash* (Alfred A. Knopf, 1967).

[2]J. Saunders Redding, *On Being Negro in America* (1951; reprint ed., Indianapolis: Bobbs-Merrill Co., 1962), 45-50. See, by way of example, Archibald Rutledge, "The Negro in the North," *South Atlantic Quarterly* 31 (January 1932): 61-69. "Every Negro under our civilization," the author said in opening, "needs a white man as his protective genius, his guardian angel."

[3]Charles Forcey, "Historians of Reform and their Consequences," unpublished paper delivered at the Organization of American Historians annual meeting, Philadelphia, April 1969, 2-3.

[4]John Hope Franklin, *From Slavery to Freedom* 3d ed. (1966; Vintage Books, 1969), 526.

[5]Harold F. Gosnell, "The Chicago 'Black Belt' as a Political Battleground," *AJS* 39 (November 1933): 335-336.

[6]James Weldon Johnson, "A Negro Looks at Politics," *American Mercury* 18 (September 1929): 88-94. This aspect of black life needs further examination. From the literature surveyed it seems certain at this juncture that the ordinary Afro-American regarded politics in much the same way as he looked upon labor organizations—with a generous measure of distrust and dislike. Certainly the Negro, as he became more and more independent of party, became more and more a political force to be reckoned with. See Herbert J. Seligman, "The Negro's Influence as a Voter," *Current History* 28 (May 1928): 230-231. Yet even after the New Deal and World War II, the black man's political clout remained limited. His recognition by the federal government may be taken as a measure. The various federal departments, wrote historian Carter Woodson, with their "Uncle Tom" in charge of Negro affairs, set up a "buffer for the head of the department who does not care to be and will not be bothered with Negroes." Carter G. Woodson, "The History of the Department of Negro Affairs," *Negro History Bulletin* 8 (May 1945): 172.

[7]John H. Burma, "The Measurement of Negro 'Passing,'" *AJS* 52 (July 1946): 18.

[8]Langston Hughes, *The Best of Simple* (Hill & Wang, 1961), 173.

[9]C. Vann Woodward, *Origins of the New South* (Louisiana State University Press, 1951), 365.

[10]"Incident," by Countee Cullen, *On These I Stand* (Harper and Brothers, 1927), 9.

[11]See, for instance, Ralph Bunche, "The Programs of Organizations Devoted to Improvement of the Status of the American Negro," *JNE* 8 (July

1939;: 539; Wilson Record, "Intellectuals in Social and Racial Movement," *Phylon* 15 (Fall 1954): 231. James Turner, "The Sociology of Black Nationalism," *Black Scholar* 1 (December 1969): 18.

[12]C. Eric Lincoln, *Black Muslims in America* (Boston: Beacon Press, 1961), 45-46.

[13]S. P. Fullinwider, *The Mind and Mood of Black America* (Homewood, Illinois: Dorsey Press, 1969), 173-174, 175.

[14]See ibid., 68-69; Elliot Rudwick, *W. E. B. DuBois* (Atheneum, 1969), 276, 282-285.

[15]Richard M. Dalfiume, "The 'Forgotten Years' of the Negro Revolution," *JAH* 55 (June 1968): 93.

BIBLIOGRAPHICAL ESSAY

THIS ATTEMPT to reach "the tone of sentiment" of the northern Negro community from 1890 to 1930—to get inside as it has been termed—has but partially exploited the sources available. While numerous scholarly articles, short stories, newspapers, monographs, novels, poems, and anthologies were explored, a rich vein of source material remains to be mined. No attempt to be comprehensive will be made here, and only a small portion of the material used will be discussed in this essay. A few general comments might be in order concerning this material, however, before turning to a topical discussion of some of the items included in this study.

An effort was made to afford some manner of systematic search into the areas thought most promising. The major black newspapers, for instance, were examined in a systematic serial fashion. For example, where the first week's issue of each month was read for, say, the *New York Age*, the second week's issue of each month was read for the corresponding period of the *Pittsburgh Courier*, the third week's issue for another, and so on. This pattern was made feasible by the supplementary nature of black newspapers and the amount of "cut-and-paste" practiced by them at this time. One can be fairly certain that no major event affecting black America would be missed in this manner. Further, the pattern was broken often enough in following a particular local story out of simple curiosity so that even changing tone in the various papers could be detected.

The best study of the black newspaper is still Frederick G. Detweiler, *The Negro Press in the United States* (College Park: McGrath, 1968), which was first printed in 1922. Lewis H. Fenderson, "Development of the Negro Press: 1827-1948" (Ph.D. dissertation, University of Pittsburgh, 1949), offers itself as a follow-on study to Detweiler, but it is not of the same league. A more recent study, Maxwell R. Brooks, "Content Analysis of Leading Negro Newspapers" (Ph.D. dissertation, Ohio State University, 1953), demonstrates how this source material may, with imagination, be exploited. The 3-M Company's reproduction program at the New York Public Library's Schomburg Collection has made this source material more readily available.

When it comes to the popular periodicals, whole runs of some were examined issue by issue for their entire lifespan, among them, *Colored American Magazine, Alexander's Magazine,* and *The Voice of the Negro.* Others, such as *The Crisis* and *The Southern Workman,* were examined issue by issue from their birth until the first issues of the early 1930s. Still other periodicals—*The Journal of Negro History, The Journal of Negro Education, Phylon, The American Sociological Review, The Journal of American History*, and *Social Forces*, to mention just a few—were checked volume by volume for pertinent articles and essays. Published bibliographies providing references to periodical literature, it was discovered quite early, would not suffice in this case because of the subject matter.

In other instances bibliographies proved invaluable, as in the case of Maxwell Whiteman, *A Century of Fiction by American Negroes, 1853-1952* (Philadelphia: Saifer, 1955), or John S. Lash, "The American Negro in American Literature," *JNE* 15 (Fall 1956). It was from such sources as these that the older novels were mined. The works of a number of prominent artists have, of course, enjoyed resurrection in paperback: McKay, Hughes, Chesnutt, and Dunbar, for example. But there were still many days spent on horribly hard chairs in the New York Public Library's main reading rooms (where many of these old novels can be found) reading yellowed copies of imaginative literature by black authors.

Especially useful here as well were the studies devoted to the literature of black American artists. Robert Bone, *The Negro Novel in America*, rev. ed. (Yale University Press, 1965), is still one of the best of these studies available today. Bone concentrated on the period following 1890 and attempted to cast the novels in their period by outlining the climate of the times in which they were written. He has been taken to task concerning this by several scholars, and his historical sense of the period is, certainly, weak in spots. Sterling Brown, *Negro Poetry and Drama* and *The Negro in Amer-*

ican Fiction (Atheneum, 1969), is a single-volume reprint of studies done in the 1930s. Bone and Brown also provide good bibliographical entry into the area, and their discussions of plot lines helped to sort out the most promising volumes for the approach being taken here.

To this same category one should add Hugh Morris Gloster, *Negro Voices in American Fiction* (University of North Carolina Press, 1948), another very lucid examination of black literature and the black in literature. *Images of the Negro in American Literature* (University of Chicago Press, 1966), edited by Seymour L. Gross and John Edward Hardy, provides a collection of critical essays concerning the Negro image and the Negro author that ranges from the colonial period through Ralph Ellison and James Baldwin. There are, as well, many specialized studies concerning black literature. Nick Aaron Ford, "The Negro Author's Use of Propaganda in Imaginative Literature" (Ph.D. dissertation, University of Iowa, 1946), asserts that racial propaganda naturally flows from the pens of black authors because of their position in the larger society. Edward Bland, "Social Forces Shaping the Negro Novel," *Negro Quarterly* 1 (Fall 1942), argues the same point, as does William T. Fontaine in, "'Social Determination' in the Writings of Negro Scholars," *AJS* 49 (January 1944). The *CLA Journal* is important in this respect for its many articles directed to individual authors, movements (for example, the Harlem Renaissance), and themes (such as the stereotyping of white characters).

The use of imaginative literature as a primary source is today quite commonplace, although the validity of doing so is still challenged from many quarters. A recent volume devoted to this topic is Nelson Manfred Blake, *Novelists' America: Fiction as History, 1910-1940* (Syracuse University Press, 1969). An imaginative use of this type of source material, and a most cogent statement of its validity as a primary source, is found in David C. McClelland, *The Achieving Society* (Van Nostrand, 1961). Of course, the usefulness of fiction as a vehicle for examining the American experience is explicit in the many anthologies that have found their way into print in recent years. *Dark Symphony: Negro Literature in America* (Free Press, 1968), edited by James A. Emanuel and Theodore L. Gross, is an excellent example. Another would be Herbert Hill, ed., *Soon, One Morning: New Writings by American Negroes, 1940-1962* (Knopf, 1963), a collection of wide-ranging excerpts, short stories, essays, and poetry that touches deeply the "blackness" of the ordinary Negro.

Paperback reprints are spreading the black facet of the American experience to ever-widening audiences as well. The Mnemosyne Publishing Company of Miami, Florida, has quite a wide listing of titles, for example, one that includes such authors as Claude McKay, Wallace Thurman, and Langston Hughes. Only a few of these works will be mentioned here.

Paul Laurence Dunbar, *The Sport of the Gods* (Arno Press, 1969), is credited as the first serious attempt to deal realistically with black urban life in the North. First published in 1902, this novel is in many ways a morality play that could have been cast in white as well as black, for it protests vigorously against all of the destructive forces that were thought inherent in city life at the time. Much more down to earth is William Attaway, *Blood on the Forge* (1941; reprint ed., Collier Books, 1970), a story of the black experience in the industrial North during World War I. The characters are rather thinly drawn, but they display a full range of reactions to conditions in the South during the period, as well as to the impact of industrial labor conditions in the North. The picture painted of Pittsburgh's black labor pool and its relationship across the color line to the white is a striking one.

The most popular story setting of the time, though, is the black Mecca of the North, Harlem. *Dark Metropolis* (Meador, 1936), by John Arthur [Arthur Joseph], examines many facets of urban living by relating the life stories of the residents of a hotel in Harlem. Arthur was not the equal of such craftsmen at Rudolph Fisher, Claude McKay, and Langston Hughes, however.

Fisher, whose short stories provide powerful insights into black life, was an artist who could employ comic realism without distorting his images. Several of his short stories seem to be almost invariably included in anthologies today. *The Walls of Jericho* (1928; reprint ed., Arno Press, 1969), is one of Fisher's highly readable works about life among the lowly in Harlem, as is his black detective novel, *The Conjure Man Dies: A Mystery Tale of Dark Harlem* (Covier-Friede, 1932).

Claude McKay was another craftsman whose work is today being reprinted. Although born in Jamaica, McKay knew the black urbanite of the North intimately and gave him voice in both his poetry and fiction. *Home to Harlem* (Harper and Brothers, 1928) is perhaps his best-known novel. It went a long way toward earning him the animosity of the black elite, he noted in his autobiography *A Long Way from Home* (1937; reprint ed., Harcourt, Brace and World, 1970), for it let the white man see the ordinary Negro as he was, and not as the upper class wanted him to be. McKay's *Gingertown* (Harper and Brothers, 1932), a collection of short stories that deals with black night life in Harlem as well as life in Europe and in the Islands, is a wide-ranging one that the elite would also question. One finds here, as John Dewey said of McKay's poetry in his introduction to *The Selected Poems of Claude McKay* (Bookman Associates, 1958), a real feeling of "the sense of being a black man in a white man's world."

Wallace Thurman, another Harlem Renaissance participant, also excited the wrath of the black elite with his choice of subject matter. As Sterling Brown notes of his 1929 novel, *The Blacker the Berry* . . . (Collier Books, 1970), Thurman "puts his finger upon one of the sorest points of the Negro bourgeoisie, its color snobbishness." In his second novel, *Infants of the Spring* (Macauley, 1932), Thurman examines a range of behavior patterns in black and white interracial contact, something George Schuyler also does in his 1931 satirical novel *Black No More* (Negro Universities Press, 1969).

The main midwestern terminus of northward migration, Chicago's Bronzeville, was another popular setting for the stories of the black experience. Waters Edward Turpin, *O Canaan* (Doubleday, Doran and Co., 1939), traces the urbanization of Joe Benson and his family during the teens and twenties of this century. Alden Bland, *Behold a Cry* (Scribner's, 1947), explores the same theme, but the story is perhaps too optimistic in tone and the characterizations too sophisticated.

The celebrated Richard Wright set some of his most effective stories in Chicago; his short autobiographical "The Man Who Went to Chicago" is an often-included item in today's anthologies. Wright's most famous work, *Native Son* (1940; reprint ed., Signet, 1964), is a novel whose title even strikes to the heart of American race relations. Wright was at home with the short story form as he was with the novel. His stories in *Eight Men* (1961; reprint ed., Pyramid Books, 1969), and *Uncle Tom's Children* (Harper & Row, 1940), all play upon the theme of being black in a white man's world and go a long way toward capturing the Negro's multiphased existence in individual black-white relations.

Not all black authors concentrated on the life experiences of the ordinary Negro, however, although life among the lowly certainly provided the more easily exploitable material. Jessie Redman Fauset, for instance, in her romances, confined her scope to the middle and upper class in the North, and in her *There Is Confusion* (Boni and Liverright, 1924), *Plum Bun* (Frederick A. Stokes, 1929), and *The Chinaberry Tree* (Frederick A. Stokes, 1931) focuses on their foibles. One can find in Fauset's novels a good pastiche of the urban life of the educated stratum and a good bit of comment on such things as the color complex. They are a bit too maudlin for today's tastes, however.

The works of the prolific Langston Hughes, which have been widely used in this study, ranged across the whole of the black social spectrum. Hughes provided many hours of purely pleasurable reading. His *Not Without Laughter* (Knopf, 1963), is a moving sketch of Negro life in a midwestern town in the years just before and during World War I. First published in 1930, Sterling Brown termed this first novel one of the best of the period. In it Hughes was especially concerned with the idea of a "job ceiling" and the role of the black woman in black-white relations.

In *The Ways of White Folks* (Knopf, 1963), a collection of short stories, Hughes presents a pastiche of the black's repertoire of responses to the white world. It displays rather pointedly just how ignorant white America has been—and is—of the black community. Hughes was especially at home with the short story vehicle. Two other widely available collections of his stories are *Something in Common and Other Stories* (Hill & Wang, 1963), and *Laughing to Keep from Crying* (1952; reprint ed., Collier, 1969).

Hughes enjoyed a fine reputation as a poet as well. His poems are found in almost every anthology of black poetry one picks up today, but he is best sampled alone, as in his *Montage of a Dream Deferred* (Henry Holt, 1951). His poems found there, as do the plays found in *Five Plays by Langston Hughes*, edited by Webster Smalley

(Indiana University Press, 1963), touch deeply upon black-on-black and black-on-white attitudes.

Hughes, who was also a columnist, published some of his most biting critiques of both the black and white worlds in his "Mr. Dooley"-style column that began in the early 1940s in the *Chicago Defender.* Arthur P. Davis's article, "Jesse B. Semple: Negro American," *Phylon* 15 (First Quarter 1954), provides an engaging introduction to Hughes's Mr. Simple. Many of Simple's comments are universal in nature, of course, but race relations was the dominant subject of his one-sided conversations, with Hughes acting as the antagonist. The columns have been collected and are readily available. *The Best of Simple* (Hill & Wang, 1961) and *Simple's Uncle Sam* (Hill and Wang, 1965) are two such samplings of Simple.

In *The Big Sea* (1940; reprint ed., Hill & Wang, 1963), and *I Wonder as I Wander* (1956; reprint ed., Hill & Wang, 1964), two autobiographical works, the late Langston Hughes rounded out his interpretations of the black man in white America. To complete the spectrum through the eyes of the autobiographical beholder, though, one should sample as well George Samuel Schuyler, *Black and Conservative* (Arlington House, 1966), Ethel Waters, *His Eye Is on the Sparrow* (Doubleday, 1951), James Weldon Johnson, *Along This Way* (Viking Press, 1933), Walter Francis White, *A Man Called White* (Viking Press, 1948), the several autobiographies of W.E.B. DuBois, and the already mentioned *A Long Way from Home,* by Claude McKay.

Each of the categories of literature mentioned above contributed to the setting up of the composite picture of the black North present here. Each contributed to the outlined climate of the times. But debts to many scholarly studies must be acknowledged as well. The debt to Robert H. Wiebe, *The Search for Order, 1877-1920* (Hill & Wang, 1967), has already been explicitly noted in the text at several points. This is obvious in the borrowing of his highly descriptive expression *search for order.* C. Vann Woodward, *Origins of the New South, 1877-1913* (Louisiana State University Press, 1951), is still the best account of the confused southern political-social scene following the end of the Reconstruction. Certainly it is the most readable. An excellent overview of the entire period is provided by

Eric F. Goldman, *Rendezvous with Destiny* (Vintage, 1955). The subtitle, *A History of Modern American Reform*, indicates its theme. John Hope Franklin, *From Slavery to Freedom—A History of American Negroes*, 3d ed. (Vintage, 1969), is probably still the best overall text devoted to black America, but it is sketchy for the period after Reconstruction. August Meier and Elliott M. Rudwick, *From Plantation to Ghetto: An Interpretive History of American Negroes* (Hill & Wang, 1966), does not live up to the promise of its title, although it is a most useful supplement to Franklin's larger work. A sociological overview is provided by E. Franklin Frazier, *The Negro in the United States* (Macmillan, 1957). The charts, diagrams, and statistics tend to get in the way, however. Also of interest is Scott Nearing, *Black America* (Schocken Books, 1969), a highly polemical examination of Negro America that was published in 1929 and that concentrates on the 1920s. The changing intellectual climate of the nation in the late nineteenth century is conveyed in Curtis Robert Grant's well-written study, "The Social Gospel and Race" (Ph.D. dissertation, Stanford University, 1968). This might be giving too much influence to a comparatively limited movement, however.

Many monographs were important to the task of setting up the background against which the ordinary northern Afro-American's ethos was to be cast. One of the very best of these is Gilbert Osofsky, *Harlem: The Making of a Ghetto* (Harper, 1963). It is an account that touches often upon ordinary black life in many of its facets. Also important in this vein is Seth M. Scheiner, *Negro Mecca: A History of the Negro in New York City, 1865-1920* (New York University Press, 1965). These studies have superseded James Weldon Johnson's still useful *Black Manhattan* (Knopf, 1930).

Other studies that examine this northern black Mecca are: Roi Ottley and William J. Weatherby, eds., *The Negro in New York: An Informal Social History* (Praeger Publishers, 1969), which was compiled from Federal Writer's Project manuscripts, and Claude McKay, *Harlem: Negro Metropolis* (Dutton, 1940). Much in both of these volumes goes beyond the time frame being considered here. McKay's work is a personal evaluation of the many facets of black life that nurtured the rise of Garveyism and subsequently the many noted cultists of the 1930s. Mary White Ovington's *Half a Man, The*

Status of the Negro in New York (1911; reprint ed., Schocken Books 1969), is a delightfully styled study that nicely demonstrates that a white can deal sensitively with the subject of blackness. The study draws together much evidence, a lot of it personally gathered, on the conditions and life-style of the urban Negro in the first decade of this century.

Three of Rudolph Fisher's short stories must be at least mentioned in passing when referring to these studies of black New York City. His "The Promised Land," *Atlantic Monthly* 139 (January 1927), provides good comment on how the black community is forced to resort to such things as the "rent party" to make ends meet in the city. His "The City of Refuge," *Atlantic Monthly* 135 (February 1925) is an often reprinted tale that reveals the ordinary black urbanite's existence as quite "normal" within his own community. There he is not a "nigger," but a father, a friend, a pusher, a sucker, whatever. The white world is kept at its distance by his protective black surroundings. The third story, "The South Lingers On," *Survey Graphic* 53 (March 1, 1925), is a collection of sketches of Harlem life that concentrates on the migrant and the vestiges of his southern rural culture: on the Reverend Taylor who followed his flock North, on the job seekers, on the young girl taken by all of the excitement, on the bootlegger carried back by the hell-fire sermons of a southern-style preacher.

The other great black city within a city, Chicago's Bronzeville, has been examined in detail as well, although not as extensively as Harlem perhaps. Alan H. Spear, *Black Chicago: The Making of a Negro Ghetto, 1890-1920* (University of Chicago Press, 1967), is the most recent. It is complementary in nature to the classic *Black Metropolis* (Harper Torchbooks, 1962) by St. Clair Drake and Horace R. Cayton, a study published first in 1945 that is still considered to be the best examination of black urban life yet published. Both are rightly classed as sociological studies; they are good social history as well. A more narrow but sharply focused look at Bronzeville is provided in William M. Tuttle, Jr., *Race Riot: Chicago in the Red Summer of 1919* (Atheneum, 1970).

Washington, D.C., was the subject of Constance McLaughlin Green's *The Secret City* (University of Princeton Press, 1967). It is a restricted, rather narrow study, however, that sees race relations in the nation's capital (to borrow from the subtitle) as being peculiar to the upper stratum of the community. [Elliott Rudwick, in his review essay "Black Metropolis—The Making of the Ghetto," *Wisconsin Magazine of History* 51 (Spring 1968), presents cogent comment on Green's *Secret City*, Spear's *Black Chicago*, and Osofsky's *Harlem*.]

Other monographs dealing with black northern urban life are W. E. B. DuBois, *The Philadelphia Negro* (Schocken Books, 1967), one of DuBois's early (1899) and best works; John Daniels, *In Freedom's Birthplace: A Study of the Boston Negroes* (Johnson Reprint, 1968), a racist-distorted study first published in 1914; Clara Alberta Hardin, "A Study of the Negroes of Philadelphia" (Ph.D. dissertation, Bryn Mawr, 1943), a study that rests upon the theme that racial consciousness lead to a press for integration but that is not very penetrating; and Richard C. Minor, "The Negro in Columbus, Ohio" (Ph.D. dissertation, Ohio State University, 1937), a most poorly written and superficial study, albeit one that provides valuable insights because of its explicit middle- and upper-class orientation. And, of course, there are also the numerous "The Negro in————" articles that are found in a wide range of periodicals. They can provide a wide variety of impressions of black life, and they were useful here in spite of the fact that the view presented is most often through the eyes of the black bourgeoisie. Thomas J. Woofter, Jr., and Associates, *Negro Problems in Cities* (1928; reprint ed., McGrath Publishing Co., 1969), is useful in integrating the data found in such articles.

Each of the studies cited to this point obviously were forced to deal with American racism and with being black in white America in one way or another. America has always been racist. This is well exhibited in Winthrop Jordan, *White Over Black* (Baltimore: Penguin Books, 1964), a thorough if overly long and repetitious study of the origins of American racial attitudes. The short article by Dante A. Puzzo, "Racism and the Western Tradition," *Journal of the History of Ideas* 25 (October-December 1964), which makes explicit the distinction between racism and ethnocentrism, is a complementary supplement to Jordan's long work. Thomas F. Gossett's *Race: The History of an Idea in America* (Schocken Books, 1965) is an excellent survey, if a bit shy on the early years of the nation's history. It, supplemented with Jordan's work and with something more definitive for the period after 1930, can provide a good comprehensive picture of American racial thought. Still, the picture would be lacking some detail without such classics as Ray Stannard Baker's *Following the Color Line* (Harper Torchbooks, 1964). Published in 1908, Baker's study today is not so important for what it says about the Negro, but for what it says about white America attitudes toward the Negro in the first decade of this century. It is still good reading in places as well, granting that today it seems very much like a too-long newspaper article dealing with contemporary race relations.

E. Franklin Frazier presents a dated but concise review of the various schools of race relations in American sociology in "Race Contacts and the Social Structure," *ASR* 14 (February 1949). It provides an excellent introduction to Thomas F. Pettigrew, *A Profile of the Negro American* (Van Nostrand Co., 1964), a mammoth work of integration. Working with a bibliography of over 500 items, Pettigrew managed to integrate a seemingly unwieldy mass of social-psychological data into quite a readable account of the Negro and his role in contemporary society. Certainly the study makes such topical discussions as E. Franklin Frazier, *The Negro Family in the United States* (University of Chicago Press, 1939), more easily handled. Andrew Billingsly's more recent *Black Families in White America* [Englewood Cliffs, N.J.: Prentice-Hall, 1968] is something of a redress of Frazier's views, but it is not in the same league.)

The standard by which all modern studies of black American life are measured is the monumental work by Gunnar Myrdal, with Richard Sterner and Arnold Rose, *An American Dilemma: The Negro Problem and Modern Democracy,* 20th anniversary edition (Harper & Row, 1962). Much in it did not bear well the weight of time, and the dilemma Myrdal saw existing between the American ideal and the actuality was not genuine, but the study is yet the most thorough examination of black life in America. (It might be added that the dilemma thesis is a cogent comment on the intellectual climate of the times.) The typescripts of the memorandums that went into the generation of this Carnegie-sponsored study are available at the Schomburg Collection, New York Public Library. Many of these have been published separately since the study was first issued. The entire collection has recently been made available through the 3-M Company's reproduction program at Schomburg.

Other studies useful in examining American racism and the experience of being black in white America are: Gordon W. Allport, *The Nature of Prejudice* (Anchor Books, 1958); Milton M. Gordon, *Assimilation in American Life; The Role of Race, Religion, and National Origins* (Oxford University Press, 1964); Arnold M. Rose, *The Negro's Morale: Group Identification and Protest* (University of Minnesota Press, 1949); and Charles S. Johnson, *Growing Up in the Black Belt: Negro Youth in the Rural South* (Washington, D.C.: Prepared for the American Youth Commission, American Council on Education, 1941). Rose's basic theme is that the last half-century or so had seen a drastic change in the general morale of the Negro— that it rose from a low in the 1890-1910 period to a peak in the late 1940s. C. S. Johnson's work, done in the best W. Lloyd Warner tradition, is especially useful because of the author's inclusion of North-South and urban-rural comparisons. Also useful in this area are a number of doctoral dissertations: Robert H. Brisbane, Jr., "The Rise of Protest Movements Among Negroes Since 1900" (Harvard University, 1949); Royal D. Colle, "The Negro Image and the Mass Media" (Cornell University, 1967); Cyril Robert Friedman, "Attitudes toward Protest Strategy and Participation in Protest Groups Among Negro Americans" (University of Connecticut, 1967); and Bernard Magubane, "The American Negro's Conception of Africa: A Study in the Ideology of Pride and Prejudice" (University of California, Los Angeles, 1967). Edward Sayler's "Negro Minority Group Strategy as a Social Movement" (Ph.D. dissertation, University of Ohio, 1948) provides some insights, but on the whole the study is a superficial one based on secondary sources. The obverse of the white racist coin is discussed in Donald L. Noel, "Correlates of Anti-White Prejudice" (Ph.D. dissertation, Cornell University, 1961). This excellent study is based on interview data and is relatively free of jargon. The sampling seems as though it might be challenged, and some of the regional comparisons made seem suspect. But these shortcomings, if they do exist, do not distract overly much from the insights it provides.

Three other works should be at least mentioned at this point. The first is *The New Negro: An Interpretation* (Arno Press, 1968), edited by Alain Locke. First published in 1925, this volume is now a classic. It is a collection of historical sketches, essays, short stories, and articles that presents with discrimination the views of the New Negro of the 1920s. Clearly integrationist in tone, it emphasizes the Negro's Americanism. The second volume is *Growing Up Black* (William Morrow, 1968), edited by Jay David. The excerpts found here are partially effective, at least, in conveying the impact of discovering one's blackness in the process of growing up in Negro America. Those selections reflecting the urban scene especially show that the "sin" of blackness is visited upon the Negro regardless of the social position into which he is born. The third volume is one of the most highly sophisticated accounts of being black in white America: J. Saunders Redding, *On Being Negro in America* (Indianapolis: Bobbs-Merrill, 1962).

While no detailed analysis of the institutional structure of the black community was attempted in this study, certain dimensions of it had to be examined to cast up the background against which the characteristic spirit of the community was depicted. Most critical to this was the black social structure and its evolution during the 1890-1930 period. As was noted in several instances in the study, though, it is most difficult to describe the social structure of black America with any precision during these years. But then the entire topic of class in America is still rather well protected by a myth of classlessness that has little grounding in fact. Milton M. Gordon, *Social Class in American Sociology* (McGraw-Hill Book Co., 1963), provides a survey and critique of the sociological research into the American class structure. He points out the uniqueness of the case of the Negro. His bibliography, although now dated, is still useful.

But the whole problem of class in black America has not been given the attention it deserves, perhaps because such attention would disturb many comfortable liberal attitudes. There are, of course, E. Franklin Frazier's *Black Bourgeoisie* (Free Press, 1957) and Nathan Hare's *The Black Anglo-Saxons* (1965; reprint ed., Collier Books, 1970), both of which caused a furor in black middle-class circles. Jay Reigle Williams, "Social Stratification and the Negro American: An Exploration of Some Problems in Social Class Measurement" (Ph.D. dissertation, Duke University, 1968), is a useful, contemporary study, but it includes indexes that seem invalid when applied to Afro-Americans. Also helpful is Adelaide C. Hill, "The Negro Upper Class in Boston—Its Development and Present Social Structures" (Ph.D. dissertation, Radcliffe College, 1952), in spite of the fact it is freighted with invitations and programs of social events, and the author felt it necessary to argue that an upper class really did exist regardless of the fact it included persons of low occupational status.

Focusing more on the period under examination in this study are the appropriate portions of Myrdal, *American Dilemma;* Drake and Cayton, *Black Metropolis;* Johnson, *Black Manhattan*; Frazier, *The Negro in the United States;* and DuBois, *The Philadelphia Negro,* all of which have already been mentioned. Norval D. Glenn, "Negro Prestige Criteria: A Case Study in the Bases of Prestige," *AJS* 68 (November 1963), is a useful analysis that encompasses a number of studies that go back to the turn-of-the-century period. Ascribed status is slighted, however, and the whole of the Negro structure is rather vague.

One of the themes of Wiebe's *The Search for Order* suggested the model for the changing northern black social structure that has been put forward in this study. The theory that changing values restructured the white community and that the changes there were reflected in the black community is found elsewhere, of course. August Meier lays the groundwork for such an approach in "Negro Class Structure and Ideology in the Age of Booker T. Washington," *Phylon* 23 (Fall 1962). He offers there, and extends more fully in *Negro Thought in America, 1880-1915: Racial Ideologies in the Age of Booker T. Washington* (University of Michigan Press, 1966) that a true Negro middle class and leadership element coalesced during this period.

But as valuable as the social-psychological inputs were, however important were the historical studies and the statistical data that was used to examine the occupational dimensions of class, the real insights into the black social structure from 1890 to 1930 are to be found in the imaginative literature. James Weldon Johnson's *The Autobiography of an Ex-Colored Man* (Hill & Wang, 1960) is one such novel. Johnson was an acute and sensitive observer, and he depicted in this 1912 novel the scope of the black social structure

around the turn of the century. The works of artists like Langston
Hughes, Claude McKay, Wallace Thurman, Rudolph Fisher, and
George Schuyler have already been mentioned.

The novels of these authors are important regarding several
peculiar aspects of the class structure as well: the color-caste system
within the black community and the status ascribed by the black
community to various occupations, for instance. Rudolph Fisher's
The Walls of Jericho and Wallace Thurman's *The Blacker the
Berry* . . . are perhaps the best examples that may be pointed to in
both cases. A more contemporary exploration of these themes is
Reba Lee [pseud.], *I Passed for White* (Longmans Green and Co.,
1955). It is a not-very-well-written rehearsal of the discovery of
blackness, self-hatred, passing, repentance, and return to the
decent world of the black community kind of sequence.

There are numerous articles and short stories that may be referred to in this regard as well. Edith Manual Durham's "Deepening
Dusk," *Crisis* 38 (January 1931), is one of the better short stories
dealing with racial consciousness and pride, and the complex conflict of values that the color caste system produced in the nation.
Others dealing with various themes of the color complex in the black
community and passing are: Fannie Barrier Williams, "Perils of the
White Negro," *Colored American Magazine* 22 (December 1907), a
story that suggests that few who give up the struggle are ever
"betrayed" by those who know their secret; "The Adventures of a
Near-White," *Independent* 75 (August 14, 1913), an unsigned, first-
person account of one who crosses and recrosses the color line; Jessie
Fauset, "Emmy," *Crisis* 5 (December 1912), a rather unconvincing
story of the impact of color on some very proper middle-class Negroes in the North; and Rudolph Fisher, "High Yaller," *Crisis* 30
(October 1925), 31 (November 1925), a story that rests on the theme
that color conflict within the race can prove so unbearable that those
who can pass are almost forced to do so.

Occupation, which provides a particularly important insight into the ordering of the black community, is also illuminated in these
novels and short stories. The real meaning of occupation as a measure of status can be found there. It is dealt with specifically and well
in Drake and Cayton, *Black Metropolis*. Some specific references in
this area are: George Edmund Haynes, *The Negro at Work in New*

236   BIBLIOGRAPHICAL ESSAY

York City: A Study in Economic Progress (Columbia University Press, 1912), Sterling Denhard Spero and Abram L. Harris, *The Black Worker: The Negro and the Labor Movement* (Columbia University, 1931), and Dean Dutcher, *The Negro in Modern Industrial Society: An Analysis of Changes in the Occupations of Negro Workers, 1910-1920* (Columbia University, 1931), plus numerous periodical articles like Elizabeth Ross Haynes, "Two Million Negro Women at Work," *Southern Workman* 52 (February 1922).

Northward-cityward migration, which so impacted upon black American life, has been the topic of much investigation. Of the studies readily available the most important are: Louise V. Kennedy, *The Negro Peasant Turns Cityward* (Columbia University Press, 1930); Carter G. Woodson, *A Century of Negro Migration* (Washington, D.C.: Association for the Study of Negro Life and History, 1918); Emmett Jay Scott, *Negro Migration During the War* (Arno Press, 1969), which was originally published in 1920; and Ira DeA. Reid, *The Negro Immigrant; His Background, Characteristics and Social Adjustment, 1899-1937* (Columbia University Press, 1939). An early examination of migration that points to the significance of the northward movement before 1900 is Frederick J. Brown, *The Northward Movement of the Colored Population: A Statistical Study* (Cushing and Co., 1897). Again there is much periodical literature on the topic, a good deal of it quite recent. For the flavor of the movement and the felt motives of the participants in the Great Migration, however, a reading of Emmett J. Scott, compiler, "Letters of Negro Migrants of 1916-18," *JNH* 4 (July and October 1919), is essential.

The violence that so many of the migrants thought they were escaping in their move to the promised land stalked it as well. Its impact is again best uncovered in the imaginative literature and in such cries of protest as Claude McKay's often reprinted poem, "If We Must Die." Several scholars have presented what might be termed anatomies of the riots that rocked the nation during the World War I era. One of the best is Elliott M. Rudwick, *Race Riot at East St. Louis, July 2, 1917* (Southern Illinois University Press, 1964). Another is the previously mentioned study of the Chicago race riot of 1919, William Tuttle's *Race Riot.* Two shorter anatomies of race violence in the early years of this century are Gilbert Osofsky's descriptive, "Race Riot, 1900: A Study of Ethnic Violence," *JNE* 32 (Winter 1963), and James L. Croutthamel, "The Springfield Race Riot of 1908," *JNH* 45 (July 1960). Specific references to racial violence can be found in practically all of the monographs mentioned, but nothing matches the descriptiveness of the NAACP's *Thirty Years of Lynching in the United States, 1889-1918* (NAACP, 1919). Along with its tabular summary and chronological listing of the victims, many enrolled only as "unknown Negro," there are one hundred "case" stories of lynchings. Walter White's *Rope and Faggot: A Biography of Judge Lynch* (Knopf, 1929) is also important in this regard, as is Allen Day Grimshaw's suggestive, "A Study of Social Violence: Urban Race Riots in the United States" (Ph.D. dissertation, University of Pennsylvania, 1959).

From the viewpoint of this study, black leadership was essentially a negative element in the community. That the ordinary Negro was suspicious of his leaders, to say the least, was emphasized in several instances. Ralph J. Bunche, for example, in his striking article of a generation ago, "The Programs of Organizations Devoted to the Improvement of the Status of the American Negro," *JNE* 8 (July 1939), asserted that all Negro organizations were narrowly racial in their interests and interpretations of events yet were unable to reach the ordinary Negro. But obviously the leadership of the period had to be considered, and in this the study relies heavily upon the previously mentioned work of August Meier, *Negro Thought in America.* It will undoubtedly remain the most definitive study of the subject for some time to come. Its theme is not restricted to black leadership, but the view is from the top down. Also important and somewhat in the same vein is S. P. Fullinwider, *The Mind and Mood of Black America: 20th Century Thought* (Homewood, Illinois: Dorsey Press, 1969).

Louis R. Harlan's recent series of articles provides the best sketch of Booker Washington we have to date: "Booker T. Washington and the White Man's Burden," *American Historical Review* 71 (January 1966); "Booker T. Washington in Biographical Perspective," *American Historical Review* 75 (October 1970); and "The Secret Life of Booker T. Washington," *Journal of Southern History* 37 (August 1971). Elliott Rudwick, *W. E. B. DuBois:*

Propagandist of the Negro Protest (Atheneum, 1969), originally published in 1960 under a slightly different title, still provides the best picture of the other great black leader of the period.

Only when it comes to Marcus Garvey does it seem that black leadership was able to reach down and touch the ordinary Negro. Otherwise the ordinary Afro-American hardly looked outside his own immediate community. E. David Cronon, *Black Moses: The Story of Marcus Garvey and the Universal Negro Improvement Association* (University of Wisconsin Press, 1955), is still the best study of Garvey and his movement, although it does not really explain satisfactorily Garvey's ability to touch the blackness of the ordinary Negro. Much better in this respect is the recent *Black Power and the Garvey Movement* (Ramparts Press, 1971), by Theodore G. Vincent. Shirley Willson Strickland, "A Functional Analysis of the Garvey Movement" (Ph.D. dissertation, University of North Carolina, 1956), is useful in many ways, but it hangs rather limply on an elaborate sociological framework that in the end seems almost wasted, and it is plagued with jargon. The periodical literature of the 1920s and the imaginative literature—much of it critical—provides the more meaningful insights into the enigmatic Marcus Garvey. Nothing, in sum, is able to touch the blackness of the ordinary Negro like the imaginative literature of the accomplished artist, a fact that is as true today as it was for the years examined in this study.

INDEX

Abbott, Lyman, 22. *See also* Social Gospel

African Methodist Episcopal (AME) Church, 61, 97

African Orthodox Church, 192

Akron, Ohio, 65-66

Allport, Gordon W., 49, 146 n. 5

American Mercury, 99

"Amos 'n' Andy", 34, 41 n. 59

Anderson, Sherwood, 35, 108

Arthur, John, 196

Association for the Study of Afro-American Life and History, 100

Attaway, William, 47

Attitudes. *See* Black Americans; Blacks on blacks; Blacks on whites; Intraracial tensions; Racial thought in America

Baker, Ray Stannard, 27, 30; *Following the Color Line*, 5-6

Baldwin, James, 124, 125

Baltimore, Maryland, 45

Bennett, Lerone, Jr., 96, 158

Black Americans: and being black in white America, 48, 49-50, 51, 76-77, 81 n. 27, 95-96, 108, 110, 118 n. 81, 121-145, 148 n. 25, 157-159, 171, 173 n.2, 191-192, 213-217; common factors in lives of, 75, 77, 121, 124-125, 213, 215; and growing up black, 125-126, 148 n. 25, 182; and growth of racial consciousness, 1-2, 22, 26, 35, 43, 50, 72, 95-111, 112 n. 11, 113 n. 25, 114 n. 31, 118 n. 81, 122, 129, 131, 145, 146 n. 2, 157, 158-159, 171, 173 n. 9, 188, 191-192, 202-203, 215-217; and interracial violence, 134-141; and a "name to go by," 110-111, 118 n. 87; and playing a role in interracial contact, 125-126, 142, 159, 214, 215-216; and racial self-hatred, 159, 161-162, 165, 176 n. 30; and social invisibleness, 123-124, 146 n. 2; and white intrusions on black life, 121-145. *See also* Blacks on blacks; Blacks on whites; Caste; Migration; Social structure

Blacks on blacks (attitudes/opinions), 157-172, 181-203; and black immigrants, 181, 192, 194-196; and color consciousness, 159-172, 175 n. 30 and 39; and economics of color consciousness, 168; influence of whites on, 159, 160, 165, 172, 181, 182, 234; and intraracial tensions, 76, 172, 181-203; North-South/urban-rural differences in, 130, 162, 175 n. 29; physical features and, 159-172, 177 n. 39; and race leadership, 197, 198-203; and social class distinctions, 162-163, 164, 167, 176 n. 30 and 33. *See also* Social structure

Blacks on whites (attitudes/opinions), 121-145; distrust of whites, 127-129, 134, 143, 145; during World War I, 31-32, 131-134; expressed in humor, 141-144; expressed in Negro newspapers, 141, 143; hatred of whites, 124-129, 131, 143, 148 n. 33, 167; and

white America, 121-122; on literature
and history, 2; on the Negro author, 3;
on passing, 169
Frazier, E. Franklin, 9, 70; and *Black
Bourgeoisie,* 176 n. 30, 185, 205 n. 17;
on class structure, 52, 69, 73-74, 75,
92 n. 161, 162, 185; on migration, 64;
on the Negro church, 191, 197. *See
also* Social structure
Fullinwider, S. P., 35, 154 n. 114, 216

Garvey, Marcus: and appeal to black
and white prejudices, 104; and color
consciousness, 202; and doctrine of
"blackness," 104, 107, 196, 216; and
growth of racial consciousness, 104,
107, 115 n. 50, 192; and importance
of Garveyism, 105, 106, 108; ordinary
black's opinion of, 106-107; as race
leader, 103-107; 202-203, 212 n. 108;
widespread appeal of, 105, 203. *See
also* Universal Negro Improvement
Association
Gladden, Washington, 22. *See also*
Social Gospel
Glazer, Nathan, 48, 81 n. 27
Glenn, Norval D., 56, 84 n. 28
Goldman, Eric, 23, 197, 201
Gordon, Milton M., 50, 80 n. 24, 96
Gossett, Thomas F., 29
Grant, Curtis R., 23, 36 n. 8
Great Depression, 34-35, 76, 111, 216
Great Migration. *See* Migration
Griggs, Sutton E., 5, 6, 97
Grimshaw, Allen D., 138, 139

Handy W. C., 166
Hare, Nathan, 202
Harlan, Louis R., 198, 201
Harlem. *See* New York City
Harlem Renaissance: black artists and,
108-109; Claude McKay on, 109-110;
as an expression of cultural national-
ism, 108; genesis of, 117 n. 70; George
S. Schuyler on, 108; H. L. Mencken

on, 34; and interracial understanding,
34, 108, 109, 110, 117 n. 77; Langston
Hughes on, 34, 109; Rudolph Fisher
on, 109
Hartt, Rollin (Reverend), 46, 87 n. 99,
102, 106
Hatred of whites. *See* Black Americans;
Blacks on whites
Hughes, Langston: and being black in
white America, 158; on black leadership, 196; on black literature, 4, 7, 9;
on employment opportunities, 75; on
the Great Depression, 34-35; on the
Harlem Renaissance, 34, 109; on
hatred of whites, 128, 143; on migration, 46, 63-64, 66, 68; on physical
features and class, 163, 164, 166, 181;
on racial consciousness, 102, 141,
203, 215; on racial self-hatred, 161;
on social classes, 163, 183, 184
Humor: and attitudes toward blacks,
167; and attitudes toward whites,
141-144; as a means of protection,
142; as a means of social critique, 142,
154 n. 104 and 114; minority group
use of, 142; in the press, 141, 143; as a
product of slavery, 142; and "putting
on" the white, 142; as a weapon,
141-144, 154 n. 114

Immigration, 22, 30-31; and color consciousness, 196, 208 n. 63; and intraracial tensions, 181, 194-196; and the
Negro church, 192; numbers, 195,
196; and race leadership, 196; and
social classes, 196
Income. *See* Employment
Intraracial tensions, 76, 172, 181-203.
See also Social structure

Jelks, William Dorsey, 28
Job ceiling. *See* Employment
Johnson, Charles S.: on being black in
white America, 50, 159; on class and
racial consciousness, 146 n. 2, 173 n.

social classes, 163, 170; white ideas about, 168, 175 n. 21, 178 n. 59. *See also* Blacks on blacks; Intraracial tensions; Social structure

Paterson, New Jersey, 71

Periodicals (Negro): *Challenge Magazine,* 134; *Colored American Magazine,* 6, 12, 91 n. 141, 97-98, 129; *Crisis,* 11, 12, 21, 32, 135, 136, 200, 201; *Messenger,* 168, 193; *Opportunity,* 12, 73, 111; as race propaganda organs, 12; as source material, 12; *Southern Workman,* 71; *Voice of the Negro,* 186; and white support, 12

Periodicals (other than Negro), 12, 60, 63, 97, 106, 160

Petry, Ann, 5, 122, 123, 127, 130-131

Pettigrew, Thomas F., 126, 205 n. 17

Philadelphia, Pennsylvania: employment in, 57; migration to, 66, 73; old elites in, 52-53, 55; racial violence in, 138; residential segregation patterns in, 45; social structure in, 51, 52, 55, 73-74

Pickens, William, 62

Pittsburgh, Pennsylvania, 44, 66, 72, 73

Poetry, propaganda and protest in, 7

Politics, 214, 218 n. 6

Pope, Liston, 190, 206 n. 38

Population: growth and religious institutions, 129, 191; growth in urban areas, 59-60, 65-66, 73, 89 n. 116 and 117, 92 n. 159; in Illinois, 59, 66; and interracial tension, 59-60, 62; in New York State, 59, 66; and relationship to white community, 59. *See also* individual place names; Migration

Populism, 26

Race leaders. *See* Leadership, racial

Race riots. *See* Racial violence

Racial consciousness. *See* Black Americans

Racial thought in America: and the abolitionist tradition, 25; biological aspects in, 22, 40 n. 42, 146 n. 5; black awareness of, 26, 28, 35, 54, 96-98, 103;

black reaction to, 100-103, 121-145, 194; and black women, 145; and Booker T. Washington, 197-201; color caste and, 24-25, 30, 33, 43, 49-50, 146 n. 5, 157, 181, 195, 197; E. Franklin Frazier on, 39 n. 29; and "Ezekielism," 144; Franz Boas and, 29, 40 n. 40; and growing racist attitudes, 24-26, 26-28, 29-30, 33-35, 38 n. 22, 96-97, 101, 103, 129, 137, 138-141, 144; and the Harlem Renaissance, 109-110; and intraracial tensions, 172, 181, 182-203; and the law, 28-29, 30, 31, 35, 143; and Marcus Garvey, 104-107; and middle-class liberals, 24-25, 27, 32, 48, 80 n. 24, 81 n. 37; and the mulatto, 160; and the Myrdal thesis, 173 n. 2; in the 1920s, 33-35; and race relations, 24-35, 81 n. 27, 82 n. 35, 95, 197-199, 213; racial hierarchies in, 22, 29, 195; and racist traditions, 24, 29, 37 n. 13, 43; and Reform Darwinists, 23; and scientific racism, 29-30; and Social Darwinism, 22; and the Social Gospel, 22-23, 36 n. 8; and solutions to the race problem, 28, 30, 34, 97, 160; and southern views of northern, 26, 27; W. E. B. DuBois on, 28, 200-201; and the press, 135; and white racist propagandists, 6, 16 n. 25, 27, 34, 38 n. 18, 141; and World War I, 30-32, 41 n. 52, 131-133, 139

Racial violence, 21, 26, 32-33, 35, 101; black resistance during, 139; causes of, 32, 62-63, 87 n. 92, 137, 138-141; Finley Peter Dunne on, 134-135; and lynching, 135-137, 140, 151 n. 72; and riots, 32, 137, 138-139, 153 n. 95; threat of, 137, 140, 189; and "wearing the mask," 124, 125, 138, 140; W. E. B. DuBois on, 33; and the white press, 135; in the World War I era, 134, 138-141

Racism. *See* Racial thought in America

Rauschenbusch, Walter, 22. *See also* Social Gospel

by, 26, 33, 38 n. 22; and *Up from Slavery,* 8-9; and W. E. B. DuBois, 200-201.

Washington, D.C., 32; employment in, 57; old elite of, 52-53; race violence in, 139; residential segregation patterns in, 45, 79 n. 9; social structure in, 163

Waters, Ethel, 34, 109, 182-183, 184

White, Walter, 169

Wiebe, Robert H., 22, 36 n. 4, 68, 194

Williams, John A., 189

Wilson, Woodrow, 30, 32, 134

Woodson, Carter G., 100, 218 n. 6

Woodward, C. Vann, 25, 38 n. 17 and 20, 197, 215

Woofter, T. J., Jr., 46

World War I: anticipated improvements in race relations during, 31-32, 133-134; black attitudes during, 131-133; and destruction of old status quo, 139-140, 145; and postwar violence, 134, 138-141; service during, 133, 150 n. 62; "work-or-fight" edicts during, 130. *See also* Employment; Migration

Wright, Richard, 7; on attitudes toward whites, 123-124; criticisms of, 4-5; and growing up black, 48, 125-126, 158; and *Native Son,* 4-5, 15 n. 19; on the term *Negro,* 110

ABOUT THE AUTHOR

David G. Nielson is an assistant professor and the director of the Liberal Arts and Sciences Programs, School of General Studies, State University of New York, Binghamton. He is presently writing a book-length work entitled *Success at the Bottom: An Informal History of the Endicott-Johnson Shoe and Leather Workers.*